RAND

Taiwan's Foreign and Defense Policies

Features and Determinants

Michael D. Swaine, James C. Mulvenon

Supported by the
Smith Richardson Foundation

Center for Asia-Pacific Policy

The research described in this report was supported by the Smith Richardson Foundation's International Security and Foreign Policy Program.

ISBN: 0-8330-3094-9

Published 2001 by RAND
1700 Main Street, P.O. Box 2138, Santa Monica, CA 90407-2138
1200 South Hayes Street, Arlington, VA 22202-5050
201 North Craig Street, Suite 102, Pittsburgh, PA 15213-1516
RAND URL: http://www.rand.org/
To order RAND documents or to obtain additional information, contact Distribution Services: Telephone: (310) 451-7002; Fax: (310) 451-6915; Email: order@rand.org

Preface

In the past few years, Taiwan (the Republic of China) has become of one of the world's most important potential flashpoints for conflict, setting the stage for a possible clash between the United States and the People's Republic of China (PRC). However, the greatest gap in our knowledge is not the strategic calculus in Washington or Beijing, but instead the strategy of the government in Taipei. This report identifies and analyzes Taiwan's evolving foreign and defense policies and assesses their implications for Asia's current and future security environment. Particular attention is paid to (1) the domestic sources of Taiwan's foreign and defense policies and related deterrence doctrine, (2) the impact upon Taiwan of China's military modernization program and external policy behavior, (3) the role played by the United States and Japan in Taiwan's foreign and defense policies, and (4) the implications for Asian stability of various possible alternative trends in Taiwan's foreign and defense policies.

This research project was conducted under the aegis of RAND's Center for Asia-Pacific Policy (CAPP), which aims to provide decision-makers with objective, cutting-edge research that aids in the formulation of more effective policies for the Asia-Pacific region. CAPP is a part of RAND's National Security Research Division, which conducts research and analysis for a broad range of clients including the U.S. Department of Defense, allied governments, the Intelligence Community, and foundations.

Funding for this effort was provided by a grant from the Smith Richardson Foundation's International Security and Foreign Policy Program, which supports research and policy projects on issues central to the strategic interests of the United States.

Contents

Table

Summary

Principal Findings

The findings of this study on the foreign and defense policies of Taiwan[1] can be divided into three sections: (1) overall assessment; (2) influences; and (3) future trajectories and implications for U.S. policy.

Overall Assessment

Taiwan's foreign and defense policies are principally focused on maintaining the security and prosperity of the territory of Taiwan and its 23 million inhabitants, in the context of a precarious and rapidly changing domestic and external environment. This environment is marked by three major features:

- The large and growing political and military threat to Taiwan's security posed by an increasingly capable Mainland Chinese regime, complicated by Taiwan's growing economic ties with the Mainland and a variety of strong ethnic and cultural connections.

- The relatively weak level of political and military assistance provided to Taiwan by foreign powers, combined with Taiwan's growing economic, social, and cultural involvement in the Asia-Pacific and beyond.

- A highly fluid domestic political and social situation, arising primarily from the ongoing democratization of Taiwan's political process, generational turnover within its society, and the growing prosperity of Taiwan's populace.

The above three basic features of Taiwan's security environment have produced a specific set of broad national security objectives and related foreign and defense policies. The Republic of China (ROC) government has five core national security objectives:

---

[1]In this study, the term "Taiwan" will be used interchangeably with the term "Republic of China" (ROC).

- To maintain domestic support as an open and democratic polity representing the interests and aspirations of the majority of the Taiwan population.

- To sustain popular confidence in the ability of the government to protect Taiwan's physical security and to ensure Taiwan's continued prosperity in the face of a growing Chinese threat.

- To maximize all possible, political and diplomatic assistance and recognition provided by the international community, especially the United States.

- To ensure Taiwan's continued access to those overseas markets and sources of materials and technologies necessary to sustain Taiwan's growth and to enhance its international influence.

- To retain an indigenous military capability and to receive military assistance and support from the United States and other Western powers, sufficient to deter the People's Republic of China (PRC) from attacking Taiwan and, if deterrence fails, to prevent the PRC from subjugating the island.

The ROC's foreign and defense policies have evolved greatly since the Nationalist Chinese movement under Chiang Kai-shek moved the seat of government to the island of Taiwan in 1949. In an ongoing effort to strengthen the internal legitimacy, international appeal, and military security of the ROC government, consecutive ROC leaders have:

- Progressively loosened the connection between national identity and statehood through the creation of a government based on popular sovereignty rather than ethnic Chinese nationalism.

- Continuously tested the existing limits on the territory's international status by adopting highly pragmatic and creative approaches to expanding Taiwan's international political and diplomatic presence, while balancing cross-Strait economic ties with attempts to integrate Taiwan more fully into the global economy.

- Sought to strengthen Taiwan's security from attack or coercion by acquiring or developing the weapons and support systems of a more efficient, modern military, and by developing closer military and political ties with the United States through arms sales and defense dialogues.

The Chen Shui-bian government has adopted a relatively low-profile, non-provocative foreign policy stance for the present, often focused on expanding Taiwan's status and support through involvement in human rights and NGO realms. In the defense policy realm, the above developments have led to growing support within Taiwan for the acquisition of weapons and support systems that could both stimulate further changes in the cross-Strait military balance and redefine the nature of the ROC-U.S. defense relationship in ways that greatly antagonize the PRC.

To better understand the future evolution of these critical aspects of Taiwan's foreign and defense policies, one must examine the following: (1) the forces of domestic change on Taiwan, including the influence exerted by the changing features of Taiwan's decision-making structure and process; (2) the influence of Chinese policy and behavior; and (3) the role played by the United States and other major powers.

The Influence of Domestic Factors

Certain common basic values and policy outlooks exist among the vast majority of Taiwan's political leadership. In the specific areas of foreign policy and defense policy, the bulk of Taiwan's political elite apparently agree on several basic principles and policy positions, reflecting the overall pragmatism and growing moderation of Taiwan's dominant political center. These policies include:

- The basic concept of flexible or pragmatic diplomacy, as opposed to dollar diplomacy.
- A more forward-oriented (some would say offensive) military strategy, designed to increase deterrence and, if necessary, degrade the ability of the Mainland to prosecute direct military action against Taiwan.

At the same time, certain critical differences or policy cleavages can be identified within the elite, though often they revolve around the emphasis and tone of policies, rather than basic substance:

- The question of national identity and treatment of the "One China" concept.
- Attitudes toward the ROC military, and military leadership in particular.
- The ultimate purpose of Taiwan's defense strategy and armed forces.
- The desired purpose and architecture of a future ballistic missile defense (BMD) system.

The formulation and implementation of ROC national strategic objectives and the major principles guiding both foreign and defense policies are marked by the following features:

- Policymaking is highly concentrated in the hands of a few senior civilian and military leaders and at times strongly influenced by the views and personality of the president.

- The process is poorly coordinated, both within the top levels of the senior leadership and between the civilian and military elite. In particular:

  — No formal, institutionalized and regularized inter-agency process or mechanism for national security strategy formulation and implementation exists that spans all the key senior civilian and military agencies and policymakers.

  — At lower levels of the policy process, no formal institutions exist to provide ongoing policy coordination and implementation of national-level grand strategies among civilian and defense policy sectors.

- As a result, national security strategy is developed either on a fragmentary basis, within individual responsible agencies, or by the president alone, through largely separate, and often private, interactions with senior civilian and military officials and advisors.

The Influence of China

China's attitudes and actions toward Taiwan constitute one of the most important factors influencing ROC foreign policy and defense policy.

- China has adopted a complex strategy of pressures and enticements to arrest Taiwan's move toward greater independence, including a "united front" strategy with the Nationalist or Kuomintang (KMT) party opposition in the Legislative Yuan (LY), a zero tolerance policy for Taiwan's attempts to increase its international space as a sovereign state, a renewed effort to reinforce its strategic relationship with Washington, and an increasing emphasis on strengthening the credibility of its military options against Taiwan.

- China has attempted to use economic ties with Taiwan to influence or pressure Taiwan businesspersons to exert pressure on the ROC government to be moderate or to accept Beijing's stance, which in turn has spurred the ROC government to place greater emphasis on expanding and diversifying its international economic activities outside the Mainland. The latter effort has enjoyed only very limited success, given the decline of Taiwan's economy.

- China has placed an increased emphasis on acquiring capabilities designed to strengthen the credibility of Beijing's military options against the island

and to deter the United States from deploying aircraft carriers in an effort to counter such options, driving Taiwan's foreign and defense policymaking apparatus to seek deeper defense commitments from the United States and greater numbers of advanced military systems, including elements of a theater ballistic missile defense system.

The Influence of the United States and Japan

The United States and Japan currently wield substantial influence over Taiwan's foreign and defense policies:

- The United States has always been Taiwan's key backer, providing critical political, military, economic, and ideological guidance and material assistance.

- Japan, by contrast, was a military opponent of the KMT on the Mainland and a colonial overlord of the island for fifty years. Like most post-colonial entities, however, Taiwan still enjoys deep ties to its former master, mainly cultural but also deeply economic and political in nature.

- On pragmatic diplomacy, both Washington and Tokyo have generally supported Taiwan's efforts to expand its presence in the international community without, however, endorsing any attempts to achieve formal recognition as a sovereign, independent state. With respect to U.S.-ROC relations, the United States has periodically sought to refine certain bilateral arrangements related to transits, meetings, and declaratory policies about Taiwan's status, especially after the crises surrounding Lee's transit through Hawaii in 1994 and his visit to Cornell University in 1995.

- On ballistic missile defense, Taiwan carefully observes Japanese moves in the BMD area for signals about American commitment to regional deployment, regional assessments of the Chinese missile threat, and calculations of PRC reactions to potentially destabilizing modernization programs, and also closely follows information on BMD and BMD-related systems that the ROC military might want to acquire.

- The United States, through both formal and informal channels of influence, is clearly the dominant influence on Taiwan's decision-making about theater ballistic missile defenses, providing various forms of information and advice that will strongly shape the course of Taiwan's BMD strategy, planning, procurement, integration, and deployment.

Future Foreign and Defense Policy Trajectories

Taiwan's foreign and defense policies display several important characteristics:

- In terms of continuities, both the KMT under Lee Teng-hui and the DPP under Chen Shui-bian have moved toward the center of the political spectrum, converging in their support for pragmatic diplomacy and at least six specific defense policies: (1) restructuring, downsizing, and streamlining of the military; (2) civilianization of defense authority; (3) strengthening rapid reaction capability; (4) augmenting air and naval defense capacities; (5) diversification of the sources of military procurement; and (6) strengthening indigenous weapons production.

- In terms of discontinuities, the Chen government has either partly or completely broken with KMT policy in three key areas:

  — *Cross-Strait Relations.* The abandonment of Lee Teng-hui's "special state-to-state formulation," combined with clear movement away from the notion that Taiwan is politically part of Mainland China or must one day reunify with the Mainland to form a sovereign Chinese state.

  — *Pragmatic Diplomacy.* A de-emphasis on so-called dollar diplomacy, and a stronger rhetorical emphasis on increasing Taiwan's involvement in non-governmental and human rights organizations and regimes.

  — *Defense Policy.* An acceleration and intensification of the effort to eliminate the influence of the KMT over the military, and the implementation of a much more offensive-oriented approach to strengthening Taiwan's deterrent, pushing the acquisition of weapons and accompanying support systems for genuine warfighting force rather than simply as political symbols of the U.S. defense commitment.

Over the next 4–5 years, Taiwan's foreign and defense policies will likely exhibit the following features:

- External relations with the United States and the rest of world will likely remain stable, with political, economic, and military ties increasing between Washington and Taipei; few major initiatives are likely on the diplomatic front, given the major advances already attained in this arena during the Lee Teng-hui era and the current impasse existing between the Chen Shui-bian government and the Legislative Yuan. However, more assertive actions cannot be ruled out.

- On cross-Strait relations, however, domestic constraints on Taipei and Beijing will likely perpetuate a policy stalemate, with both sides appealing to outside constituencies to facilitate a deal. Given the reluctance of Washington to directly mediate talks between the two sides, there is little prospect for improvement in ties in the short-term.

- On defense policy, the Chen government will seek to obtain quantitatively and qualitatively greater levels of weaponry and related military assistance from the United States, and to develop closer military and political relations between Taipei and Washington. Yet internal debates will continue to rage over the dangers, costs, and opportunities presented by Chen's policy proposals, such as the adoption of offensive strike capabilities and/or the construction of sophisticated active defense measures such as various types of BMD systems.

Ballistic Missile Defenses

- Political considerations are paramount in Taiwan. The top priorities of the government are (1) reassurance of the public, (2) maintenance of positive relations with the United States, and (3) minimizing the potential Chinese reaction to the systems.

- The pace, tempo, level of support for BMD within Taiwan are heavily influenced by bureaucratic and budgetary issues.

- The acquisition of some Lower Tier (LT) systems is under way, but more sophisticated Upper Tier (UT) systems face significant obstacles.

- The timeline for the deployment of key systems is very long, even 10–20 years for limited coverage systems.

- The systems integration requirements are enormous, with reforms of air defense and command, control, communications and intelligence (C3I) systems posing the most vexing challenges.

As a result of these factors, Taiwan's BMD policy is likely to have five major features:

- Taiwan will seek to acquire LT interceptors, as well as both LT- and UT-capable early warning systems and C3I infrastructure.

- Taiwan will avoid open advocacy of U.S.-ROC integration, but will favor closer ties, particularly in the military-to-military realm.

- Taipei will likely delay decisions on acquiring UT systems, avoiding public statements on the issue.

- The ROC will likely avoid R&D cooperation on Upper Tier. If the United States presses, Taiwan will likely promise to "study" the problem.

- Internal pressure will cause the government to "hedge its bets" and proceed with the development of an offensive tactical missile.

- Overall, we expect token, slow acquisition of UT at most, probably following the U.S. lead. Taiwan is likely to avoid any decision on UT until the United States deploys, assuming that the United States deploys by 2007 as planned. The deployment of the systems is unlikely to alter the strategic balance in Northeast Asia, because such systems will be deployed too slowly and remain relatively modest in capability, especially given China's ballistic missile capabilities. But BMD deployment could alter the political balance, especially Chinese perceptions of the regional security environment in Asia.

Implications for U.S. Policy

Taiwan's evolving foreign and defense policies will continue to exert a profound impact on American relations with both Taiwan and China. Our specific policy recommendations include:

- Taiwan's policymakers believe that there are strong differences between Congress and the Executive Branch regarding Taiwan policy. The Bush administration should seek to forge a united front with Congress on cross-Strait policy, reducing the incentives of those who would seek to exploit cleavages in the system.

- Taiwan's foreign and defense policymakers rely on U.S. military intervention as a key assumption in their planning. Although such U.S. intervention will likely take place in the event of what the United States views as an unprovoked attack by the Mainland, U.S. policy should be calibrated to deter or prevent any Taiwan leader from undertaking political actions that Washington believes might provoke a Chinese attack.

- Significant benefit is gained by preserving ambiguity over U.S. intentions towards Taiwan's security and international status. The U.S. government should maintain a public allegiance to the notion of "One China" as originally defined in the normalization agreements, combined with a posture of public ambiguity regarding the level of the U.S. commitment to defend

Taiwan. Taiwan should not be treated as a security partner of the United States.

- Privately, the United States should make it clear to Beijing that it will by necessity respond militarily in the event of a Chinese attack, while stating privately to Taipei that the United States will prevent what it views as any unilateral attempt to secure an independent status for Taiwan. American support for Taiwan's democratic development should not equate with support for independence.

Beijing will not accept a mere avoidance of a formal declaration of independence by Taiwan as sufficient to guarantee "no independence"; Taiwan could take other actions, with U.S. support, that Beijing would view as dangerous—and Taiwan would be more inclined to do so if the United States provides a public defense guarantee.

- On BMD, we offer five policy recommendations for missile defenses and Taiwan:

  — The United States should not press Taiwan to participate in joint development of the systems. The technical and financial benefits would be minimal, while the potential damage to Sino-U.S. relations would be high. Moreover, Taiwan itself does not seek this type of development, and it should not be forced upon them for fiscal reasons.

  — Taiwan should be discouraged from making any UT-related announcements. There is no useful purpose served by such an action.

  — A clear distinction should be made between UT interceptors and support systems. Regarding the latter, high priority should be placed on a careful evaluation of the implications of a UT system for ROC-U.S. C3I integration.

  — The best option seems to be Lower Tier with long-range radar, plus the indigenous Sky Bow system. This configuration requires much better C3I integration than Taiwan currently possesses.

  — Any Evolved Advanced Combat System (EACS) or AEGIS sale should explicitly preclude future UT capability.

Interviews in Taiwan suggest that there is an active program of research on a tactical ballistic missile with maximum 1,000-km range, plus a possible land-attack variant of the Hsiung-Feng II cruise missile. While the U.S. government would likely detect any testing or deployment of these missiles and could press to stop the program, policymakers in Washington should be alerted to the possibility that the program is actually a "card" to be dealt away in exchange for specific weapons systems (AEGIS or Upper Tier) or enhanced defense commitments.

Acknowledgments

The authors wish to thank their RAND colleague Kevin Pollpeter for his significant substantive contribution to the research on the project, especially his detailed and thoughtful responses to a wide range of queries during the course of the work. They also thank the many generous interlocutors in Taiwan and the United States who shared their insights with the research team, although most will remain anonymous to protect the confidentiality of their remarks. We also wish to thank the reviewers, Shelley Rigger and Robert Suettinger, for their close reading of the manuscript and insightful comments. Finally, the authors acknowledge the leadership of Rachel Swanger, who served as Acting Director of the Center for Asia-Pacific Policy during the course of the research and was a principal force behind the initiation, implementation, and completion of this effort.

1. Introduction

In the past few years, Taiwan (the Republic of China, or ROC) has become one of the world's most important potential flashpoints for conflict, setting the stage for a possible clash between the United States and the People's Republic of China (PRC). This dangerous situation has emerged largely as a result of the interaction between (a) Taiwan's ongoing democratization process, which has generated an assertive Taiwan national identity separate from the Mainland; (b) China's efforts to counter this perceived "pro-independence" trend through political, diplomatic and military means; and (c) America's steadfast commitment to a peaceful resolution of the resulting China-Taiwan confrontation through efforts to preserve the self-defense capacities of the ROC government while simultaneously acknowledging the notion that both sides are part of a single Chinese nation. Within this complex equation, Taiwan's political, diplomatic, and military actions have arguably exerted an increasingly significant impact on the calculations of both China and the United States. In particular, Taiwan's search for greater international respect as a separate, sovereign political entity, the apparent rejection by many Taiwan citizens of the notion of reunification with the Mainland, the growing contrast—in the eyes of many Americans—between Taiwan's unruly yet increasingly democratic brand of domestic politics and the often repressive aspects of Mainland rule, and Taiwan's cultivation of closer political and military ties with the United States together intensify both Chinese efforts to prevent the "loss of Taiwan" and American efforts to protect a "beleaguered democratic friend" while maintaining constructive relations with Beijing.

Many observers thus believe that Taiwan's future behavior could prove to be the most critical variable influencing whether, and in what manner, U.S.-China-Taiwan tensions might intensify and thereby threaten overall stability in Asia. A military conflict between the United States and China prompted by Taiwan's actions would severely challenge the U.S.-Japan security alliance and greatly threaten Asian stability. More broadly, such a clash would likely result in a prolonged confrontation between China and the United States and hence fundamentally alter the strategic landscape in Asia. To avoid these outcomes, this study seeks to broaden our understanding of Taiwan's evolving foreign and defense policies and assess their implications for Asia's current and future security environment.

The Structure of the Study

The report focuses on four main sets of factors: (1) the historical background and context of Taiwan's foreign and defense policies; (2) the domestic sources of Taiwan's foreign and defense policies and related deterrence doctrine; (3) the impact upon Taiwan of China's military modernization program and external policy behavior; and (4) the role played by the United States and Japan in Taiwan's foreign and defense policies. The report concludes with brief observations on the possible future evolution of Taiwan's foreign and defense policies and approach to cross-Strait relations and their implications for the United States.

Two comparative cases will be examined from the perspectives of Taiwan participants to illuminate the major features of these four issues. The first case is Taiwan's policy of "pragmatic diplomacy," by which Taipei uses the various tools at its disposal, primarily financial, to generate more international support. Past applications of this policy include the financial wooing of smaller countries to switch their formal diplomatic recognition from the PRC to Taiwan, Taiwan's attempts to reclaim a seat in the United Nations, participation in a variety of official and unofficial multilateral fora ranging from the Olympics to the World Trade Organization (WTO), and efforts to increase Taiwan's political contacts with the major powers, especially the United States and Japan.

The second issue is the possible deployment of ballistic missile defenses (BMD) on Taiwan, which could be the most important development in the security dynamic between Beijing and Taipei. An effective BMD system in Taiwan would strongly influence security policymaking across the Taiwan Strait, because it would fundamentally change China's current security calculus. Specifically, BMD would undermine China's most effective leverage point against Taiwan—the threat of missile attack—and thus reduce the level of pressure on Taiwan to settle the issue of reunification. To forestall this outcome, China might well greatly increase its production of short-range ballistic missiles in order to overwhelm the ROC's BMD system, and thereby further destabilize the entire region. Worse yet, Beijing might conceivably conclude that it must act militarily to "resolve" the Taiwan problem before any BMD system is deployed by or on behalf of Taipei.

Both "pragmatic diplomacy" and BMD cut across the above four factors in a number of important ways. On the Taiwan domestic front, pragmatic diplomacy was a key pillar of former President Lee Teng-hui's popular support, appealing to the sense of pride and entitlement of the Taiwan population regardless of their stand on the issue of formal independence, and thereby weakening popular support for the opposition movement. In the past, this political reality, combined with the perceived support the policy received from sectors of the U.S. Congress and the impressive prosperity of the Taiwan economy, at times gave Taipei sufficient political leverage to challenge the status quo and provided the Taipei government with a strong incentive to continue actions that unintentionally raise the level of tension with the PRC. Elements of this dynamic continue under the current Chen Shui-bian government, despite clear signs of internal political deadlock, a growing dependence on economic links with the Mainland, and declining domestic prosperity.

BMD, on the other hand, is a controversial issue among the Taiwan population. Many ordinary citizens support the notion of missile defense in principle but do not want any BMD sites to be located near their homes. Likewise, many members of Taiwan's political and military elite welcome the positive political implications of U.S. BMD deployments on the island, but think that BMD is militarily ineffective and too expensive. In terms of Chinese behavior and military modernization, Taiwan's pursuit of pragmatic diplomacy and BMD are both important drivers of more aggressive policies by Beijing. Pragmatic diplomacy's attempts to create more "international space" for Taiwan have aroused the nationalist ire of Beijing, which has responded by placing even greater pressure on targeted countries and international fora. Likewise, BMD potentially undermines China's missile advantage, prompting Beijing to increase the level of pressure on Taiwan and the countries that supply Taipei with military systems, most notably the United States.

Third, pragmatic diplomacy and BMD deployments are closely linked to the role of the United States and Japan in Taiwan's foreign and defense policies, both because the United States and Japan are perceived by Beijing to encourage the attempts by Taipei to carve out more international space and because Taiwan deployment of BMD is often discussed in parallel with BMD deployments in Japan.

Finally, both pragmatic diplomacy and BMD are key factors in the formulation of several possible trajectories in Taiwan's foreign and defense policies, given the extent to which both issues negatively affect the decision calculus of the PRC.

2. General Context

Basic Principles and Features

Taiwan's foreign and defense policies are focused on maintaining the security and prosperity of the territory of Taiwan[1] and its 23 million inhabitants, in the context of a precarious and rapidly changing domestic and external environment. This environment is marked by three major features:

- The large and growing political and military threat to Taiwan's security posed by an increasingly capable Mainland Chinese regime, complicated by Taiwan's growing economic ties with the Mainland and a variety of strong ethnic and cultural connections.

- The relatively weak level of political and military assistance provided to Taiwan by foreign powers, combined with Taiwan's growing economic, social, and cultural involvement in the Asia-Pacific and beyond.

- A highly fluid domestic political and social situation, arising primarily from the ongoing democratization of Taiwan's political process, generational turnover within society, and the growing prosperity of Taiwan's populace.

The threat posed by Mainland China is rooted in the fact that Taiwan is considered by the People's Republic of China to be Chinese territory that has been under the control or influence of either foreign imperialist or rival Chinese powers since the end of the 19th century.[2] The island is regarded by many Chinese as the last major portion of China's sovereign territory remaining to be reunited with China proper, following the reversion of Hong Kong and Macau in the nineties and the earlier "recovery" in the fifties of larger regions such as Tibet and Xinjiang in the west and northwest. Hence, for many Chinese citizens, the reunification of Taiwan with the Mainland constitutes a final "sacred task" of Chinese nationalism symbolizing the full attainment of Chinese unity, dignity, and pride in the modern era. For China's civilian and military leaders, the ability of the Chinese government and the People's Liberation Army (PLA) to reunify Taiwan with the Mainland—or at the very least to prevent its permanent

---

[1]This territory consists of the main island of Taiwan, the island of Penghu (also know as the Pescadores), and several smaller offshore islands near the Chinese mainland.

[2]By imperial Japan from 1895 to 1945, and by Nationalist China from 1945 to the present.

separation—is thus also viewed as a critical indicator of the capacity and the legitimacy of the PRC regime as the defender of China's nationalist interests and aspirations. The permanent "loss" of Taiwan would thus be perceived by Chinese leaders and many Chinese citizens as a catastrophic event that could generate severe political and social instability.

Although the PRC regime has been willing to accept the existence of an autonomous, rival Nationalist Party (Kuomintang, or KMT) government on Taiwan since the fifties (largely because of the protection afforded to that government by the United States), it is entirely unwilling to accept the emergence of a *de jure* independent Taiwan state and has repeatedly indicated that it will employ force to prevent such an outcome. Chinese concerns in this regard have increased significantly since the late eighties as a result of the democratization process on Taiwan. This process has led to a steady decrease in the influence of conservative, pro-reunification Mainlanders within the KMT Party in favor of Taiwan-born leaders such as former ROC President Lee Teng-hui, a concurrent shift in political power toward independence-minded forces associated with the native Taiwan-dominated Democratic Progressive Party (DPP), and increasing levels of support from democratic countries such as the United States. Moreover, past high economic growth rates, expanding levels of foreign trade and investment across the region, and the accumulation of enormous foreign exchange reserves have given Taiwan new avenues for asserting its influence in the regional and global arena. These developments, and especially Beijing's growing fear that the United States is directly or indirectly supportive of Taiwan's movement toward independence, have served to strengthen China's sense of concern over Taiwan and increase its willingness to use coercive diplomacy, if not outright force, to prevent the island from achieving permanent independence.

In addition, the threat posed to Taiwan by the Mainland has been increasing in recent years as a result of enormous changes in China's capabilities and external influence brought about by the introduction of wide-ranging economic and social reforms in the late seventies. China's resulting high economic growth rates and increasing involvement in the international community (in the form of an expanding array of economic, political, social, and military links with foreign countries and international bodies) have permitted China to acquire greater military capabilities of concern to Taiwan, significantly increased China's access to and influence within the international community, and increased the desire of other countries to maintain good relations with China and to support China's position regarding the status of Taiwan.

Finally, in addition to the above factors, Mainland China's ability to influence, if not coerce, Taiwan arguably has increased significantly since the early nineties as a result of the rapid emergence and deepening of a broad range of economic and financial ties between the island and the Mainland. Rapid increases in investment and trade with the Mainland by a large number of Taiwan companies have threatened to create a level of strategic dependence by Taiwan on the Mainland that could be used by Beijing in an attempt to coerce Taipei to accept its terms for political association.

The growing threat to Taiwan posed by the Mainland is significantly compounded by the relatively low level of political and military support provided to Taipei by foreign powers or international bodies. Taiwan is not formally recognized diplomatically by any of the major or medium-sized powers. It has no presence in the United Nations or other major international organizations that require sovereign statehood status for membership. Although Taipei participates in many international, non-governmental economic, social, and cultural bodies, its status in such bodies is formally below that of a sovereign state. Moreover, those countries that recognize Taiwan diplomatically consist exclusively of small Central American or African states, and their reasons for providing such recognition are largely economic, i.e., they receive financial assistance from Taiwan in return. Most states formally recognize Taiwan as a part of China or acknowledge the Mainland Chinese position regarding Taiwan, and hence view Taiwan as in principle subject to PRC sovereignty and/or as a "nonstate" in the international system. They are thus—with the sole exception of the United States—extremely reluctant to provide Taiwan with weapons of any kind.

From a political and military perspective, Taiwan remains heavily dependent on the support provided by the United States. Yet American support and assistance for Taiwan are not founded on a security alliance or any unambiguous security guarantees, nor are they based on a formal diplomatic relationship. Taiwan's formal military and political ties with the United States were terminated when Washington established diplomatic relations with Beijing in 1979. Hence, Washington does not recognize Taiwan as a sovereign, independent state. The United States government is required by U.S. law—in the form of the Taiwan Relations Act (TRA) of 1979—only to assist Taiwan in maintaining its own defense against possible armed coercion by Beijing, and to ensure that the resolution of the China-Taiwan issue is ultimately peaceful and mutually agreed upon. It is not obligated to come to the assistance of Taiwan in the event of a confrontation with Beijing.[3] Moreover, U.S. strategy and tactics in upholding its commitments to Taiwan are heavily influenced by Washington's larger strategic, economic, and political interests in Asia and concerning China in particular, including the desire to prevent the Taiwan issue from fundamentally destabilizing Sino-U.S. relations. As a result, the United States does not support unilateral political or military actions by Taiwan that might precipitate a conflict across the Taiwan Strait, and opposes efforts by Taiwan to acquire potentially destabilizing weapons of mass destruction (such as nuclear arms) or less devastating offensive conventional weapons (such as surface-to-surface ballistic missiles) as a means of deterring an attack from the Mainland. Thus, while Taiwan is highly dependent on U.S. support, such support remains limited and somewhat ambiguous in nature.

Finally, Taiwan's potential vulnerability is accentuated by its high level of dependence on overseas markets, products, and technology for continued economic growth and prosperity. In other words, Taiwan is a trading state and hence must maintain access to regional and global resources and markets to survive. At the same time, Taiwan's economic links with the Asia-Pacific and beyond provide it with an important potential source of political influence, as long as the level and scope of its foreign economic power remain high.

Taiwan's security environment, including both the threat posed by Mainland China and Taipei's ability to generate support from the international community, has been greatly influenced over the past decade by a host of radical changes occurring in Taiwan's polity and society. Since the late eighties, the democratization process has brought about a steady erosion of the state's identification with the ideals and objectives of the Nationalist KMT Party and ended the long-standing monopoly over political and social life exercised by the Mainlander minority over the indigenous Taiwan majority. These features have been largely replaced by a new identity and basis for state authority—a concept of popular sovereignty based upon the individual's association with a free, democratic and prosperous Taiwan, not necessarily the larger Chinese state or a Chinese ethnic or cultural community. As a result of this process, discussed in greater detail below, Taiwan's connections with the Mainland have been steadily reduced and delimited to encompass only general historical, cultural, economic, and social ties, and the past claim of the Republic of China as a political entity

---

[3]The TRA merely indicates that any use of force against Taiwan by the PRC would be viewed with "grave concern" by Washington, and that, if Mainland China poses a military threat to Taiwan's security, the President should consult with the Congress as to how to respond. For the full text of the TRA, see Paul H. Tai, ed., *United States, China, and Taiwan: Bridges for a New Millennium*, Public Policy Institute, Southern Illinois University, Carbondale, Illinois, 1999, pp. 237–251.

exercising sovereign authority over both Mainland China and Taiwan has been jettisoned by the ROC government.

This transformation in Taiwan's self-identity and foundation of governmental authority has led to a belief by a majority of both the elite and the populace in the de facto independence and separateness of the ROC state and an unwillingness to contemplate reunification with the Mainland on any basis other than between two equal, prosperous, and democratic political entities.[4] At the same time, Taiwan's democratic transformation has strengthened political support for Taiwan among Western industrial democracies, especially the United States. Many Westerners now see a growing contrast between an economically vibrant yet still politically repressive and increasingly obsolete PRC regime and an increasingly democratic, prosperous, and forward-looking Taiwan regime. This development has greatly heightened Chinese fears that Taiwan will eventually attain a position of permanent separation from the Mainland as a *de jure* independent state supported by the major powers of the international community.

The above three basic features of Taiwan's security environment have produced a specific set of broad national security objectives and related foreign and defense policies. The ROC government has five core national security objectives:

- To maintain domestic support as an open and democratic polity representing the interests and aspirations of the majority of the Taiwan population.

- To sustain popular confidence in the ability of the government to protect Taiwan's physical security and to ensure Taiwan's continued prosperity in the face of a growing Chinese threat.[5]

- To maximize all possible political and diplomatic assistance and recognition provided by the international community, especially the United States.

- To ensure Taiwan's continued access to those overseas markets and sources of materials and technologies necessary to sustain Taiwan's growth and to enhance its international influence.

---

[4]However, such a stance does not necessarily preclude the possibility of Taiwan agreeing to an eventual "loose" form of reunification that preserves its political (i.e., state-based) autonomy while acknowledging its nonpolitical (i.e., nation-based) association with the Mainland. Indeed, some observers believe that the ongoing separation of statehood from nationhood will likely make the bulk of Taiwan's populace more receptive to a future confederation with the Mainland.

[5]This objective and the preceding one require the ROC government to walk a fine line between ensuring the strength, dignity, and de facto independence of Taiwan and its populace and avoiding any provocation of the PRC regime that could result in a potentially disastrous assault from the Mainland.

- To retain an indigenous military capability and to receive military assistance and support from the United States and other Western powers, sufficient to deter China from attacking Taiwan and, if deterrence fails, to prevent China from subjugating the island.[6]

These five core national security objectives determine a more specific set of foreign and defense policies. In the foreign policy realm, these include efforts to maintain and, if possible, expand Taiwan's political-diplomatic-economic presence in and value to the international community. On the broadest level, since the mid-eighties, this objective has required a rather unconventional approach to conducting foreign relations, based on a rejection of the past, narrow "zero-sum" PRC-ROC competition over diplomatic recognition and participation in international bodies of the fifties, sixties, and seventies in favor of a highly flexible and pragmatic "positive-sum" approach that tolerates a wide variety of international contacts. In the area of formal diplomatic relations, this approach has resulted in the pursuit of a de facto "dual recognition" or "two Chinas" strategy, marked by a willingness to establish diplomatic relations with states irrespective of their existing relations with Beijing, using a variety of enticements, especially economic. This approach has also included a general stress on establishing and expanding a wide range of both official and unofficial, nondiplomatic "substantive" political, cultural, and economic ties with other states and international bodies, using a variety of formulations and mechanisms. In the economic and trade arena, this approach has focused on efforts to facilitate the expansion of Taiwan's access to overseas markets and sources of technology and resources.

These broad foreign policy efforts have significantly improved Taiwan's international position in certain respects and thus arguably enhanced Taiwan's security. However, it is the relationship with the United States that remains in many ways the core of Taiwan's foreign (and defense) policies. Taipei's overriding foreign policy objective is to strengthen the U.S. commitment to Taiwan's security and prosperity without provoking a major conflict or tension with Mainland China. This effort requires maintaining a strong U.S. fealty to the Taiwan Relations Act and to the so-called Six Assurances,[7] which together

---

[6]Regarding the United States, this includes efforts to strengthen Washington's willingness, if deemed necessary by Taipei, to intervene directly with its military forces in a future cross-Strait military crisis.

[7]The Six Assurances were six points proposed by the ROC government to the U.S. government in 1982 as guidelines for the latter to use in conducting U.S.-Taiwan relations. The points were accepted by Washington. They state that: (1) the United States will not set a date for termination of arms sales to Taiwan; (2) the United States will not alter the terms of the Taiwan Relations Act; (3) the United States will not consult with China in advance before making decisions about U.S. arms sales to Taiwan; (4) the United States will not mediate between Taiwan and China; (5) the United States will

provide the basis of U.S. political and military support for Taiwan. Thus, Taiwan's policy clearly implies a desire to expand the degree of support for Taiwan provided by U.S. political and economic elites, especially members of Congress and important business leaders. It also implies efforts to improve the level and type of U.S. military assistance provided to Taiwan, in order both to strengthen Taiwan's military capabilities vis-à-vis the Mainland and to convey an impression of America's heightened commitment to the security of Taiwan and to the peaceful resolution of the China-Taiwan imbroglio. Finally, although rarely openly acknowledged, Taiwan's policy toward the United States also includes efforts to prevent Washington from improving relations with Mainland China or otherwise striking a "deal" with Beijing that might compromise Taiwan's interests.

Taiwan employs a variety of means to achieve the above foreign policy objectives toward the United States. These include, first and foremost, a reliance on strong relationships with key U.S. decision-makers, based on a wide variety of factors, including long-standing personal ties, economic enticements, special interests, and basic moral and political values. As indicated above, in recent years, these ties have been reinforced by appeals made to both American elites and the American public to support Taiwan as a burgeoning democracy and a strong proponent of human rights whose behavior and outlook contrasts greatly with the PRC regime. Such efforts are ultimately focused on attaining widespread recognition within the United States of the importance to U.S. national interests of preserving a prosperous, free and democratic Taiwan.

Although not formally considered within the arena of foreign relations, Taiwan's interactions with the Mainland clearly influence Taiwan's overall foreign (and defense) policy objectives. In this regard, Taiwan's primary objective since the late eighties has been to expand and improve economic, social and cultural contacts with the People's Republic of China in order to assist Taiwan's development and to lower tensions and hence avoid a cross-Strait conflict while also encouraging the development of a more free and open polity and society on the Mainland. At the same time, Taiwan also desires to avoid being placed in a position whereby Mainland China can use its growing links with Taiwan to pressure Taipei to accept its approach to reunification or otherwise increase pressure on Taiwan to "come to terms" with Beijing in a manner that compromises Taiwan's interests. On the most fundamental level, this requires

---

not alter its position about the sovereignty of Taiwan—which was that the question was one to be decided peacefully by the Chinese themselves—and would not pressure Taiwan to enter into negotiations with China; and (6) the United States will not formally recognize Chinese sovereignty over Taiwan. See Tai, 1999, pp. 260–261.

Taipei to approach Beijing as a separate but equal political entity, and not on the basis of the "one country, two systems" approach to relations favored by the Chinese leadership.[8]

In the realm of defense policy, Taiwan is pursuing a variety of objectives, keyed to the need to deter the Mainland and to reassure the Taiwan public that it is secure from attack. On the most basic level, Taipei desires to possess a credible deterrent or other adequate countermeasures against all likely PRC military threats, through the formulation of an appropriate military doctrine and related operational guidelines for the ROC military and the maintenance of a corresponding force structure and command, control, communications, computers, and intelligence (C4I)/logistics infrastructure.[9]

In the early nineties, when the ROC government formally abolished its long-standing emphasis on retaking the Chinese Mainland, Taiwan's military doctrine shifted from an emphasis on unified offensive-defensive operations (*gong shou yi ti*) to a purely defensive-oriented concept (*shoushi fangyu*) which excludes provocative or preemptive military actions against the Mainland.[10] This purely defensive posture contains two strategic notions: "resolute defense" (*fangwei gushou*) and "effective deterrence" (*youxiao hezu*). The former concept is largely political and defensive, connoting the determination of the Taiwan military to defend all the areas directly under its control without giving up any territory. The latter concept is more active and forward-oriented, connoting the commitment to building and maintaining a military capability sufficient to severely punish any threatening or attacking force and to deny such a force the attainment of its objectives, thereby deterring it from initiating an assault against Taiwan.[11]

The implementation of these strategic concepts presents enormous challenges, because (a) China is a very large potential adversary possessing significant resources, (b) the main island of Taiwan is located less than 100 nautical miles from China, and (c) Taiwan is a long, narrow island offering little opportunity for

---

[8]This long-standing Chinese formula for reunification would supposedly permit Taiwan to preserve its existing social, economic, cultural, and political systems and forms within the structure of an overarching single national sovereignty exercised by a central government on the Mainland.

[9]Much of the following description of Taiwan's defense doctrine and related military policies is excerpted from Michael D. Swaine, *Taiwan's National Security, Defense Policy, and Weapons Procurement Process*, RAND, MR-1128-OSD, Santa Monica, California, 1999, pp. 51–61.

[10]Alexander Chieh-cheng Huang, "Taiwan's View of Military Balance and the Challenge It Presents," in James R. Lilley and Chuck Downs, eds., *Crisis in the Taiwan Strait*, National Defense University Press, Washington D.C., September 1997, pp. 282–283.

[11]Alexander Huang, 1997, pp. 284–285.

maneuver and defense in depth.[12] As a result, the Taiwan military must have the capability to conduct significant offshore operations in the event of a serious threat from China. Taiwan's defense planners thus employ a four-layer defense-in-depth strategy, consisting of (1) a front line that encompasses the defense of ROC territory in close proximity to the Chinese Mainland, including the highly fortified islands of Kinmen and Matsu; (2) the middle line of the Taiwan Strait, which has served for over forty years as an unofficial but mutually understood "boundary" separating PRC and ROC air and naval forces; (3) Taiwan's coastline, which must be successfully defended to ensure the defeat of any invasion force; and (4) the western plain of Taiwan, which must be successfully defended to prevent any invading forces from securing Taiwan's north-south Chongshan Highway and thereby gaining rapid access to the entire island.[13]

To implement this strategy, Taiwan's military forces must be able to succeed in carrying out three key missions, listed in general order of priority: (1) air superiority (*zhikong*) for the ROC Air Force; (2) sea denial (*zhihai*) for the ROC Navy; and (3) anti-landing warfare (*fandenglu*) for the ROC Army.[14] Each of these missions is generally viewed by each service as constituting a relatively separate and distinct task. In other words, Taiwan's defense strategy is not currently based upon the concept of joint warfighting. This is reportedly due in part to the small size of the ROC military, the limited expanse of the battlespaces involved, the limited technical capabilities of Taiwan's weapons systems, and the purely defensive nature of the mission given to each service. It also reflects the severe restrictions on operational capabilities imposed by Taiwan's relatively small defense budget, which does not permit even the most basic, individual mission of each service to be fully implemented.[15] More broadly, the separate warfighting

---

[12]On the third point, Taiwan has a total area of 36,000 square kilometers, measuring only 394 kilometers from north to south, and 144 kilometers from east to west. Its long and narrow shape is not conducive to defense. Moreover, about two-thirds of the island is mountainous, and almost all inhabitants and military bases are concentrated on the plains and undulating hills. The great density of the population also makes it difficult for Taiwan to deploy and move its army in times of war. See Yuan Lin, "The Taiwan Strait is No Longer a Natural Barrier—PLA Strategies for Attacking Taiwan," *Kuang Chiao Ching*, 16 April 1996.

[13]Ibid., pp. 286–288.

[14]The first two missions reportedly enjoy the highest priority, given the importance of air and sea denial capabilities to preventing air or missile attacks, blockades, and invasions and the fact that Beijing is currently stressing the improvement of its air and naval power projection capabilities.

[15]Taiwan's defense budget fluctuates between US$8 billion and US$10 billion, whereas the PRC defense budget is generally estimated by most well-informed analysts as somewhere in the range of US$30 billion–US$35 billion. Moreover, due to the increasing cost of social welfare programs and infrastructure investment, the share of Taiwan's defense budget as a percentage of both total government expenditures and GDP has fallen in recent years. And much of Taiwan's defense budget is taken up by huge personnel costs, which greatly exceed both operational costs and military purchases. In the FY99 defense budget, these three categories of expenditure respectively accounted for 50.5 percent, 19.09 percent, and 30.86 percent. Moreover, arms acquisitions represent only a very small portion of overall military purchases. See Ding and Huang, pp. 2–3.

missions of each military service reflect the larger "stovepiped" nature of the ROC military structure as a whole.[16]

Although the notion of "resolute defense" has usually taken precedence in the above strategic formulation, in recent years military planners and political leaders have placed an increasing emphasis upon the development of a more robust military deterrence, in response to the growing capabilities of the PRC. For most observers, this shift in emphasis implies a focus on the acquisition of a capable air and missile defense system and a significant number of surface and subsurface naval assets, to deal with the threat to Taiwan's security posed by the growing possibility of air or missile displays or attacks, naval harassment or blockades, and amphibious and air-based invasions of territory under ROC control. For some observers, it also implies the acquisition of more offensive weapons systems designed to strike at Mainland Chinese ports, airbases, and missile launchers.

To successfully implement the above military strategies, Taiwan must augment its limited indigenous military systems by obtaining critical weapons, support infrastructure, and military technology and training from the outside. Perhaps even more important, as indicated above, Taipei's political leaders must also strive to ensure that the United States will provide direct military assistance to Taiwan in the event of a serious threat from the Mainland.[17] In support of these objectives, Taiwan's defense policy thus aims at increasing the size and scope of arms acquisitions and technical assistance obtained from the outside and the level and type of professional military interactions with foreign powers, especially the U.S. military. The latter is accomplished through efforts to expand both formal and informal military dialogues with foreign senior military officers and strategists, Taiwan's participation in foreign military education programs, direct contacts between military operators (through training, exchanges, etc.), and, whenever possible, combined unit exercises of various types.

Finally, Taiwan's defense policy also includes efforts to streamline, restructure, and strengthen the organization of the ROC military, in order to ensure more

---

[16]In recent years, however, a greater emphasis has been placed on developing joint operations capabilities. Specifically, efforts to develop joint operations have made some significant headway in the areas of C3I and early warning and reconnaissance, where jointness is becoming increasingly necessary. For further details, see Swaine, 1999.

[17]Officially, the concepts of "resolute defense" and "effective deterrence" suggest that Taiwan must acquire the capability to carry out the above three military missions successfully without outside assistance. In reality, however, ROC defense planners realize that Taiwan is almost certainly incapable of effectively resisting an all-out and prolonged attack from the PRC without help from the United States. Therefore, Taiwan's defense strategy is primarily designed, on the operational level, to hold out and give the U.S. ample time to intervene. In fact, for some Taiwan observers, ensuring prompt U.S. support in the event of a conflict with the Mainland takes precedence over all other security objectives.

effective civilian control over the armed forces, to more effectively integrate defense planning with the larger priorities of the government's national security policies, to eliminate waste, corruption, and inefficiency in military procurement and readiness, and to increase the military's overall combat effectiveness. These goals are to be accomplished largely through the promulgation and implementation of an extensive set of organizational reform laws and military restructuring programs.[18]

Historical Context

The above major features of Taiwan's foreign and defense policies were by no means fully in place when the ROC government retreated to Taiwan in 1949. While some elements of these policies reflect the enduring realities of Taiwan's basic security problem, centered on its long-standing hostile relationship with the PRC regime, others have gradually emerged throughout the sixties, seventies, eighties, and nineties, in response to major changes in Taiwan's external and domestic political, social, economic, and military environments. It is necessary to examine how those policies have evolved over time, in order to gain a better understanding of how they might evolve in the future.

During the fifties and sixties, the ROC government under Chiang Kai-shek enjoyed widespread international recognition as the sole legitimate government of China, largely because of its historical links to the nationalist movement of Dr. Sun Yat-sen that had inherited power from the imperial order in 1912, and because it was then receiving critical support and protection from the United States. The latter largely emerged as a result of the ongoing Sino-American confrontation that had been precipitated by the Korean War. American assistance during this period (and well into the seventies) was expressed in (1) the U.S.-ROC Mutual Security Treaty of 1954, which brought Taiwan into America's larger security strategy in Asia, primarily as a forward base for U.S. forces in the region; and (2) via Washington's critical backing of the ROC government in the United Nations as the sole legitimate government of China and member of the UN Security Council. Although the Nationalist regime had been soundly defeated by the communists in 1947–1948, Chiang persisted during the initial years of his rule on Taiwan in the belief that his government could use the island as a base from which to launch a military counterattack to regain the Mainland, with the support of the United States and the bulk of the international community. During the Chiang Kai-shek era, Taiwan's strategy was thus focused

---

[18]See Swaine 1999, for details.

on "recovering the Mainland by force" (*fangong dalu*), an explicitly "offensive" defense policy dedicated to full-scale operations on the continent. In the meantime, the exiled Nationalist regime on Taiwan continued to function as if it represented the entire Chinese nation and thus maintained a high level of autocratic control over the local Taiwan population. The level of international recognition provided to the Nationalist regime, as well as the continued threat posed by the communists to U.S. interests in Asia, served to justify and permit such controls.[19]

Taiwan's basic foreign and defense policies in the fifties and early sixties thus centered on four core efforts: (1) to oppose and eventually remove the communist regime on the Mainland from power; and, prior to that event, (2) to strengthen the international standing of the Taiwan regime as the sole legitimate government of China; (3) to maintain the essential military and political backing Taipei received from the United States; and (4) to ensure the domestic survival of the minority KMT-centered ROC regime and its system of autocratic rule over the indigenous Taiwanese[20] majority.

In support of these objectives, Chiang Kai-shek's foreign policy rigidly adhered to the notion of "One China" and thus opposed any international or domestic policies or actions that served to advance the idea of "two separate Chinas," "One China, one Taiwan," or "an independent Taiwan republic." During this period, the ROC government would scarcely enter into any relations with any countries that supported communist ideology or had contacts with the PRC regime. Moreover, as indicated above, although Taiwan's defense policy was ostensibly focused on maintaining a defensive capability to protect Taiwan against a communist assault while preparing for a military counterattack to recover the Mainland, in reality, Taiwan's diplomatic and military postures were highly dependent upon and coordinated with the United States. Even though Washington sought to preserve the ROC government's international status and posture, from at least the mid-fifties it consistently prevented the ROC from attacking the Mainland or otherwise provoking the Beijing regime into a military confrontation across the Strait.[21]

---

[19]Hsieh, Chiao Chiao, *Strategy for Survival: The Foreign Policy and External Relations of the Republic of China on Taiwan, 1949–79*, The Sherwood Press, London, 1985, pp. 78–79; Dennis Van Vranken Hickey, "U.S. Policy and Taiwan's Reintegration into the Global Community," *Journal of Northeast Asian Studies*, Vol. 11, Spring 1992, pp. 18–32.

[20]Throughout this study, the term "Taiwanese" refers primarily to citizens of Taiwan whose ancestors over several generations were born on the island. The term "Mainlander" refers to those residents who were born in Mainland China or whose parents were born on the Mainland.

[21]Hsieh, 1985, pp. 280–282, 286–287.

By the late fifties, the continued lack of any U.S. support for an ROC attack on the Mainland, combined with the consolidation of PRC rule, together prompted the ROC government to shift its Mainland recovery program from an all-out offensive military confrontation to a long-term political struggle. Taipei thus substituted the notion of "political counterattack" (*zhengzhi fangong*) for the earlier policy of military counterattack, and the struggle with the Mainland was now termed 70 percent political and only 30 percent military.[22] Over time, the ROC government greatly downplayed any references to retaking the Mainland in favor of building support among Chinese in the PRC for Sun Yat-sen's political doctrine—the Three Principles of the People (*San Min Chu Yi*).[23] Although such a shift implied a partial reorientation of Taiwan's defense policy and a restructuring of its armed forces toward a more defensive posture less centered on the ROC Army, in reality, little change occurred in these areas.[24]

This shift toward a more-defensive political security strategy was followed in the sixties by more notable adjustments in Taiwan's foreign policy, largely as a result of growing concerns over the loss of international support for the ROC government. By this time, China had made some significant headway in its continuous effort to replace the ROC as China's sole legitimate government in the United Nations (UN). Equally important, Taipei also feared that U.S. support for the island might be flagging. These developments produced some subtle policy adjustments. Although the ROC leadership continued to stress the basic policies of anti-communism, Mainland recovery, and the "One China" principle (i.e., Taipei continued to break relations with any state that recognized Beijing), they also sought to generate broader international support (and hopefully reduce the ROC's level of political dependence on the United States), elicit a greater recognition among China's citizens of the superiority of Taiwan's political system over communism, and strengthen the ROC's domestic legitimacy on Taiwan by building the island into a model Chinese province of stability and prosperity and a de facto permanent power base for the ROC.[25]

In the diplomatic arena, the ROC government also embarked in the sixties on a program of foreign aid and agricultural diplomacy toward the Third World (especially the newly independent states in Africa and some nearby Asian states) and even tentatively explored links with the Soviet Union. While ostensibly

---

[22]Hsieh, 1985, pp. 88, 127–128.

[23]Hsieh, 1985, p. 287.

[24]This was partly because the ROC Army enjoyed a clearly predominant position, both bureaucratically and politically, among the three armed services, and because Taiwan's defense posture and force planning remained wedded to the larger strategy and structure of the U.S. military.

[25]Hsieh, 1985, p. 289.

involving efforts to de-emphasize Taiwan's total dependence on the United States, these foreign policy initiatives were primarily aimed at countering China's UN drive and challenging the PRC for diplomatic recognition in Africa. This entire effort was only partly effective, however, and did not stop the overall trend toward greater support for the PRC in the United Nations.[26]

Further, more significant changes in Taiwan's foreign policies occurred in the seventies, in response to a series of major external and internal developments. The Sino-U.S. rapprochement and subsequent ejection of Taipei from the United Nations in the early seventies, followed, in the late seventies, by Washington's formal diplomatic de-recognition of Taiwan and accompanying abrogation of the ROC-U.S. Mutual Security Treaty, along with the advent of China's market-led economic reforms and open door policies together created a dual crisis for the ROC government. Externally, Taipei faced the potential loss of U.S. military and political support,[27] diplomatic isolation, and significant increases in China's international influence and military-economic capabilities.[28] Internally, Taipei's loss of international backing, combined with the fact that the ROC government remained an undemocratic, authoritarian regime, severely weakened Taipei's claim to authority over Mainland China, greatly reduced the likelihood that the ROC would eventually regain its position on the Mainland through political and/or military means, and bolstered the views of those on Taiwan who criticized the ROC government as a despotic, occupying power. Overall, these developments dealt a serious blow to both the security and the international and domestic legitimacy of the ROC government.

Further impetus for change in the ROC government's foreign policy occurred as a result of less direct causes, including the effect of generational change on Taiwan and prolonged economic growth, based on extensive foreign trade and technology transfers. These changes resulted in the gradual development, on the one hand, of a moribund and obsolescent KMT old guard less able to defend the conservative policies of the Chiang Kai-shek regime, and, on the other hand, of a new middle class and a strong business community that argued for greater

---

[26]Hsieh, 1985, pp. 140, 155–158, 171, 182, 290.

[27]By the late seventies, Taipei was also pressured by intense U.S. criticism of Taiwan's unequal trade practices and human rights abuses, as well as its continued enforcement of martial law. Economic friction between Taiwan and the United States peaked in the late 1980s when the U.S.-ROC trade deficit rose tremendously, from US$2.3 billion in 1979 to US$19 billion in 1987. This exceeded even the U.S.-Japan trade imbalance on a per capita basis. Such trade problems finally triggered a comprehensive tariff reduction program. See Richard Bush, "Taiwan's International Role: Implications for U.S. Policy," in Robert G. Sutter and William R. Johnson, eds., *Taiwan in World Affairs*, Westview Press, Boulder, Colorado, 1994, pp. 305–306.

[28]The accelerated growth of the Chinese economy served not only to attract industrial powers to China, but also presented China with the opportunity to improve its military capabilities and thereby potentially increase its ability to coerce Taiwan.

international respect for Taiwan and more expansive contacts with the international economy.[29]

Chiang Kai-shek's son, Chiang Ching-guo,[30] clearly recognized the challenges to Taiwan's survival, prosperity, and domestic unity posed by these developments and implemented a range of significant, albeit limited, domestic and foreign policy initiatives to strengthen the political legitimacy and authority of the ROC government and the security of the island.[31] Internally, Chiang initiated a multifaceted reform program designed to build a stronger political, economic and social base of support for the Nationalist regime. The key elements of this program included government efforts to foster rapid economic development and modernization, involving a relatively equitable distribution of wealth and social-educational benefits; the cessation of gross discrimination in favor of Mainlanders within the ruling KMT party and the KMT-controlled government (including the military);[32] and, beginning in the mid-eighties, a program of gradual political liberalization involving the expansion of local, provincial, and national elections, in order both to select some top decision-makers in government and to serve as indirect referenda on the state of KMT rule.[33] Although the political liberalization movement was partly prompted by American criticism of the Nationalist regime's human rights record and structure of autocratic rule, the most critical motivating factors were the actions of progressive individuals within the KMT and the challenge to the authoritarian system presented by the emerging pro-democracy *"dangwai"* movement of opposition politicians.[34]

---

[29]Michael Yahuda, "The Foreign Relations of Greater China," in David Shambaugh, ed., *Greater China: The Next Superpower?* Oxford University Press, 1995, Oxford, p. 47, and Chyuan-jeng Shiau, "Civil Society and Democratization," in Steve Tsang and Hung-mao Tien, eds., *Democratization in Taiwan: Implications for China,* St. Martin's Press, Inc., New York, 1999, pp. 110–111.

[30]Chiang ruled as ROC premier for several years prior to his father's death in 1975 and as ROC president from 1978 to 1988.

[31]Robert Sutter, "Taiwan's Role in World Affairs: Background, Status, and Prospects," in Robert G. Sutter and William R. Johnson, eds., *Taiwan in World Affairs,* Westview Press, Boulder, Colorado, 1994, pp. 5–6.

[32]By the mid-eighties, more than 70 percent of the KMT's 2.2 million members were native Taiwanese, and decision-making had moved to a generation that had come to political maturity on the island. This new wave of Taiwanization, unlike in the past, was not confined to the lower ranks of the party. See Christopher Hughes, *Taiwan and Chinese Nationalism,* Routledge Press, London, 1997, p. 51.

[33]Sutter, 1994, p. 6. In July 1987, Chiang lifted martial law and removed the existing ban on organizing new political parties, and in December, he announced a plan to reform Taiwan's parliamentary bodies. See Shao-chuan Leng and Cheng-yi Lin, "Political Change on Taiwan: Transition to Democracy?" in David Shambaugh, ed., *Greater China: The Next Superpower?* Oxford University Press, 1995, Oxford, p. 154.

[34]Richard Bush, 1994, p. 286. Opposition politicians expressed a growing popular mood of unfairness and frustration toward the one-party rule of the Mainlander-dominated government that had emerged in the seventies as part of a coherent native Taiwanese identity and in response to growing demands for democracy. Such opposition sentiments were fueled by (1) the authoritarian rule of the ROC government, which prohibited popular elections for all key offices and suppressed

In the area of foreign policy, Premier Chiang in early 1973 launched a strategy of "total diplomacy" (*zhongti waijiao*) that provided the foundation for subsequent efforts at "pragmatic diplomacy" (*wushi waijiao*). "Total diplomacy" called for the mobilization of all available resources, including political, economic, scientific, technological, cultural, and sports exchanges, to maintain or develop substantial links with states that had transferred diplomatic recognition to Beijing. The goal of this pragmatic, opportunistic strategy was to employ every possible means to escape political and diplomatic isolation in the international arena and to utilize Taiwan's international standing to gain political advantage.[35] Under this strategy, Taiwan continued aid to some states that had recognized the PRC, encouraged unofficial contacts with the outside world and sought to participate more extensively in both international governmental and non-governmental organizations. In particular, the economic component of this strategy involved an attempt to enmesh other states in a network of trade, investment, and technological relations so that it would be harmful to their interests for the PRC to attempt to subjugate Taiwan. Finally, and perhaps most significantly, this strategy also sought to retain semiofficial contacts with countries such as Japan, through the exchange of non-governmental representative and trade offices.[36]

In the related area of cross-Strait relations, growing pressure for new initiatives in Taiwan's policy toward the Mainland were answered by allowing a wide variety of indirect contacts. By 1984, Taiwan had accepted economic contacts with China, and some journalists had traveled to Mainland China. An agreement had been reached for Taiwan and the PRC to send teams to the 1984 Olympics, and reports of the drab conditions on the Mainland helped prompt the ROC authorities to break the taboo on visits to PRC. One of the final acts of Chiang Ching-kuo before his death in January 1988 was to authorize visits by Taiwan residents to the Mainland for family reunions. More than a million such visits had been made by 1991.[37]

These changes in the ROC government's approach to foreign relations and cross-Strait relations served to dilute, in practice, the original meaning of the "One China" principle by suggesting the emergence of a de facto "two Chinas"

---

many freedoms and basic human rights; (2) the imposition of an official high culture, exemplified by the exclusive use of Mandarin in public; and (3) the creation of a culturally advantaged Mainlander group vis-à-vis the less advantaged Taiwanese group. See Fiorella Allio, "The Dynamics of the Identity Issue in Taiwan," *China Perspectives*, No. 28, March–April 2000, French Centre for Research on Contemporary China, Hong Kong, p. 66.

[35]Michael Yahuda, "The International Standing of the Republic of China on Taiwan," *The China Quarterly*, No. 148, December 1996, p. 1330; and Hughes, 1997, p. 131.

[36]Hsieh, 1985, pp. 287, 290, 292.

[37]Yahuda, 1995, p. 48; Hughes, 1997, p. 50.

situation in which Taipei coexisted alongside Beijing in the international arena.[38]
Despite such implications, the ROC government continued to adhere formally to
a narrow definition of the "One China" principle, thus widening the gap between
Chinese nationalist claims and political practice. In particular, Chiang Ching-kuo
continued to rule out a political solution with Beijing, rejected any recognition of
Taiwan as a separate state, and continued to insist that the ROC government
obtained its legitimacy from elections held on the Chinese Mainland under a
constitution designed for all of China.[39] Moreover, Chiang's response to PRC
efforts in the early eighties to entice Taiwan into peaceful reunification
negotiations was the "Three Nos" policy: no contacts, no negotiations, and no
compromises with the Mainland.[40]

In the area of defense policy, Washington's de-recognition of Taipei, combined
with the abrogation of the U.S.-ROC Mutual Security Treaty, led to the
withdrawal of U.S. forces from Taiwan and the cessation of substantive contacts
between the American and Taiwan military forces. The Taiwan Relations Act
compensated, to some degree, for these losses by providing a basis for both the
provision by the United States of continued defensive-oriented military
assistance to Taiwan (in the form of arms sales and technology transfers), and the
possible future intervention of the U.S. military in the event of an attack from the
Mainland. However, on balance, Taiwan's military situation had obviously
become far more precarious, presumably requiring the ROC armed forces to
develop a more potent, independent capacity to defend the island. Hence, during
the Chiang Ching-kuo era, a greater emphasis was placed on the acquisition of
defensive armaments, and concerted efforts were undertaken, with some success,
to purchase major weapons systems from the United States and other Western
powers. However, this era did not witness a fundamental conceptual shift in
Taiwan's defense policy. In general, the ROC military continued to emphasize
the need to both defend Taiwan against attack and to prepare, if possible, for an
eventual effort to retake the Mainland. Chiang modified his father's defense
strategy to "converging offense with defense" (*gongshou yiti*), which was not
focused on, but did not rule out, a military offensive against the Mainland. Thus,

---

[38]Hsieh, 1985, p. 293.

[39]Before abolishing the legal foundations for martial law in July 1987, Chiang declared that new
parties would only be legal if they respected the constitution and did not advocate independence.
Also, the Chiang regime maintained a National Security Law that stipulated that freedom of
assembly or association should not violate the constitution or be used to advocate communism or
separatism. See Hughes, 1997, pp. 46, 50–51; and Peter R. Moody, Jr., *Political Change on Taiwan*,
Praeger, New York, 1992, p. 92.

[40]Cal Clark, "The Republic of China's Bid for UN Membership," *American Asian Review*, Vol. 13,
No. 2, Summer 1995, p. 8.

Taiwan's military continued to stress the implementation of unified offensive-defensive operations.[41]

Chiang Ching-kuo's successor, Lee Teng-hui—the first native Taiwan-born citizen to serve as president of the ROC—eventually carried out far more radical changes in the areas of Mainland policy, foreign policy, and domestic reform, while also greatly advancing the basic shift in Taiwan's defense policy toward the construction of a more capable, defensive-oriented military. Lee's actions were presumably motivated by a variety of factors, including (1) the need to co-opt the rising tide of support within Taiwan (and across much of Asia) for democracy and popular sovereignty and thereby establish a more legitimate political base for the ROC government rooted in the values and interests of the majority of the Taiwan populace; (2) the need to improve Taiwan's ability to cope with a stronger, more globally active Mainland Chinese regime by increasing the international, and especially the American, commitment to the security and prosperity of Taiwan; and (3) a desire to establish his personal legacy on Taiwan as the man who led the effort to forge a modern, democratic, and sovereign nation-state largely unencumbered by the beliefs and political structures of conservative Chinese Nationalists associated with the Chiang Kai-shek regime.

These objectives of course were closely interrelated, e.g., increased international (and especially Western) support for Taiwan relied in part on the establishment of an open, democratic, and free trade–based polity and economy worthy of such support, and the ROC government's ability to withstand growing pressure from the Mainland and create the foundations for economic prosperity and social order depended greatly on the success of its efforts to attain genuinely popular support for its policies. Both of these objectives in turn required a major reduction in the influence of Nationalist conservatives on foreign and domestic policies.[42]

In fact, in carrying out these objectives, Lee and his supporters had to contend with powerful political forces on both the right and the left: the former committed to maintaining an increasingly precarious conservative status quo in both cross-Strait and state-society relations, and the latter committed to rapidly creating a fully democratic and independent Republic of Taiwan, an act that

---

[41]The absence of a major shift in Taiwan's defense doctrine at this time probably resulted from the continued influence exerted by conservative Mainlanders within the senior echelons of the civilian and military leadership, as well as Chiang Ching-kuo's desire to maintain some fealty to the ultimate military objective of "retaking the Mainland." One additional factor might have been the military stance of the PRC regime. Following the normalization of relations with Washington, the Chinese government reduced significantly its military deployments along the Taiwan Strait.

[42]Hughes, 1997, p. 53.

would almost certainly prompt a violent response from the Mainland.[43] Lee also had to deal with the consequences of intensifying social and economic ties with the Mainland, precipitated by Chiang Ching-kuo's reforms. These links both strengthened domestic support for deeper and more amicable cross-Strait relations while raising concerns about the security implications of increasing economic dependence on the Mainland.[44]

Lee's response to this complex set of objectives and conditions was fourfold:

- In the area of domestic reform, to create the legal, political, and procedural bases for a government based primarily on democracy and popular sovereignty by the citizens of Taiwan while retaining broad constitutional, historical and cultural links to the Chinese nation that offered the prospect of some type of future association across the Strait.

- In the area of cross-Strait relations, to expand greatly all forms of cultural, economic, social, and (if possible) political contact with the Mainland while avoiding levels of economic/trade dependence and various types of political interaction that might increase Beijing's leverage over Taipei or otherwise compel Taipei to accept unequal or disadvantageous forms of political association.

- In the area of foreign policy, to adopt a highly pragmatic, opportunistic approach to relations with foreign states and international bodies, intended to increase Taiwan's overall support and influence within the international community without provoking a conflict with the Mainland.

- In the area of defense policy, to intensify Taiwan's fundamental shift to a military strategy and accompanying force structure keyed to protecting the existing territory under the jurisdiction of the ROC government from a Mainland attack and to securing greater U.S. defense assistance, while also commencing efforts to seek ROC participation in regional security dialogues and structures, to the extent possible.

In the first area, Lee Teng-hui sought to build popular support, and hence legitimacy, for the KMT, co-opt the views of the rising pro-independence DPP, and at the same time avoid destroying altogether the legitimizing Chinese nationalist beliefs of the KMT's original Mainlander supporters. In other words, he sought to promote popular sovereignty and self-determination and yet

---

[43]Cal Clark, 1995, p. 13; Bush, 1994, pp. 287–288.

[44]For statistics on the rapid expansion of cross-Strait trade and investment ties and the growing synergies between the Taiwan and Mainland economies, see Hughes, 1997, pp. 109, 111, and the more detailed discussion below.

uphold some type of Chinese identity. He accomplished this by stressing economic performance, political liberalization, and eventually democracy, and by fundamentally redefining (i.e., loosening) the meaning of "One China."

To attain the former objectives (economic performance and political liberalization), Lee and KMT government leaders encouraged continued high rates of economic growth through expanded trade, technology, and investment ties with Mainland China and the rest of Asia, especially Southeast Asia.[45] Of even greater importance, Lee also undertook major democratic reforms of all national government bodies. By December 1991, all legislators and National Assembly (NA) members elected on the Mainland over 40 years earlier were retired, and newly elected NA members representing predominantly people from Taiwan undertook to amend the constitution to facilitate further democratic reforms. In late 1992, an election to make the Legislative Yuan predominantly representative of the people of Taiwan took place, and by 1996, the democratic election of a new president of the ROC occurred, under the terms of the revised constitution.[46]

To attain the latter objective (a redefinition of the "One China" concept), Lee asserted the existence of two Chinese states or governments within the framework of a single Chinese nation, each exercising entirely separate jurisdictions and with vastly different political systems and levels of development.[47] ROC citizenship was thus based upon a popular identification with Taiwan alone, not with Chinese territory or Chinese ethnicity (i.e., what had been the traditional Chinese nationalist basis for allegiance to the ROC). Moreover, any links with the Mainland were based solely upon the common history, culture, and language of the two sides, not any notion of a single political sovereignty exercised by a single government. For Lee, reunification, if it were to occur, must therefore take place on the basis of political and economic compatibility between the two sides and with the full concurrence of the citizens of Taiwan. In practical terms, this meant that political reunification would require an acceptance by the Mainland government and people of a variant of the Taiwan example of democratization and free market expansion. In the meantime,

---

[45]However, over time, economic links with the Mainland became a source of growing concern to Lee Teng-hui, as indicated above, and prompted efforts by him to restrict such links and balance them with ties to other Asian states.

[46]Sutter, 1994, p. 6. Also see Hung-mao Tien and Yun-han Chu, "Building Democracy in Taiwan," *The China Quarterly*, No. 148, December 1996, pp. 1157–1170.

[47]Clark, 1995, p. 10; Hughes, 1997, p. 54; Yahuda, 1996, p. 1323. This was a variation of the German formula.

24

Lee insisted that Taipei could only conduct direct negotiations with the Mainland on an equal footing.[48]

This was clearly a "one country, two governments," or "one country, two entities" approach that redefined the meaning of "One China" in the present as a vague entity essentially unrelated to any notion of political sovereignty.[49] Instead, for Lee Teng-hui and his supporters both inside and outside the KMT, "One China" became a non-statist, *Gemeinschaft*-like concept linked to Chinese ethnicity. This notion thus blurred the edges between national identity and statehood and gave Taiwan the flexibility to carve out a new identity and status for itself. Although the existence of something called "One China" could be acknowledged by Lee Teng-hui, this was to be interpreted as an entity other than the nation-state as traditionally understood in international society.[50]

In this manner, the Lee Teng-hui regime gradually shifted its main source of legitimation for the ROC government from the claim that it represented all of China to the performance-based claim that it had brought about economic power and prosperity for Taiwan's citizens, and the claim that it represents the interests and views of the vast majority of Taiwan's population.[51] In addition, this redefinition of the "One China" concept also permitted Lee and his supporters among the public to argue that Taiwan was already a de facto independent state and should be recognized by the international community as the Republic of China on Taiwan (ROCOT).[52]

The elimination of the political connection between Chinese identity and the ROC state allowed the Lee Teng-hui regime to embark on an unprecedented expansion in cross-Strait contacts without implying a movement toward political association.[53] Such increased contacts were deemed essential for a variety of practical reasons: to reduce tensions with Beijing as Lee proceeded to dilute the meaning of "One China" and embark on a more vigorous foreign policy strategy (discussed below); to buy time necessary to develop a viable approach for dealing with Beijing over the long term; and to help build Taiwan's economic power and influence.[54]

---

[48]Yahuda, 1996, p. 1323; Clark 1995, p. 13; Hughes, 1997, p. 54.

[49]Hughes, 1997, p. 89; Sutter, 1994, p. 11, p. 21, footnote 12.

[50]Hughes, 1997, pp. 143–144.

[51]Hughes, 1997, p. 177. Lee began to clarify the ideological implications of this latter view in May 1994 when he began to advocate the doctrine of popular sovereignty by the people of Taiwan, not the people of China. For a further discussion, see Hughes, 1997, pp. 96–98.

[52]Yahuda, 1996, p. 1323.

[53]Hughes, 1997, p. 100.

[54]Sutter, 1994, pp. 8–9.

As an essential prerequisite to further expansion in cross-Strait contacts, in May 1991 Lee Teng-hui formally ended the state of war between the ROC and the PRC, officially dropped Taipei's claim to retake the Mainland by military means, and urged all concerned to accept the reality that, within overall Chinese boundaries, there exist two political entities that exercise jurisdiction over two separate parts of China.[55] In the early nineties, Lee also proposed government-to-government contacts between the two "political entities" in Beijing and Taipei,[56] established three new organs for coordinating Mainland affairs (the National Unification Council, the Mainland Affairs Council, and the "non-governmental" Straits Exchange Foundation), and enunciated specific guidelines for national unification.[57]

The resulting explosion in the number and type of cross-Strait contacts that took place during the Lee Teng-hui era had two notable consequences. On the one hand, it confirmed, for many Taiwan residents, the enormous disparities in living standards and political systems between the two sides and thus served to reinforce the inherently cautious approach that most ROC citizens adopted toward the reunification issue. On the other hand, increasing contacts led to closer economic ties across the Strait, involving a steady outflow of Taiwan capital and a rapidly growing trade relationship. Lee Teng-hui initially encouraged what at first appeared to be a trend toward economic interdependence and provided support for a "westward" policy that stressed economic ties with coastal China, both to allow for a quick pullout if necessary, and to influence China's reforms process. However, the ROC government eventually came to express growing fears of excessive Taiwan dependence and attempted to limit the scope of economic ties with the Mainland. This effort produced significant resistance from major Taiwan businessmen and has therefore led to some backtracking.[58]

In the area of foreign relations, the Lee Teng-hui regime greatly expanded and deepened the existing policy of "total diplomacy," initially labeling the new strategy "flexible diplomacy" (*tanxing waijiao*), and then "pragmatic diplomacy" (*wushi waijiao*). Although similar in its general thrust to the policy of the Chiang Ching-kuo era, this strategy embodied a far more relaxed stance on the

---

[55]Yahuda, 1996, p. 1324.

[56]Clark, 1995, p. 10.

[57]Chong-pin Lin, "Beijing and Taipei: Dialectics in Post-Tiananmen Interactions," in David Shambaugh, ed., *Greater China: The Next Superpower?* Oxford University Press, 1995, Oxford, p. 126; John Fuh-sheng Hsieh, "Chiefs, Staffers, Indians, and Others: How Was Taiwan's Mainland China Policy Made?" in Tun-jen Cheng, Chi Huang, and Samuel S.G. Wu, *Inherited Rivalry: Conflict Across the Taiwan Strait*, Lynne Rienner Publishers, Boulder, Colorado, 1995; Clark, 1995, p. 13.

[58]Hughes, 1997, pp. 112, 114. More on this point below.

sovereignty issue and employed more extensive, more sophisticated, and more unconventional means to advance Taiwan's international influence and to legitimize the ROC government in the international order.[59] The strategy had three major components.

First, in the area of bilateral interstate relations, pragmatic diplomacy completely jettisoned Taipei's past zero-sum diplomatic competition with Beijing and accepted all manner of ties and contacts with foreign governments, from full and formal diplomatic representation (either exclusively or on the basis of some form of "dual recognition" of both the ROC and the PRC), to extremely informal and unofficial contacts and relationships. The former type of contacts began in 1988, shortly after Lee Teng-hui came to power, when Taiwan established formal diplomatic ties with Grenada even though that state continued to enjoy formal ties with Beijing.[60] The latter included efforts at so-called "vacation diplomacy," in which senior ROC political leaders would travel to foreign countries and meet with foreign leaders under the guise of unofficial vacation trips.[61]

As indicated above, this strategy amounted to an explicit rejection of the past "One China" approach to diplomatic relations in favor of a de facto "two Chinas" or "One China, two governments/political entities" approach. Although initially resisted by both conservatives within the KMT and some traditionalists among the professional ranks of the ROC Foreign Ministry, the first ROC Foreign Policy White Paper (published in January 1993) drove home the point that Taipei's pursuit of substantive international relations was based on the "One China, two political entities" principle (i.e., the dual-recognition formula).[62]

In support of such new forms of international contact, the ROC government also strengthened considerably its efforts to court influential political and economic elites within key nations, especially the United States. The ROC government had maintained close personal and professional connections to American businessmen and political decision-makers after the U.S. government broke

---

[59]Samuel S. Kim, "Taiwan and the International System: The Challenge of Legitimation," in Robert G. Sutter and William R. Johnson, eds., *Taiwan in World Affairs*, Westview Press, Boulder, Colorado, 1994, p. 151; Hughes, 1997, pp. 54, 131; Lin, 1995, p. 121; Yahuda, 1996, p. 1330. Also see the appendix on Taiwan's Pragmatic Diplomacy contained in Congressional Research Service (CRS) Report 90-11 F, *Taiwan's Elections: Implications for Taiwan's Development and U.S. Interests*, by Robert Sutter, December 7, 1989.

[60]Hickey, 1992, p. 20. A less extensive form of recognition was termed "reciprocal recognition" (*xianghu chengren*). It included virtually all of the forms of full diplomatic relations but without full recognition; although ambassadors were not exchanged, each state would treat the other in conformity with the principles of international law, especially concerning economic, trade, and cultural contacts. Hughes, 1997, pp. 130–131. Also see Yahuda, 1995, pp. 56–57. Yahuda, 1996, p. 1326.

[61]Dennis Van Vranken Hickey, *Taiwan's Security in the Changing International System*, Lynne Rienner Publishers, Boulder, Colorado, 1997, p. 120.

[62]Kim, 1994, p. 175.

diplomatic relations in 1979. However, under the Lee Teng-hui regime, these links were significantly strengthened and expanded, especially those with members of the U.S. Congress. As a result, during the Lee Teng-hui era, ROC officials would at times use their influence in the Congress to attain specific policy objectives which the ROC government believed were resisted or opposed by the Clinton administration.

Second, Lee Teng-hui's new foreign policy strategy employed Taiwan's growing economic strength and trading ties to increase the incentives of other states and international bodies to support Taiwan politically and economically. Specifically, bilateral, foreign investment, trade, and technology links, as well as offers of ROC economic aid, loans, and technical assistance to individual countries were used to obtain or reinforce diplomatic ties, to gain greater access to regional and global economic bodies, and generally to increase Taiwan's leverage and influence in the international arena. This approach, termed "dollar diplomacy" by some observers, also included efforts to use major economic projects to entice greater contacts with foreign economic officials and to upgrade political and economic relations with states. Such projects included the development of a highly ambitious infrastructure development plan involving foreign bidding, the creation of a Asia-Pacific Regional Operations Center to integrate Taiwan with the region in a variety of areas (sea and air transport, financial services, telecommunications, etc.), and the establishment of an International Economic Cooperation Development Fund to assist friendly countries to develop their economies.[63] Finally, this component of Taiwan's foreign policy strategy also included efforts to avoid excessive economic dependence on the Mainland (noted above) by expanding economic ties with other regions in Asia, especially Southeast Asia. This so-called "southward" policy (*nanxiang zhengce*) began in 1993–1994 and produced a significant amount of Taiwan investment and trade with Southeast Asia, and, as a consequence, some notable expressions of political support for the ROC government in that region.[64]

The third major component of Lee Teng-hui's foreign policy involved a major push to expand Taipei's participation in both international non-governmental organizations (NGOs) and international governmental organizations (IGOs), including the General Agreement of Tariffs and Trade (GATT) and the United Nations. Although this initiative as a whole obviously was undertaken to increase international support for Taiwan, the UN bid in particular was rooted

---

[63]Sutter, 1994, p. 10; Hickey, 1992, pp. 27–28; Hughes, 1997, p. 131; Yahuda, 1995, pp. 56–57; Yahuda, 1996, p. 1332.

[64]Hughes, 1997, p. 133; Yahuda, 1996, p. 1334; Yu-Shan Wu, "Taiwan in 1994," *Asian Survey*, Vol. 35, January 1995, p. 63.

primarily in domestic concerns.[65] Taiwan's movement away from the Chinese nationalist definition of the "One China" concept under the Lee Teng-hui regime, combined with growing pride in the island's economic successes, had increased pressure from the opposition and society in general to do something to raise Taiwan's international status. The DPP in particular, apparently motivated by a desire both to embarrass the KMT for Taiwan's diplomatic isolation and to raise questions about the legitimacy of a Mainlander-dominated government, obtained significant political advantage by calling for a bid to enter the United Nations as the Republic of Taiwan.[66] At first, the ROC government resisted such pressure, citing the "One China" policy and strong support in the UN for the PRC position. As suggested above, many conservative KMT leaders were committed to a "zero-sum" definition of "One China" and hence opposed any effort by the ROC to attempt to participate in the UN as either a "second China" or as a totally separate and independent state. However, in mid-1991, the Legislative Yuan (LY) approved a draft resolution stating that the government should seek to rejoin the UN at an appropriate time as the ROC, and over 60 percent of the public supported the bid for UN membership. These developments, combined with the departure of many key conservatives from the KMT, enabled the Lee Teng-hui government to initiate a bid to enter the UN in spring 1993.[67] More than any other foreign policy decision, this effort was a way of demonstrating that the ROC government was responsive to the people while at the same time serving to neutralize DPP influence and hopefully dampen public support for secession.[68] Moreover, the UN bid allowed the KMT regime to develop a new type of political partnership with the DPP in a first-ever common foreign policy objective.[69]

In the area of defense policy, in the early 1990s the Lee Teng-hui regime finally formally abolished the ROC government's long-standing emphasis on reoccupying the Chinese Mainland and adopted in its place a defensive military strategy ("pure defense," or *shoushi fangyu*) keyed to protecting the territories under ROC control from attack by an increasingly capable Mainland, and to increasing the level of military and political support provided by the United

---

[65]This is not to deny that the bid did not have an important, and obvious, international component. It first emerged in part in 1991 in response to the entrance of the two Koreas into the United Nations. See Kim, 1994, p. 164.

[66]Clark, 1995, pp. 11–12.

[67]In June 1995, the ROC government offered to provide one billion dollars in assistance to developing nations if it was allowed to reenter the United Nations. See Hickey, 1997, p. 122.

[68]Clark, 1995, pp. 11–12; Kim, 1994, pp. 164–165; Hughes, 1997, pp. 140–141; Yahuda, 1995, p. 58.

[69]Hung-mao Tien and Yun-han Chu, "Building Democracy in Taiwan," *The China Quarterly*, No. 148, December 1996, p. 1169.

States. In changing this policy, Lee Teng-hui basically bowed to pressure from the rising opposition Democratic Progressive Party, which sought to rein in the excesses and scandals in military procurement by reducing Taiwan's defense budget. In support of this basic shift, the ROC government also inaugurated a far-reaching set of restructuring programs for the armed forces aimed at simplifying and strengthening the civilian command structure over the military and constructing a smaller, more streamlined, and robust military force capable of responding quickly and powerfully to any type of military attack from the Mainland. Moreover, under Lee Teng-hui, increased efforts were undertaken to acquire more advanced weapons systems from the West, both to augment Taiwan's warfighting capabilities and to strengthen political-military relations with powers such as the United States. As an ancillary to this overall strategy, the ROC government also supported the creation, with ROC involvement, of a comprehensive system of security cooperation across the Asia-Pacific region, and sought to increase contacts with Taiwan's military counterparts in Asia, Europe, and especially the United States. This formal shift in military strategy, and many of its supporting elements, was clearly laid out in Taiwan's first Defense White Paper, published in February 1992, and in subsequent annual White Papers.[70]

During the later years of the Lee Teng-hui regime, and largely in response to improvements in Chinese military capabilities, Taiwan's defense policy and military strategy witnessed three notable developments. First, China's resort to missile "tests" and military exercises in 1995–1996 allowed Lee to advocate a new strategy entitled "resolute defense, effective deterrence" (*fangwei gushou, youxiao hezu*). This concept placed an explicit—albeit secondary—emphasis on deterrence capabilities; such capabilities could theoretically include offensive weapons like surface-to-surface ballistic missiles and air strikes against the Mainland. Tension arising from Lee's "special state-to-state formulation," as well as a concern by the military that "deterrence" should now precede "defense," led to the re-formulation of the strategy as "effective deterrence, resolute defense" (*youxiao hezu, fangwei gushou*). This reordering of priorities was formally enshrined in the ROC 2000 Defense White Paper.[71] For some Taiwan defense planners, this new emphasis on strategic deterrence—in contrast to a more passive defense-centered concept—requires the acquisition of specific offensive capabilities against the Chinese Mainland, such as surface-to-surface ballistic missiles, mine-laying submarines, and aircraft capable of conducting extensive strikes against ground targets on the Mainland. Such a reformulation is thus perceived by many as a

---

[70]Kim, 1994, p. 174; Stephen S.F. Chen, "The Republic of China on Taiwan: Building Bridges for Peace and Prosperity," in Tai, 1999, p. 31. Also see Swaine 1999 for further details.

[71]*2000 National Defense Report*, ROC Ministry of National Defense, Taipei, Taiwan, July 2000.

more assertive or even confrontational posture than in the past. However, considerable debate exists within ROC defense circles over whether Taiwan should acquire or develop more-potent offensive capabilities, and to what specific end.[72]

Second, partly in response to the limitations presented by an offensive-based deterrent and the potential opportunities afforded by technological advances in the West, other ROC military strategists and political leaders became increasingly focused on developing and/or acquiring more potent active defensive measures. These especially include various types of BMD systems,[73] along with more capable naval air defense, early warning, and C3I systems.[74] However, BMD systems in particular also raise a host of major problems and concerns, not only regarding their feasibility, cost, and complexity of operation, but also their potentially adverse impact on the Chinese threat.[75]

The changes in Taiwan's foreign and defense policies that occurred during the Lee Teng-hui era culminated in the overall features summarized at the beginning of this chapter. In the foreign policy realm, Taiwan's efforts to expand its international presence, raise its international profile, and strengthen the level of support it receives from the international community through the policy of pragmatic diplomacy achieved some notable successes. For example, a wide variety of states significantly increased their level of economic, social, and cultural contact with and support for Taiwan during the nineties (establishing what the ROC government refers to as "substantive relations"), and many small states were enticed to establish formal diplomatic relations with Taipei. Taiwan also greatly increased its presence in international non-governmental organizations, ranging from scientific and technological to sports and cultural bodies. Of greatest significance, however, was Taiwan's development during the Lee Teng-hui era of more substantive political relations with the United States. This has included increases in the status of U.S. officials visiting Taiwan, a steady expansion in the number of congressional visits, sister state agreements, and state trade offices established, growing social and cultural bonds, and the passage of

---

[72]See subsequent chapters for further details on this debate.

[73]Such a system is designed to intercept ballistic missiles at both low and high altitudes, and would thus constitute a much more sophisticated and capable anti-missile system than the existing so-called PAC 2+ variant of the Patriot system already supplied to Taiwan. The latter is essentially a limited-range, "point" defense system primarily designed to intercept enemy aircraft.

[74]See, for example, "Taiwan Experts Want Bigger Anti-Missile Budget," Reuters, August 16, 2000.

[75]See Thomas J. Christensen, "Theater Missile Defense and Taiwan's Security," Orbis, Winter 2000, pp. 79–90. The perspectives and concerns of the Taiwan leadership regarding ballistic missile defense are discussed in greater detail below.

both binding and non-binding congressional legislation designed to express support for Taiwan.[76]

In the defense policy realm, the ROC government's shift to a purely defensive military stance, and its attempts to increase the size and scope of arms acquisitions, technical assistance, and military know-how obtained from the outside have all enjoyed significant success. Most notable have been increases in the quality and quantity of weapons sold to Taipei by the United States and other Western powers, and in the level and type of contacts between the Taiwan and American militaries.[77]

These successes were not simply the consequence of Taiwan's policies during the Lee Teng-hui era, however. They became possible largely because of three basic sets of political, strategic, and economic considerations. First, the precipitous decline in China's prestige that occurred as a result of the Tiananmen incident of 1989 and the subsequent increase in human rights violations by the PRC regime during the nineties contrasted enormously with the simultaneous emergence of a multiparty democracy on Taiwan, thus generating more political (and in some cases military) support for Taiwan in the international community. Second, the reduction in China's strategic importance to the United States and other Western governments due to the collapse of the Soviet Union opened the door to improved relations with Taiwan and the West. At the same time, increases in Chinese military deployments along the Taiwan Strait in the nineties further encouraged U.S. military support for Taiwan and facilitated initial efforts to upgrade and improve the ROC military. Third, the continued, enormous expansion of Taiwan's aggregate economic power and the scope and level of its trade, investment, and technology links with the outside world significantly increased the attraction, leverage, and basic presence of the ROC government in the international community. In fact, Taiwan's financial and economic clout was arguably the main driving force behind the above-mentioned successes attained in the diplomatic arena.[78]

Despite such successes, however, Lee Teng-hui's policy of pragmatic diplomacy had little effect in reversing Taiwan's diplomatic isolation. Those states that established diplomatic relations with the island are "either geographically small, economically less developed, or both," and "are concentrated in Central and

---

[76]Hughes, 1997, pp. 135–138; Hickey, 1992, pp. 20–22; Hickey, 1997, pp. 116–125.

[77]Sutter, 1994, p. 18; Bush, 1994, p. 290. For a detailed summary of the major weapons system sold to Taiwan by the United States during the Lee Teng-hui era (and earlier), see T.Y. Wang, "United States Arms Sales Policy Toward Taiwan: A Review of Two Decades of Implementation," in Tai, 1999, pp. 122–129.

[78]Hickey, 1992, pp. 25–26, 28.

South America, the Caribbean, Africa, the Pacific Islands, and the Holy See."[79] Moreover, most of these states established relations with the ROC government to obtain lucrative economic benefits, and many of them have switched recognition back and forth between Taipei and Beijing in order to maximize such benefits. Some larger states have also reduced their level of contact with Taiwan in response to Chinese protests and pressures; France is perhaps the foremost example of such a state. And all major countries placed clear limits on the size and scope of their contacts with Taipei, in order to maintain good relations with the PRC, for both geopolitical and economic reasons. Also, Taiwan's participation in international organizations was almost always limited to a form of representation short of sovereign statehood. For example, Beijing has successfully prevented Taiwan from joining GATT and its successor, the WTO, before China can enter and in any capacity that implies statehood. Perhaps most notably, Taiwan's repeated efforts during the Lee Teng-hui era to enter the United Nations were easily rebuffed; the case has never been placed on the UN agenda.[80]

In the defense policy realm, the effort to restructure and streamline Taiwan's military and to improve relationships of command and control between the civilian and military leadership achieved few concrete results during the Lee Teng-hui era. This was in part because of the extensive time required to develop and pass appropriate legislation, and because of major personal and bureaucratic concerns and disputes within the ROC military and between the ROC military, the executive leadership, and the legislature. In addition, the basic effort to improve the overall fighting capabilities of Taiwan's armed forces met with mixed results at best, for a wide variety of reasons, such as budgetary and manpower limitations, technical constraints, leadership preferences, the hesitancy of most foreign suppliers to provide specific weapons systems, limitations on the development of adequate skill levels as a result of Taiwan's short, two-year conscription system, and the lack of a professional, non-commissioned officer (NCO) corps.[81]

Finally, despite significant increases in cross-Strait contacts, including an explosion in trade and investment ties, Lee Teng-hui's foreign and defense policies have clearly contributed to a significant increase in tensions between Taipei and Beijing during the nineties. China was greatly alarmed and angered by Lee's efforts to dilute the basic meaning of "One China" and espouse in its

---

[79]Hughes, 1997, p. 130.

[80]Hughes, 1997, pp. 139–142.

[81]Swaine 1999, p. 60.

place a concept of "One China, two political entities," as the core of a strategy designed to establish popular sovereignty as the primary legitimizing principle of the ROC government, to build public support for the KMT by adopting many of the policy positions of the DPP, to use Taiwan's financial resources to raise the island's international status, to increase contacts with Western and Japanese officials, and to significantly accelerate efforts to obtain more advanced arms from the United States and other major powers and increase military contacts with them. Beijing's leaders were also shocked by various remarks made by Lee Teng-hui during his term as president on the subject of Chinese nationalism, Japan, sovereignty, and PRC-ROC relations.[82]

Lee clearly attempted to soften Beijing's response to such actions and statements by coordinating their occurrence with the launching of significant overtures to or contacts with the Mainland.[83] For example, he strongly supported the initiation of a non-governmental yet authoritative cross-strait dialogue, which led to a series of interactions between the ROC Straits Exchange Foundation (SEF) and the PRC Association for Relations Across the Taiwan Strait (ARATS). The most significant of these contacts consisted of a historic public meeting between the heads of the two organizations—ARATS's Wang Daohan and SEF's Koo Chen-fu—held in Singapore in April 1993 following a preparatory meeting in 1992. During the 1992 meeting, the two sides reportedly reached an understanding that each side of the Taiwan Strait could adhere to its own interpretation of the meaning of "One China." This understanding paved the way for the subsequent Singapore meeting by allowing both sides to set aside their differences over the political or sovereignty implications of "One China" and to focus instead on strengthening two-way cultural, trade, and economic exchanges. Wang and Koo thus signed four agreements on bilateral exchanges during their Singapore talks and established an institutionalized channel of communications for the settlement of disputes arising from cross-Strait activities.

However, Lee's overtures to the Mainland ultimately produced mixed results at best. For example, increased Taiwan-China business ties and contacts had the reverse effect of serving to constrain Lee's behavior, as many Taiwan businessmen with huge stakes in cross-Strait commerce urged the ROC

---

[82]Hughes, 1997, p. 89. In the above-mentioned 1994 interview with a Japanese journalist, Lee stated that the implications of "China" are not clear, that sovereignty is a dangerous concept, and that he had a close affinity to Japan. He also described the notion that Taiwan is a part of the PRC as a "strange dream." In July 1999, Lee also remarked in an interview with a German journalist that relations between the PRC and Taiwan must be understood as "special state-to-state" relations, thus setting off a furor with Beijing.

[83]Hughes, 1997, pp. 124–125.

government to avoid provoking the Mainland.[84] Moreover, at the political level, the Wang-Koo contacts eventually stalled as a result of intensified frictions between the two sides in 1995–1996 and 1999 (the former centered on the U.S.-China confrontation precipitated by Lee Teng-hui's visit to the United States in June 1995 and the latter deriving from Lee Teng-hui's public characterization of Mainland-Taiwan relations as a "special state-to-state relationship—more on these points below). Indeed, Lee's overtures certainly did not prevent Beijing from exerting pressure on Taiwan through political and military means, including armed displays and thinly veiled threats during the 1995–1996 Taiwan Strait crisis.[85] Although Beijing says it remains committed to a peaceful resolution of the Taiwan issue as a first priority, there are indications that the PRC leadership is becoming increasingly pessimistic toward the evolving situation, and is certainly undertaking efforts to increase the ability of its military forces to deter movement by the ROC government toward more explicit forms of independence and to resolve the situation in Beijing's favor if a use of force becomes necessary.[86]

Taiwan's 2000 presidential campaign marked a new stage in the public discussion of Taiwan's defense strategy, as each of the three candidates put forward comprehensive proposals that seemed to revise or reject past defense concepts. KMT candidate Lien Chan advocated the notion of "active defense, effective deterrence" (*jiji fangyu, youxiao hezu*), calling for a more explicit emphasis on tactical offense measures such as long-range surface-to-surface missiles.[87] Independent (and later People First Party leader) James Soong agreed with Lien's move towards "active defense," but explicitly opposed the idea of missiles, believing that Taiwan did not have the requisite technological capability and fearing that the move would undermine the island's international support. Emphasizing Taiwan's ability to preemptively deter invasion and extend its depth of defense by pushing the defense line westward, Soong put forward the concept of "active deterrence and effective defense" (*jiji hezu, youxiao fangwei*), and advocated enhancement of early warning, crisis management, and the

---

[84]Hughes, 1997, pp. 114–116.

[85]At the same time, Taiwan businessmen also told Beijing that military pressure hurt China's economy by damaging Taiwan business and investment confidence. This apparently led Beijing to be more reassuring during the Strait crisis. Hughes, 1997, p. 117.

[86]For a further discussion of Beijing's changing calculus toward Taiwan, see below, and Michael D. Swaine, "Chinese Decision-Making Toward Taiwan, 1978–98," in David M. Lampton, ed., *The Making of Chinese Foreign and National Security Policy in the Era of Reform: 1978–2000*, Stanford University Press, Stanford, California, 2001.

[87]See Presidential Office News Release, 8 December 1999, and Lien Chan, *Lien Chan's Policy Views* [Lien Chan de zhuzhuang], The Commonwealth Publishing, Taipei, 2000, p. 12.

capability to either preempt or retaliate against the Mainland with land attack cruise missiles and submarines.[88]

DPP candidate Chen Shui-bian introduced perhaps the most forward-leaning policy, calling for a change from "pure defense" to "offensive defense" (*gongshi fangyu*). This formulation explicitly abandoned the "old concept of attrition warfare" in favor of an emphasis on "paralyzing the enemy's warfighting capability" and "keeping the war away from Taiwan as far as possible."[89] A key principle of Chen's platform is "decisive offshore campaign" or "decision campaign beyond boundaries" (*jingwai juezhan*), calling for Taiwan's military to "actively build up capability that can strike against the source of the threat" using enhanced naval and air forces as well as joint operations and information warfare.[90] These various defense concepts are bundled together under the rubric "preemptive defense," which is marked by the maintenance of a strong deterrence posture during peacetime through the development of information warfare and long-range precision strike capabilities. During wartime, however, preemptive measures are necessary, including the suppression of Chinese C4I systems, anti-submarine warfare, and anti-blockade warfare.[91]

As Alexander Huang has argued,[92] there were some important commonalities among these three campaign platforms. First, the logic of their defense policies appears to be more offensive in nature, especially when compared with earlier eras. They all agreed that Taiwan should actively seek the initiative in military operations against the PRC. In a war with the Mainland, preemptive and/or retaliatory measures are not excluded from their policy options. There is consensus that the primary area of operations in a cross-Strait military conflict should be as far away from Taiwan as possible. Finally, they all emphasized naval and air power as well as information warfare. One critical discontinuity among the proposed strategies was the debate over the utility of medium- and long-range surface-to-surface missiles, which were seen by Lien as a key feature of enhanced deterrence but were rejected by Soong and Chen as too provocative.

---

[88]James Soong and Chao-hsiung Chang, *Soong-Chang National Policy Guideline for the 21st Century* [Soong-Chang kuashiji guojia zhengce gangling], The Soong-Chang Presidential Campaign Headquarters, Taipei, 2000, pp. 43–47.

[89]Chen Shui-bian, *New Century, New Future: Chen Shui-bian's Blueprint for the Nation – Volume I: National Security* [Xinshiji xinchulu: Chen Shui-bian guojia lantu – diyice: guojia anquan], Chen Shui-bian Presidential Campaign Headquarters, Taipei, 1999, pp. 50–51.

[90]Ibid, pp. 50–51.

[91]Ibid, pp. 74–75.

[92]Alexander Huang, "Homeland Defense with Taiwanese Characteristics: On President Chen Shui-bian's New Defense Concept," draft paper prepared for the 11th Annual PLA Conference, U.S. Army War College, Carlisle Barracks, PA, December 1–3, 2000.

The unexpected election of DPP leader Chen Shui-bian to the post of ROC president in March 2000 has raised the prospect of further significant changes in the ROC's foreign and defense policies, and perhaps greater tensions with the Mainland. On the broadest level, however, there appears to be significant continuity between the policies of the Lee Teng-hui regime and those of the Chen Shui-bian government. This in part reflects the fact that the KMT under Lee and the DPP both moved toward the center of the political spectrum during the mid-nineties, and thus converged on many policy issues. Such continuity also to some extent derives from the fact that the Chen government has been unable to undertake any significant policy initiatives since it took power, largely because the KMT-dominated Legislative Yuan has repeatedly sought to obstruct and paralyze the government.

At the level of grand strategy, Chen's government clearly sides with the political opposition in its desire to maintain Taiwan's high rate of economic advance, strengthen the democratic process, raise Taiwan's international stature and influence, and improve Taiwan's security through the development of a stronger military and the establishment of closer relations with democratic industrial powers. According to ROC Foreign Minister Tien Hung-mao, the strategic goals of Taiwan's current policy are "to maintain the sovereignty and dignity of the ROC, to ensure its survival and development, and to guarantee the safety and benefits its citizens deserve from the international community."[93] On a parallel economic track, also in a manner similar to the Lee Teng-hui government, the Chen regime seeks to diversify Taiwan's international economic contacts and resist excessive dependence on the Mainland.[94] At the same time, Taipei remains committed to regional and multilateral economic groups, such as the Asia-Pacific Economic Cooperation forum (APEC) and the Asian Development Bank (ADB). Taiwan hopes that the process of WTO accession, which highlights the strengths of the island's economy and subtly reminds the global markets of their interdependence, will further legitimate Taiwan's international position.

In the defense arena, the Chen government also supports many of the policies initiated by the Lee regime, including the restructuring, downsizing, and streamlining of the military, efforts to place the armed forces more clearly under the jurisdiction of the civilian government, a greater emphasis on strengthening the rapid-reaction and air and naval defense capacities of the military, continued

---

[93]"The Current State of ROC Diplomacy, An Abridgment of the Report by Foreign Minister Dr. Hung-mao Tien to the Foreign and Overseas Chinese Affairs Committee of the Legislative Yuan, June 5, 2000." See http://www.mofa.gov.tw/emofa/emofa8965.htm.

[94]However, as discussed in greater detail below, this policy line has been significantly undermined in recent months as a result of Taiwan's economic decline and the increasing pull exerted by the robust PRC economy.

strong support for ballistic missile defense, and efforts to diversify the sources of military procurement and strengthen the indigenous production of weapons.[95]

However, several significant differences in foreign and defense policy are also evident. First, official positions taken by the DPP leadership in the past as well as more recent statements made by government officials indicate that the Chen regime has dropped so-called dollar diplomacy, i.e., the effort to use Taiwan's economic power to purchase international access. This strategy is apparently regarded by Chen and the DPP as relatively ineffective and excessively costly, especially given the recent downturn in the Taiwan economy.

Second, Chen's inauguration remarks and subsequent statements made by senior ROC officials suggest that his government is attempting to place a strong emphasis on promoting democracy and increasing Taiwan's involvement in non-governmental and human rights organizations and regimes. The hope is that participation in such NGOs will allow Taiwan to play the role of a "sincere and active participant" in the international order and to replace the mistaken impression of being a "trouble maker."[96] While arguably less provocative than direct and immediate efforts at achieving international recognition of Taiwan as a sovereign, independent state,[97] such an emphasis is apparently intended to increase further international respect for Taiwan among liberal democracies and thereby hopefully strengthen the commitment of the United States, Japan, and other Asian and Western democratic states to the security and prosperity of the island. This was of course a major objective of the Lee Teng-hui regime, but was largely pursued by Lee via domestic democratization and reform.

Third, the Chen government apparently intends to accelerate and intensify the effort, begun during the Lee Teng-hui era, to eliminate the influence of the KMT over the military. Little progress has occurred in this area to date, largely because Chen Shui-bian has had to focus his energies on more urgent issues, such as dealing with the opposition-dominated LY and a declining economy. However, such an effort—once undertaken—will likely produce considerable friction, given the long history of KMT dominance of the officer corps, deriving from the original purpose of the ROC military as a "party-army" serving the interests of the Chinese Nationalist Movement.

---

[95]Interviews, Taipei, May–June 2000. Current ROC policies in many of these areas are discussed in greater detail below.

[96]"The Current State of ROC Diplomacy: An Abridgment of the Report by Foreign Minister Dr. Hung-mao Tien to the Foreign and Overseas Chinese Affairs Committee, Legislative Yuan, 5 June 2000."

[97]Taiwan is continuing its long-standing effort to become a full member of United Nations. However, this goal is clearly relegated to the long term.

Finally, the ascension of the DPP's Chen to the presidency has also resulted in certain modifications of Taiwan's BMD strategy. For example, the Chen government seems highly focused on protecting Taiwan's civilian and military facilities from the first waves of Chinese missile strikes, mainly as preparation for expected counterstrikes by Taiwan. In August 2001, Minister of Defense Wu Shih-wen outlined the logic for the Chen government's renewed concern about civil defense, arguing that effective dispersion and evacuation would limit the damage from missile attacks. However, if a missile were to strike Taiwan, Wu admitted that panic might ensue, even if the material destructiveness was limited. Therefore, the people's will to resist will be a key factor.[98] "BMD is a political issue."[99] Equally important, Chen Shui-bian has reportedly stated that Taiwan should establish a joint ballistic missile defense system with the United States and Japan.[100] To our knowledge, such a proposal was not publicly advocated by the Lee Teng-hui government.

Perhaps the most significant shift in the orientation of the Chen Shui-bian government thus far has occurred in an area of indirect, albeit critical, importance to foreign and defense policies, i.e., re cross-Strait relations and the "One China" issue. Since taking office, Chen has stated repeatedly what have become known as the "Five Nos": no declaration of independence; no change in the name of the nation (Republic of China); no insertion in the ROC constitution of Lee Teng-hui's so-called "state-to-state" concept; no national referendum to determine the level of popular support for an independent Taiwan; and no abolition of the National Unification Council or the Guidelines for National Unification.[101] At the same time, after some initial resistance, Chen now supports the establishment of direct links with the Mainland in air and sea transport, postal and telecommunications (the so-called Three Links—*san tong*)[102] and has indicated his willingness to travel to China for a summit meeting without any preconditions beyond the need for both sides to interact as two equal entities.

---

[98]Fang Wen-hung, "DefMin Wu Shih-wen Says Taiwan to Continue To Try To Obtain Early Warning System," Central News Agency, 31 August 2000.

[99]Huang Ching-lung, Kuo Chung-lun, Hsia Chen, Lu Chao-lung, and Wu Chung-tao, "Defense Minister Wu Shih-wen Says: The Nationalist Forces Now All Know that President Chen Will Not Stand for Taiwan Independence," *Zhongguo shibao*, 2 July 2000.

[100]Brian Hsu, "Military Says US National Missile Defense An Option," *Taipei Times*, July 18, 2001.

[101]Harvey Sicherman, "Taiwan's New President: One If and Five Nos," Foreign Policy Research Institute, June 2, 2000.

[102]Chen's increased support for direct links occurred in part as a result of growing pressure from Taiwan's business community. The influential chairman of the powerful Formosa Plastic Group, Wang Yung-ching, urged the Chen government to adopt a more open attitude toward economic contacts with the Mainland. He also reportedly pressed Chen to reduce political uncertainties between the two sides by explicitly endorsing the alleged 1992 cross-Strait agreement in support of the notion of One China with separate definitions. "Tycoons Urge Chen to Pen Cross-Strait Links," Central News Agency, Taipei, November 26, 2000.

These actions constitute a rejection of Lee Teng-hui's more cautious approach to government-to-government contacts with the Mainland, an implicit repudiation of Lee's above-mentioned "two-state" concept, and an apparent promise to maintain the status quo, which, in the Unification Guidelines, still declares Taiwan's objective to be unification, that is, "One China."[103]

However, in contrast to the Lee Teng-hui regime, Chen Shui-bian has not explicitly endorsed the Unification Guidelines and has refused to unambiguously support the notion that Taiwan might one day reunify with the Mainland, or even that the ROC government has its own understanding of "One China." He has not clearly affirmed his support for the implied definition of that concept found in the ROC constitution.[104] Instead, he has at most agreed merely to discuss the notion of a "future One China" with Mainland authorities and supported the convening of a multiparty task force to forge a national consensus on cross-Strait relations. His government has also denied that any understanding was reached with Beijing during the famous 1992 Wang-Koo talks regarding the "One China" concept, in contrast to the view of participants in the talks such as former Mainland Affairs Council Vice Chairman Kao Koong-lian.[105] In the meanwhile, Chen emphasizes the need to further advance the concept of a "New Taiwan Identity" distinct from the Chinese identity. Finally, as a form of deterrence against the PRC regime, Chen has stated repeatedly that the ROC government would abrogate the above "Five Nos" and declare independence immediately if the Mainland were to attack Taiwan.

The resulting uncertainties created by the basic contrast between the conception of "One China" implied or contained in the ROC constitution and Unification Guidelines and the evasive stance of the new Chen regime presents serious implications for the future of Taiwan's foreign and defense policies. Chen has attempted to allay some of the concerns that have emerged in China and elsewhere as a result of these uncertainties by asserting—in line with the recommendations of a cross-Strait task force convened in late 2000—that his government's approach to the "One China" issue will remain consistent with the ROC constitution. Moreover, in his subsequent New Year's Eve address of December 2000, Chen also identified "political integration" with the Mainland as one possible goal. While reassuring to some observers, these statements have not, however, fundamentally altered the intense suspicion with which the Chinese

---

[103]Sicherman, 2000.

[104]The ROC constitution implies the concept of "One China" as denoting a single political entity by encompassing the Republic of China's claim of sovereignty over both Taiwan and the Mainland.

[105]"Taiwan Won't Offer More On 'One China,'" Reuters, July 19, 2000; "No 1992 Consensus, MAC Chief Says," China Post, October 20, 2000.

government regards the Chen Shui-bian government. Although Beijing has thus far adopted a "wait-and-see" stance toward the policies and actions of the Chen regime, many outside observers believe that the Chinese leadership has become more pessimistic about the prospects for an eventual peaceful resolution of the Taiwan issue. Such observers argue that, absent a renewed cross-Strait political dialogue leading to a new modus vivendi regarding the status of Taiwan, the chances of an eventual armed conflict will increase over time.

Conclusions

The ROC's foreign and defense policies have evolved greatly since the Nationalist Chinese movement under Chiang Kai-shek moved the seat of government to the island of Taiwan in 1949. In an ongoing effort to strengthen the internal legitimacy, international appeal, and military security of the ROC government, consecutive ROC leaders have:

- Progressively loosened the connection between national identity and statehood through the creation of a government based on popular sovereignty rather than ethnic Chinese nationalism.

- Continuously tested the existing limits on the territory's international status by adopting highly pragmatic and creative approaches to expanding Taiwan's international political and diplomatic presence, while balancing cross-Strait economic ties with attempts to integrate Taiwan more fully into the global economy.

- Sought to strengthen Taiwan's security from attack or coercion by acquiring or developing the weapons and support systems of a more efficient, modern military, and by developing closer military ties with the United States through arms sales and defense dialogues.

In the foreign policy realm, these developments ultimately amount to a claim that Taiwan ought to be represented internationally and unambiguously supported by all democratic states because its political and economic achievements entitle it to such representation and support, as a "partner nation" of the West in Asia.[106] This burgeoning appeal constitutes one of the most serious reasons why the PRC regime is increasingly pessimistic about the prospects for a peaceful resolution of the Taiwan issue.[107] Whether and in what

---

[106]Hughes, 1997, pp. 143–144.

[107]The other major reason for Beijing's pessimism is the belief that an increase in Sino-American rivalry resulting from China's continued economic and military development will prompt greater

manner the ROC government is able to capitalize on its appeal as a democratic and prosperous entity and gain greater support from Western states and Japan constitutes the central issue in Taipei's future foreign policy. In the defense policy realm, the above developments have led to growing support within Taiwan for the acquisition of weapons and support systems that could both stimulate further changes in the cross-Strait military balance and redefine the nature of the ROC-U.S. defense relationship in ways that greatly antagonize the PRC.

To better understand the future evolution of these critical aspects of Taiwan's foreign and defense policies, one must examine the following: (1) the forces of domestic change on Taiwan, including the influence exerted by the changing features of Taiwan's decision-making structure and process; (2) the influence of Chinese policy and behavior; and (3) the role played by the United States and other major powers. Chapters 3, 4, and 5 will examine these critical factors in greater detail.

U.S. support for a policy designed to permanently detach Taiwan from the Mainland, for basic geostrategic reasons.

3. The Influence of Domestic Politics and the Decision-Making Process

Four interrelated aspects of Taiwan's domestic environment exert a decisive influence on foreign and defense policies:

- *The Political Process.* The structural dynamics of a rapidly changing, competitive multiparty system marked by increasing numbers of political actors, intense political struggles, contending policy views, and a weak commitment to the norms of the democratic process.

- *Senior Elite Composition and Outlook.* The changing makeup and values of political and military leaders in response to the forces of democratization, institutional evolution, generational change, and economic development.

- *Societal Views.* The growing influence on the polity of public opinion and interest groups, especially concerning critical issues such as state identity, cross-Strait relations, national security, and specific foreign and defense policies.

- *The Decision-Making Apparatus.* The structural dynamics of an increasingly complex and in some ways uncoordinated pattern of decision-making concerning national security, foreign, and defense policies.

This chapter discusses the major features of each of these four areas as they have evolved in recent years and their general policy implications. The chapter concludes with an overall assessment of the present and likely future influence exerted by Taiwan's domestic environment on foreign and defense policies, especially regarding pragmatic diplomacy and ballistic missile defense.

The Political Process

As indicated in the previous chapter, the democratization process on Taiwan has produced major changes in the ROC political system. These changes hold significant implications for the content and direction of ROC policies in general and for foreign and defense policies in particular.

During the fifties, sixties, seventies, and most of the eighties, the ROC political system was dominated by a single political party—the KMT—and the views and activities of a single paramount leader—first, Chiang Kai-shek and then his son Chiang Ching-kuo. The KMT was for most of this period a Leninist-type party organization. Hence, the party and its predominantly Mainland Chinese leadership controlled the major activities of all key government agencies and supervised a network of cadres charged with carrying out its policies. The KMT controlled all major spheres of political and social life, and all key decisions, government appointments, and policies were decided through the party's organizational procedures. Party membership was especially high in the civil service, farmers' groups, and the ROC military. In particular, a strong KMT political commissar system was constructed by Chiang Ching-kuo within the armed forces. This ensured party control of the military and greatly reduced the possibility of coups. The KMT also played a key role in various socialization functions, co-opted significant local elites, monopolized the media and educational systems, and generally sought to mobilize the population behind the regime and to propagate the ROC government's policies and ideology. At times, however, the KMT regime also relied on brute force to ensure obedience, suppress resistance and prevent the emergence of genuine opposition political movements.[1]

This single-party power structure—labeled by some observers as a kind of developmental authoritarian dictatorship—provided a mechanism for rule by the minority of Mainland Chinese who had fled to Taiwan in the late forties. Although the KMT expanded its membership over the years to include a clear majority of native Taiwanese, few of these individuals reached high office until the later years of the Chiang Ching-kuo era. Moreover, despite extensive Taiwanization, the party remained under the ultimate control of Mainlanders and hence the regime reflected the interests of this minority segment of the population throughout most of this period.

Within the KMT leadership, ultimate power was exercised by the party chairman and discipline at lower levels was enforced through observance of the Leninist principle of democratic centralism.[2] Chiang Kai-shek held the post of KMT chairman from 1949 until 1975, and Chiang Ching-kuo held the post from 1975 until 1988, when Lee Teng-hui—a native Taiwanese and a technocrat—became chairman. Prior to 1988, the KMT-led ROC regime was a highly personalistic

---

[1]This paragraph is based on Keith Maguire, *The Rise of Modern Taiwan*, Ashgate Publishing, Hampshire, England, 1998, pp. 32–33. Also see Tien Hung-mao, *The Great Transition: Political and Social Change in the Republic of China*, Hoover Institution, Stanford, 1989; and Thomas B. Gold, "Domestic Roots of Taiwan's Influence in World Affairs," in Robert G. Summer and William R. Johnson, eds., *Taiwan in World Affairs*, Westview Press, Boulder, Colorado, 1994, p. 197.

[2]This principle permitted scope for considerable internal party debate over key issues. But once the debate had concluded and a decision was made, the party and its members were bound by the policy.

political system. Both Chiang Kai-shek and Chiang Ching-kuo (but especially the former) ruled through personal prestige and by balancing various internal KMT party factions and ROC government institutions. Hence, although the political system was not entirely monolithic, Chiang Kai-shek ensured ultimate control by deliberately providing the only link between the many contending parts of the KMT regime. The extensive diffusion of power and overlapping of party and state functions also served to strengthen the power of the paramount leader.[3]

Beginning in the mid-eighties under Chiang Ching-kuo, and especially under Lee Teng-hui, Taiwan's political system gradually evolved toward a representative democracy. This process was marked by (1) a gradual increase in open political competition, leading to the creation of a competitive multiparty system; (2) the emergence of the National Assembly and Legislative Yuan into fully representative parliamentary bodies entirely elected by the ROC population; (3) the removal of restrictions on freedom of the press and of information and on the evolution of independent civil-interest groups; (4) a steady reduction in the influence exerted by the KMT over the government, the military, and the media and the accompanying gradual Taiwanization of the power structure; (5) concerted efforts to mobilize Taiwan society in support of the regime through the expansion of local elections; and (6) the overall increasing importance of public opinion to decision-making and leadership interactions.[4]

As briefly discussed in the previous chapter, the mainstream KMT under Lee Teng-hui sought to maintain its legitimacy and control while guiding and encouraging a process of democratization and constitutional reform. Lee initially maneuvered against both die-hard conservative factions within the KMT, who clung to the original nationalist beliefs of the Chiang Kai-shek era, and radical proponents of Taiwan democratization and independence, primarily represented by the DPP. He sought to build legitimacy for the KMT by simultaneously co-opting the views of the rising DPP and weakening the influence exercised by conservative Chinese nationalists while avoiding repudiating the beliefs of the KMT's original Mainlander supporters.[5] In this effort, Lee faced a dilemma: On

---

[3]Peter R. Moody, Jr., *Political Change on Taiwan*, Praeger, New York, 1992, pp. 19–25.

[4]Most of these points are adapted from Jürgen Domes, "Electoral and Party Politics in Democratization," in Steve Tsang and Hung-mao Tien, eds., *Democratization in Taiwan: Implications for China*, St. Martin's Press, Inc., New York, 1999, p. 49. For a useful overview of the democratization movement in Taiwan, also see Samuel S. Kim, "Taiwan and the International System: The Challenge of Legitimation," in Robert G. Sutter and William R. Johnson, eds., *Taiwan in World Affairs*, Westview Press, Boulder, Colorado, 1994, pp. 170–175. We are also indebted to Shelley Rigger for bringing to our attention the efforts undertaken by the KMT government in the eighties to promote local elections and in general to mobilize Taiwanese in support of the ROC regime, as part of an overall pattern of "mobilizational authoritarianism."

[5]As KMT-sponsored democratization proceeded in the late eighties and early nineties, the DPP emphasis switched from stressing democratization to advocating a somewhat more ambiguous "self-

one hand, a continuation of the past policy based on a rigid understanding of the "One China" concept would have prevented the expansion of cross-Strait ties, possibly alienated much of the population, and dragged the ROC into a self-imposed diplomatic isolation. On the other hand, rejecting the "One China" concept outright would have probably split the KMT and possibly set off a civil war. In other words, Lee was forced to maneuver between the apparent goals of independence and reunification, keeping the KMT right wing, the PRC, and the DPP off-balance. He ". . . chose to square the circle of promoting independence and upholding a Chinese identity by suggesting that there should be two states within the framework of one Chinese nation."[6]

Over time, the dynamics of the struggle over power and policy produced an array of political parties and internal party groupings representing both contending personalities and different approaches to basic issues such as Taiwan's national identity, relations with Mainland China, aspects of foreign and defense policy, and domestic reform. The KMT initially split into two parties: the majority, mainstream KMT under Lee Teng-hui, which championed continued democratization and a highly diluted "One China" concept, and the minority New Party (NP), dominated largely by second-generation Mainlander Chinese nationalists who were unhappy both with corruption in the KMT and with what they viewed as the "Taiwanization" of KMT ideology and leadership.[7] Subsequently, the mainstream KMT split yet again, largely on the basis of a political and personal dispute between Lee Teng-hui and James Soong Chu-yu, the highly popular former governor of Taiwan. Soong had strongly resisted Lee's efforts to eliminate the provincial governorship post—as part of the latter's general effort to end the political expressions of Taiwan's status as a part of present-day China—and also did not accept Lee's decision to support the relatively unpopular former ROC Premier Lien Chan as his successor for the presidency. When Soong announced in late 1999 that he would compete with Lien Chan in the March 2000 presidential election, he was ejected from the KMT and eventually established the New Taiwan People's Party, which was subsequently renamed the People's First Party (PFP).

---

determination," which many read as a codeword for independence. The conservative, anti-mainstream KMT, in contrast, stressed the necessity to maintain the constitutional order and hinted that the ROC military might not defend Taiwan if an independent republic were proclaimed. Each side accused the other of treason, i.e., the conservatives accused the DPP of betraying the bedrock beliefs of the ROC regime and the DPP accused the KMT of selling out to Beijing. See Cal Clark, "The Republic of China's Bid for UN Membership," *American Asian Review*, Vol. 13, No. 2, Summer 1995, pp. 12–14.

[6]Michael Yahuda, "The International Standing of the Republic of China on Taiwan," in *The China Quarterly*, No. 148, December 1996, p. 1333.

[7]The Chinese New Party was formed in August 1993. Its policy positions are discussed below.

More recently, the humiliating defeat of Lien Chan in the March 2000 election has produced a further, even more important division of the KMT: between pro–Lee Teng-hui and pro–Lien Chan groups. Lien Chan's supporters blamed Lee for Lien's loss in the March 2000 election and distanced themselves from the former president, especially after he was forced to resign as head of the party. Lee Teng-hui in turn became increasingly critical of Lien and the KMT leadership, including the efforts of the KMT-led LY to obstruct and undermine the activities of the Chen Shui-bian government. Lee's increasing sympathy for the Chen government and especially his open support for a newly formed rival to the KMT—the Taiwan Solidarity Union (TSU)[8]—led the KMT to expel him from the party in September 2001. This development has further weakened the KMT.

The original DPP has also fragmented over time, largely as a result of internal differences over the issue of Taiwan independence. The majority of the DPP membership eventually adopted a more moderate and diverse policy stance keyed to democratization, social and political reform, and a reduced emphasis on independence (discussed further below). In protest, a minority of more radical, pro-independence members left the party to form the Taiwan Independence (or National Construction) Party in December 1996.[9] Hence, both minority parties— the New Party and the Taiwan Independence Party—emerged largely due to dissatisfaction over the more moderate stances on self-determination and independence adopted by the mainstream of the KMT and DPP in their efforts to build or consolidate public support and amass political power.[10]

In addition to this overall fragmentation of the political spectrum, Taiwan's major political parties—the KMT and DPP—have become subject to a variety of specific internal and external pressures and divisions that significantly influence political and policy behavior.

In the case of the KMT, the internal defection from the mainstream KMT that eventually resulted in the People's First Party began as an internal dispute between Lee Teng-hui and James Soong, as indicated above. This division still resonates within the KMT today (more on this point below). Moreover, the departure of Lee Teng-hui from the KMT has led many observers to conclude that a new, more popular political figure must replace Lien Chan if the party has any chance of regaining power. One possible candidate is the popular KMT

---

[8]This new political party—formed in August 2001—includes many former KMT members and regards Lee Teng-hui as its spiritual mentor.

[9]Other, smaller political parties have also emerged in the process of democratization and political maneuver, but they exert little influence over the distribution of power in the system.

[10]I-chou Liu, "The Development of the Opposition," in Steve Tsang and Hung-mao Tien, eds., *Democratization in Taiwan: Implications for China*, St. Martin's Press, Inc., New York, 1999, pp. 72–73.

mayor of Taipei, Ma Ying-jeou. As Minister of Justice in the early nineties, Ma moved forcefully against criminal elements in Taiwan society and has consistently taken a strong stand against party corruption. He has also distanced himself from corrupt elements associated with Lien Chan and the more pro-independence leanings of some of Lee Teng-hui's followers, and is an advocate of deeper political reform, including a review of Taiwan's electoral system. Hence, Ma to some degree represents the forces for greater domestic reform and greater restraint on the independence issue within the KMT. However, Ma's popularity is largely limited to Taipei, and he reportedly angered many KMT members during the 2000 presidential election when he appeared to support the anti–Lien Chan, anti–Lee Teng-hui demonstrators who gathered around KMT headquarters at that time.[11]

Opposition to any further movement toward independence has arguably grown significantly within the KMT since the departure of Lee Teng-hui from the party. Conservative or cautious party members largely oppose what they view as further efforts by the KMT to establish the political, legal, and conceptual foundations for Taiwan's permanent separation from the Mainland. Some party members, perhaps including leaders such as Ma Ying-jeou, apparently oppose the actions taken by Lee Teng-hui near the end of his rule to advance Taiwan's independent status, such as the promulgation in July 1999 of the "two states" concept.[12] It is unclear to what extent Lien Chan currently supports this concept. Lien's views on cross-Strait issues and foreign and defense policy have been very close to those of Lee Teng-hui, since Lien served as the latter's foreign affairs minister, premier, and vice president. However, he has been more explicit than Lee in voicing support for eventual reunification, under conditions of common democracy, freedom, and prosperity. And Lien has been less vocal than Lee about alternatives to unification.[13] Lee Teng-hui's ejection from the KMT has resulted in the further repudiation of many of Lee's views by pro–Lien Chan KMT officials.

The KMT is also significantly influenced by the political realities of a corrupted power base. During the authoritarian era, the party co-opted local political factions to control the limited electoral process in place at the local level. These KMT-dominated factions relied heavily on institutionalized vote-buying mechanisms to secure electoral support, using funds obtained through local

---

[11]We are indebted to Shelley Rigger for this observation.

[12]In an interview with a German journalist given on July 9, 1999, Lee stated that the relationships between the ROC and the PRC was a "special state-to-state relationship." This provoked a strong reaction from Beijing, as well as from some non-Chinese observers, who declared that such a remark was tantamount to the explicit repudiation of the notion of "One China."

[13]We are indebted to Shelley Rigger for this point.

governments' procurement and regulatory authority, as well as through land speculation. During the eighties, as opposition candidates received greater public support and the effectiveness of vote-buying declined, many local factions recruited criminal elements to protect their electoral bases and demanded significant pay-offs from the KMT leadership in return for their support. The party also became increasingly dependent upon support from the growing business community and privileged business operations that generate many millions of dollars a year in dividends. As a result, the former institutional insulation that had existed between the party-state leadership and the business sector has disappeared, and major scandals of corruption, bid-rigging, and shady financial deals involving KMT politicians, government officials, and business magnates have become commonplace. With the expansion of electoral competition, this overall pattern of corruption has been transmitted into national representative bodies. The Legislative Yuan has become an arena of bargaining between groups that act as surrogates for local factions and business interests, and many LY members now have links with criminal elements.[14]

The KMT's increased reliance on what is known as "money politics" or "black gold" has presented it with a major dilemma: If it undertakes major efforts to end the KMT's corrupt relations with local factions, open up the internal decision-making system, and liquidates its corporate holdings, it will likely garner notable public support; however, such efforts could also significantly weaken its political base.[15] This issue has led to divisions within the KMT over the pace and scope of the internal reform process. Lee Teng-hui's mainstream faction, which began from a weaker power base within the party-state apparatus than the conservative Mainlander faction, relied extensively on the business community, local factions, and criminal elements. Hence, both Lien Chan's supporters and former Lee Teng-hui supporters—especially the gangster-politicians among them—are undoubtedly less enthusiastic about carrying out major structural reforms in the future than emergent pro-reform leaders such as Ma Ying-jeou.

For the KMT, these internal factors are complicated by external pressures from those above-mentioned former KMT members or groups that split from the party during the Lee Teng-hui era, for both ideological and political reasons. The defection of conservatives to form the Chinese New Party was the main cause for

---

[14]Tien Hung-mao and Yun-han Chu, "Building Democracy in Taiwan," *The China Quarterly*, No. 148, December 1996, p. 1150. Also see Yun-han Chu, "The Challenges of Democratic Consolidation," in Steve Tsang and Hung-mao Tien, eds., *Democratization in Taiwan: Implications for China*," St. Martin's Press, Inc., New York, 1999, pp. 152–153, 155; Yun-han Chu, "Taiwan's Unique Challenges," *Journal of Democracy*, Vol. 7, No. 3, 1996, pp. 69–82; and Hughes, pp. 86–88.

[15]Julian Baum, "Under My Thumb," *Far Eastern Economic Review*, Vol. 161, February 26, 1998, p. 26.

the loss of voter support for the KMT in the December 1995 Legislative Yuan and March 1996 National Assembly elections.[16] The New Party developed a significant following in the early nineties by championing both reconciliation with the Mainland and, equally important, clean government.[17] By the mid-nineties, it constituted roughly 14 percent of the electorate. About half of its support came from traditional KMT strongholds (Mainlander families, public-sector employees, and military veterans). But it had also developed significant support among the young and emerging educated middle class in the urban areas, as well as among many women, suggesting that it represented many elements of the new, united Taiwan.[18] Although the New Party's fortunes have declined significantly in recent years as a result of internal divisions and continued public skepticism toward its unificationist orientation,[19] it continues to exert some political leverage in the LY, competes with the DPP and KMT among independent voters, and thus represents a potential coalition partner for the KMT under some circumstances. Hence, the KMT cannot ignore its views and influence. This has become especially true since the DPP won the presidency in March 2000.

The People's First Party represents a more significant source of pressure on the KMT, albeit one that might prove to be short-lived. It enjoys considerable—and likely growing—influence largely due to the popularity of its leader and founder, James Soong. Despite being a Mainlander and having served as a senior party operative for the KMT in the eighties and during most of the nineties, Soong managed to develop enormous public and local factional support as provincial governor. He speaks the local Taiwanese dialect, has traveled widely around the island, attempts to understand and represent the views and desires of local communities, and used his office to develop a clientelist base among local KMT leaders. He also expresses a pragmatic view toward relations with the Mainland that appears to resonate with many ROC citizens.[20] He favors efforts to reduce

---

[16]Hung-mao Tien and Yun-han Chu, "Building Democracy in Taiwan," *The China Quarterly*, No. 148, December 1996, p. 1159.

[17]The New Party does not favor quick reunification, but is more conciliatory than the KMT toward relations with the Mainland. Unlike the mainstream KMT and the DPP, it supports the rapid establishment of direct links across the Strait and favors the "one country, several seats" (*yiguo, duoxi*) concept of United Nations representation. It also supports the negotiation of a confederate entity, followed by a federation embracing the two Chinese states. See Jean-Pierre Cabestan, "Taiwan's Mainland Policy: Normalization, Yes; Reunification, Later," *The China Quarterly*, No. 148, December 1996 pp. 1274–1275.

[18]Steven M. Goldstein, *Taiwan Faces the Twenty-First Century: Continuing the 'Miracle,'* The Foreign Policy Association, Headline Series, No. 312, June 1997, p. 65.

[19]According to Goldstein (p. 65), the New Party is united ". . . simply around the issue of opposition to what the KMT government has become under Lee Teng-hui."

[20]At the same time, a significant number of Taiwan citizens apparently regard Soong as above all a political opportunist, willing to modify his policy stance for personal power. They point to the

tensions with the PRC, including cross-Strait negotiations, a thirty-year non-aggression agreement, an all-party conference to build a national consensus on how to improve relations with the PRC, and a lessening of inflammatory rhetoric on both sides.[21] The PFP under Soong does not have the power base and contacts of the KMT, however.[22] It is composed primarily of former KMT and CNP members who supported Soong's presidential bid. Thus, the PFP will likely lose influence or disappear altogether if Soong's popularity declines or he leaves the political stage. Moreover, the coalition that backs him contains highly contradictory elements, such as groups strongly opposed to corruption (e.g., many urban intellectuals) as well as corrupt local officials. However, over at least the short term, the PFP represents a significant political force in Taiwan politics, especially given the demoralized state of the KMT following its humiliating defeat in the March 2000 presidential election and the general unpopularity of KMT head Lien Chan.

The newly formed Taiwan Solidarity Union arguably constitutes an even more serious source of potential pressure on the KMT than the PFP, especially if it emerges as a vehicle for the establishment of a Lee Teng-hui–Chen Shui-bian anti-KMT coalition. The TSU has introduced 39 candidates for the December 2001 legislative elections and espouses a political platform that largely reflects the views of Lee Teng-hui. This includes a stress on the "special ethnic relationship" between China and Taiwan, the pursuit of "constructive engagement" between the two sides that is peaceful, equal, and mutually beneficial, and a close identification, in domestic, foreign, and defense matters, with the interests of Taiwan as an independent political entity.[23]

Thus, although KMT legislators continue to hold by far the most seats in the Legislative Yuan, the party runs the risk of becoming even more divided, pressured, and out of step with public sentiment on many issues, and could lose badly in future elections. Overall, the KMT must thus work with both the NP and the PFP to shore up its declining influence, and yet not abandon the political center to the DPP or a DPP-TSU coalition. In this effort, the KMT must eventually confront more squarely the above-mentioned dilemma posed by its continued reliance on money politics, and generally reflect more effectively the increasingly

---

fact that Soong had been an extremely loyal supporter of Lee Teng-hui—and increased his power as a result—prior to the falling out between the two leaders.

[21]For example, Soong is opposed to the provocative "Two States" theory espoused by Lee Teng-hui in July 1999.

[22]Moreover, Soong likely lost support as a result of the abolition of the Provincial Assembly. That body was arguably Soong's strongest institutional base.

[23]See "New Taiwan Solidarity Union gets big-name support," Taiwan Government Information Office, at http://publish.gio.gov.tw/FCJ/past/01082423.html.

sophisticated middle class values of the populace.[24] It will probably also be forced to reassess its obstructionist stance toward the Chen Shui-bian government, which is viewed by significant numbers of Taiwan's citizens as excessively disruptive.

The DPP also confronts a range of internal and external pressures and divisions. The party has been characterized by factional rifts since its formation in the late eighties. The departure from the DPP of radical pro-independence elements to establish the Taiwan Nation Building Party in October 1996 did not end—or even appreciably reduce—the DPP's internal divisions. Many factions still exist within the DPP today, including the Justice Alliance, the Progressive Alliance, New Era, New Energy, the Welfare State Alliance, and the New Tide Faction. In general, factional members are primarily organized on the basis of personal associations, not policy views. However, differences do exist over critical issues. Some members are increasingly moderate on the critical issue of independence: although certainly sympathetic to the pro-independence movement, many do not want to press the issue in ways that threaten stability across the Strait. Such sentiments in part reflect the interests of strong business elements, especially groups involved in trade with the Mainland. In contrast, groups such as the New Tide faction generally support the independence movement (indeed, some more radical members of the New Tide faction remain very assertive on the issue of independence), are less influenced by business interests, and are more concerned with corruption and social reform issues.[25]

The overall moderation of the mainstream DPP (discussed below) and a trend toward the greater institutionalization of party factions have combined to reduce the intensity of factional strife in recent years. However, a number of high-ranking party leaders continue to openly advocate independence for Taiwan, sometimes using rather provocative language. This has become a more significant problem ever since Chen Shui-bian was elected president, by a very slim plurality of votes, in the March 2000 election. Holding a relatively weak mandate and facing a legislature dominated by largely anti-DPP forces, Chen has been forced to move further and further toward the moderate center of Taiwan politics and thereby risk antagonizing the more radical elements of the DPP. Moreover, the DPP increasingly faces its own internal difficulties with the "money politics" phenomenon described above. Although Chen's presidential

---

[24]Robert Sutter, "Taiwan's Role in World Affairs: Background, Status, and Prospects," in Robert G. Sutter and William R. Johnson, eds., *Taiwan in World Affairs*, Westview Press, Boulder, Colorado, 1994, p. 15.

[25]John Fuh-sheng Hsieh, "Chiefs, Staffers, Indians, and Others: How Was Taiwan's Mainland China Policy Made?" in Tun-jen Cheng, Chi Huang, and Samuel S.G. Wu, *Inherited Rivalry: Conflict Across the Taiwan Strait*, Lynne Rienner Publishers, Boulder, Colorado, 1995, pp. 144–145.

victory has led to a rapid growth in the DPP's membership, many of its new members are opportunists and individuals associated with corrupt personal political machines operating at the local level.[26]

The DPP's internal challenges are compounded by the external difficulties it faces in the effort to consolidate its political and social base and become Taiwan's majority party. The DPP originally built significant public support by championing democracy, independence, and the Taiwanization of the political process, thus at first providing a stark counterpoint to the undemocratic, conservative, pro-Chinese, KMT-dominated power structure. However, by the mid-nineties, the DPP's appeal to democratic ideals and a separate Taiwan identity had exhausted much of its electoral utility in the face of Lee Teng-hui's successful effort to co-opt many of its pro-democracy positions and to Taiwanize much of the KMT leadership, and after the unexpected rejection by the public of the DPP's radical independence platform during the 1991 National Assembly elections. The DPP realized at that time that it might lock itself into a position of permanent opposition by continuing to emphasize the creation of an independent Taiwan republic; such a position was viewed as excessively dangerous by the largely pragmatic Taiwan electorate and especially by stability-minded business elites and the growing middle class (more on these groups below).[27] Even the DPP's drive for Taiwan to enter the United Nations lost steam when Lee Teng-hui decided to co-opt the UN membership campaign in 1993. Over time, DPP and mainstream KMT views in a variety of areas—including domestic reform, Mainland policy and foreign policy—became increasingly convergent.[28] Such DPP moderation led to the formation of the explicitly pro-independence Taiwan Nation Building Party (*Jianguo Dang*) mentioned above. However, this party has garnered little support among the Taiwan electorate.

Thus, in order to maintain its public support, the DPP has focused less on national identity and independence in recent years and more on those domestic issues that the KMT has been less willing and able to address, such as social welfare, the environment, and corruption.[29] However, the DPP has thus far generally failed to appropriate such basic social issues and translate them into a

---

[26]We are indebted to Shelley Rigger for this observation.

[27]Hung-mao Tien and Yun-han Chu, "Building Democracy in Taiwan," *The China Quarterly*, No. 148, December 1996, pp. 1148–1149. The DPP introduced a "welfare state" platform in the 1992 LY campaign.

[28]For example, the DPP endorsed Lee Teng-hui's effort to resist pressure for lifting the ban on direct air and sea links with the PRC. See Hung-mao Tien and Yun-han Chu, "Building Democracy in Taiwan," *The China Quarterly*, No. 148, December 1996, p. 1148. Also see Moody, pp. 164–165. More on this point in the next section.

[29]Hughes, p. 86.

stable and growing base of support.[30] This is partly because these issues have also been strongly championed by minority parties such as the PFP, as well as by individual KMT members such as Ma Ying-jeou. The party has also been unable to shake voter suspicion that it has an excessively provocative stance on the independence issue, and that its leaders do not possess enough experience and knowledge to rule Taiwan. The notion that the DPP lacks sufficient competence to govern Taiwan has arguably been strengthened as a consequence of the many political problems that have plagued the Chen Shui-bian presidency. As a result of all the above factors, the DPP is rarely able to garner more than 30 percent of the vote in national elections and continues to hold a relatively small number of seats in the LY. However, the pro–Lee Teng-hui Taiwan Solidarity Union might provide critical political support and governmental experience to the DPP as a partner in a future DPP-TSU coalition.

A final feature of Taiwan's evolving political system that merits consideration is its lack of maturity as a democratic, constitutional order with well-defined and commonly observed rules of the game. As Chu Yun-han asserts, the above political parties, factions, and individual leaders contend with one another in a near free-for-all environment marked by ". . . a lack of fairness and transparency in the election process, politicians' non-compliance with the democratic process, lack of protection for opposition parties' rights to participate in government, the administrative bias of the state machinery, the bias of the state-owned media, and the lack of autonomy in the private sector and the quality of candidates."[31] Such features derive from a basic lack of trust, in which every major political player works to actively undermine each perceived opponent and thus avoids seeking a basis for political cooperation. This "zero-sum" approach to politics perceives all major aspects of the political system, including constitutional principles, as bargaining chips in the power struggle. The immature features of Taiwan's political system also reflect the continued influence exerted by KMT control mechanisms over the state apparatus, despite the fact that the KMT is now only one of several political parties and no longer directs the executive branch of government.

This focus on partisan political advantage, combined with the persistence of KMT influence over the state, has contributed not only to the creation of an acutely contentious and frequently unethical political process, but also to the emergence of an unstable constitutional order with uncertain lines of authority between key governmental players. In the mid-nineties, intense political

---

[30]Moody, p. 165.

[31]Chu Yun-han, "Consolidating Taiwan's Democracy," *Taipei Times*, May 20, 2000.

struggles between the parties influenced the process of constitutional revision undertaken by Lee Teng-hui. This process led to basic changes in the balance of power between the executive and legislative branches of government, from a parliamentary-style system to a French-style semipresidential system in which a popularly elected president shares executive power with an appointed premier. Under this system, the president has the authority to appoint the premier and the cabinet without the formal approval of the legislature. Yet the views of the premier and the cabinet are expected to reflect the preferences of a majority of lawmakers. When this is not the case, the LY can propose a no-confidence vote against the premier. Under such a circumstance, the president can dismiss the legislature and force re-elections. However, unlike the French system, the president cannot dissolve the legislature in the absence of a no-confidence vote by the legislature. Hence, under this hybrid system, the president exercises considerable power when he is from the same party as the majority party in the legislature. But the system can also produce deadlocks or unpredictable consequences when the majority party in the LY is different from the president's party (i.e., in a situation of "cohabitation"), or when no party holds a majority, or when the president appoints a premier and a cabinet without consulting the legislature. Such a deadlock in fact emerged following the presidential election of March 2000, which resulted in a DPP president and a legislature dominated by the KMT.[32] Hence, as Chu Yun-han argues, the president can exercise the power of appointment of the premier at his free will only when his party enjoys the majority control of the LY or it is too fragmented to act against the president. In the end, the LY has gained the most out of the realignment of power.[33]

Finally, we should add that, under Chen Shui-bian, the power of the president has resided more completely in the institution, whereas the power of past presidents Chiang Kai-shek and Chiang Ching-kuo derived primarily from their positions as head of the KMT party apparatus and their personal relationships with key party and bureaucratic leaders. This is another reason why the Chen presidency is so weak compared to its predecessors.[34]

---

[32]Yun-han Chu, "The Challenges of Democratic Consolidation," in Steve Tsang and Hung-mao Tien, eds., *Democratization in Taiwan: Implications for China,*" St. Martin's Press, Inc., New York, 1999, p. 151; Stephanie Low, "Scholars say Constitution at Heart of Political Crisis," *Taipei Times,* November 27, 2000.

[33]Yun-han Chu, p. 164.

[34]We are indebted to Shelley Rigger for this point.

Senior Elite Composition and Outlook

The combination of democratization, institutional evolution, generational change, and economic development has brought about a basic transformation in the composition, outlook, and background of Taiwan's political and military leadership, posing major implications for foreign and defense policies.

This basic transformation began in the seventies, largely in response to the government's need to strengthen legitimacy through accelerated economic development and the establishment of closer contacts with the native Taiwan populace. At that time, Chiang Ching-kuo initiated an effort to raise the overall educational level of KMT members, expand local elections, promote the notion of the Republic of China to ordinary Taiwan citizens, and in the process enrolled larger numbers of native Taiwanese and intellectuals into the middle and lower ranks of the party.[35] By 1974, Taiwanese constituted a majority of the KMT, and they comprised over 55 percent of the party in 1976. Among new recruits, the share of Taiwanese was over 75 percent.[36] This transformation gradually expanded upwards, during the Lee Teng-hui era, to include the most senior levels of the KMT political elite. Li Cheng and Lynn White highlight the dramatic decrease in average age, increases in educational level, and rise in the percentage of native Taiwanese in the ROC cabinet and KMT Central Standing Committee (CSC) in the eighties.[37] However, this development has thus far not extended in a major way into the leadership of the ROC armed forces, which is still dominated by Mainlanders or individuals from Mainlander families. Over time, younger, better educated, more pragmatic and specialized civilian leaders and bureaucrats who were more oriented toward the local affairs of Taiwan and the requirements for economic and social development largely replaced the traditional Mainlander elite of ideologues, party professionals, and military men.[38] A large number of these leaders held advanced college degrees—many from the United States—in the natural sciences, engineering, and especially the social sciences, humanities, and the law, and few had any meaningful experience in the armed forces.[39] This development gave the KMT "... the resources it needed to shift its main efforts from its original revolutionary goals (that is, retaking the Mainland) to running

---

[35]Li Cheng and Lynn White, "Elite Transformation and Modern Change in Mainland China and Taiwan: Empirical Data and the Theory of Technocracy," *The China Quarterly*, Number 121, March 1990, p. 7; Dickson, pp. 114–115.

[36]Dickson, p. 127.

[37]Li Cheng and Lynn White, 1990, p. 9.

[38]Gold, p. 188; Dickson, pp. 114–115.

[39]Moody, p. 107.

local elections and developing Taiwan's economy."[40] As a whole, the largest occupational groups in the KMT remain government and party officials and workers, while the number of soldiers in the party has declined significantly since the early seventies, indicating a trend away from military objectives.[41]

Equally important to the above developments, as a result of deepening democratization and the retirement of aging KMT conservatives in the late eighties and early nineties, party leaders at all levels gradually became representative politicians whose power derived from the support of the voters, not the party organization.[42] This development led to the introduction of a wide variety of individuals into leadership posts, not only in the KMT, but also among the newly formed opposition parties and of course within the Legislative Yuan. Members of the emergent Taiwan middle class, professionals from various walks of life, and successful businessmen ran for office in all parties. As a result of this development, the internal composition of the political parties has mattered less than their share of the popular vote, their basic record and policy platform, and the views and connections of individual candidates. At the same time, it should be noted that some party leaders—especially within the KMT—continue to emphasize traditional personalized relationships and patterns of rule and to resist the emergence of new leaders more attuned to popular sentiment.

Several general conclusions relevant to ROC foreign and defense policies can be drawn from these basic changes in the Taiwan political elite.

First, geographical origins have become much less relevant as an indicator of party policies and general political outlook, at least between the two major political parties. Overall, the strategies of representatives and parties are increasingly linked to public opinion and elections and less concerned with party traditions and ideology.[43] Second, the general inclusion of more Taiwan-born descendants of native Taiwanese families among these parties suggests increasing support among the political elite as a whole for the development of a separate Taiwan identity. Third, the expansion among party ranks of both intellectuals and technocrats on the one hand and public-oriented politicians on the other hand arguably increases the possibility of tensions not only among politicians with differing political and policy agendas, but also between

---

[40]Dickson, p. 125. In the economic sphere, the inclusion of young intellectuals into the KMT coincided with and reinforced a shift in the KMT's economic strategy, toward export-oriented industrialization.

[41]Dickson, pp. 128–129.

[42]Dickson, p. 115.

[43]Dickson, pp. 116, 129.

politicians and professional career bureaucrats.[44] Fourth, the growing gap between civilian, native Taiwanese politicians and Mainlander-oriented military officers creates strong mutual suspicions, as discussed in greater detail below.

The above basic transformation in Taiwan's political elite, along with the broader impact of rapid economic development, democratization, and the growing threat from the Mainland, has created certain common basic values and policy outlooks among the vast majority of Taiwan's new leadership.[45] In general, the majority of Taiwan's elite desire to maintain Taiwan's high rate of economic advance, to strengthen the democratic process, to raise Taiwan's international stature and influence, and to improve Taiwan's security through the development of a stronger military and the establishment of closer relations with democratic industrial powers. These attitudes are largely reflected in the views of Taiwan's public, as indicated below.

In the specific areas of foreign policy and defense policy, the bulk of Taiwan's political elite apparently agree on a wide range of basic principles and policy positions, reflecting the overall pragmatism and growing moderation of Taiwan's dominant political center.

In the foreign policy arena, these principles include the following:

- Widespread agreement that ROC foreign policy should uphold Taiwan's basic existence as a sovereign, independent state. Hence, all political parties—except possibly the New Party—believe that Taiwan should enjoy full membership in the United Nations as a sovereign state, and should generally strive to expand its overall level of political and diplomatic presence as a sovereign state in the international arena, including participation in as many international organizations as possible.

- Broad acceptance of the notion that foreign policy and foreign relations should include a wide variety of activities and interactions, both formal and informal, governmental and non-governmental, and should not focus exclusively or even primarily on the advancement of Taiwan's formal diplomatic status. This notion was a basic pillar of Lee Teng-hui's policy of pragmatic diplomacy and is still widely recognized by elites today.

---

[44]At least one analyst has drawn attention to the apparent shift that occurred during the Lee Teng-hui era in the makeup and outlook of those in charge of cross-Strait policy, from experienced professionals to politicians and nonprofessional elites. See Tse-Kang Leng, p. 75. Other observers have noted the tensions that apparently existed during the Lee Teng-hui era in the foreign policy area between Lee and his political advisors and the professional foreign policy establishment.

[45]The following general discussion of leadership views within Taiwan's political parties presents the mainstream viewpoint in each case. It is recognized that extreme, non-mainstream views are also held by some party members.

- Support by most political elites for the development of close ties with as many Asian states as possible, and the strengthening of relationships with key players in the region, especially the United States and Japan.

- Recognition that Taiwan's regional and global economic presence and influence should be used to expand international political support for the ROC and to reduce economic dependence on the Mainland; at the same time, support has dropped in recent years for the specific strategy of "dollar diplomacy" as practiced by the Lee Teng-hui government.

- Support by the leaders of both major parties for greater transparency in the conduct of foreign affairs, partly to reduce suspicions that the government continues to engage in "dollar diplomacy" in its efforts to attract new allies and to retain established ones.

- Stress by both major parties on increased people-to-people contacts and greater efforts by Taiwan to communicate its message to the international community, to gain the support and understanding of ordinary people around the world.

- In the related area of cross-Strait relations, support by most elites for efforts to increase understanding with the Mainland, to encourage democracy in China, and to deal with China on the basis of equality and mutual respect. Although leaders encourage trade and investment with the Mainland, they do not want such contacts to provide China with political leverage, as indicated above. Hence, they strongly support efforts to diversify and deepen Taiwan's foreign economic relationships beyond China.[46]

In the area of defense policy, there are many similarities in outlook among Taiwan's political elite, especially the leaders of the KMT and the DPP. First, and perhaps foremost, all ROC leaders are clearly committed to the development and maintenance of an effective military. However, it is unclear whether they support a strong military primarily for *political* purposes as part of a larger political strategy towards Beijing and Washington, or primarily for genuine *warfighting* purposes to deter or defeat a possible attack from the Mainland. Each viewpoint suggests a different approach to military development and defense strategy.[47]

The former perspective would largely derive from three key assumptions. First, Taiwan's security rests primarily upon the level of political and military support it receives from the United States and Japan. Second, any conflict with the

---

[46]"Lien Promotes 'Peace Zone' Concept," *United Daily News,* February 1, 2000.

[47]The following three paragraphs are taken from Michael D. Swaine, *Taiwan's National Security, Defense Policy, and Weapons Procurement Process*, RAND, MR-1128-OSD, Santa Monica, California, 1999, pp. 31–33.

Mainland would almost certainly require swift and forceful intervention by the United States if Taiwan were to survive, since Taiwan likely would not be able to mount an effective defense on its own for more than a few days or weeks at most. Third, Beijing recognizes that any use of force against Taiwan would pose dire consequences for regional stability and prosperity and hence seriously undermine its larger regional goals. As a result of these assumptions, Beijing is viewed as highly unlikely to use direct military force against Taiwan, as long as the possibility of a strong and swift U.S. reaction exists—and would be at least very reticent to do so under almost any circumstances. Hence, at present, the military threat from Beijing is viewed as being largely political in nature, i.e., as part of a broader PRC strategy of coercive diplomacy designed to deter movement toward greater independence and to weaken U.S. political and military support for the island (in part by convincing the United States that the Taiwan issue is a matter of war or peace for Beijing). However, this type of "threat" (some would say bluff) does not presuppose an actual intention to attack Taiwan.

From this perspective, a strong ROC military is viewed primarily as a political instrument, i.e., to convey Taiwan's defiance, to reassure the Taiwan public that they are secure from Chinese military intimidation and coercion, and, most important, to strengthen U.S. ties with Taiwan. The last objective becomes increasingly important as China's capabilities increase and Taiwan's relative ability to provide for its own defense declines. Hence, Taiwan's armed forces are primarily seen as symbols of reassurance and resolve, not as key components of a larger force structure designed to attain genuine warfighting objectives; U.S. weapons systems are valued primarily as critical indicators of greater American support for the island. As a result of these assumptions, Taiwan should primarily emphasize the acquisition of highly visible and/or sophisticated weapons platforms, preferably from the United States, and not less-visible support systems and other forms of "software" essential to the creation of a serious warfighting capability.[48]

The latter (warfighting) perspective would derive from an assumption that Beijing sees the utility of employing direct force against Taiwan and may indeed be preparing, not just threatening, to use such force in the future, and that the United States might not respond to a Chinese attack swiftly and forcefully enough to limit escalation and ensure Taiwan's security in the early stages of a conflict. Moreover, such a viewpoint probably also assumes that Beijing's willingness and ability to employ force will likely increase over time, thus

---

[48]Interviews in Taipei, June–July 1998.

potentially increasing the likelihood of a miscalculation leading to war. The logical conclusion drawn from this perspective is that Taiwan must create and maintain a military capable of repelling an attack from the Mainland and of holding on for an appreciable period of time, presumably until the United States arrives. Hence, from this perspective, major foreign weapons platforms and their support systems should be evaluated on the basis of their true capability to successfully sustain military resistance against a Mainland attack. Many interviewees strongly suspect that most ROC politicians adhere to the former viewpoint regarding the military threat from Beijing and how best to deal with it, whereas most military leaders adhere to the latter viewpoint.

Second, both the KMT and the DPP have advocated the acquisition by Taiwan of medium-range surface-to-surface missiles, more potent offensive naval weapons such as submarines, and greater force projection capabilities overall, to deter, preempt, or degrade a Chinese military attack. Lien Chan has even stressed the importance of offensive missiles as the pillar of a second-strike capability. This concept implies a more active and outward-oriented defense strategy in place of Taiwan's traditional concept of resolute defense or a purely defensive posture. In particular, this strategy reportedly emphasizes the conduct of warfare beyond the main island of Taiwan,[49] and to some observers implies the acquisition of capabilities to retaliate against targets such as Shanghai and Beijing.

Third, both the KMT and the DPP support consideration of confidence building measures (CBMs) to defuse misunderstandings and misperceptions between the two sides of the Taiwan Strait, including notification of military exercises and the establishment of a hot line. James Soong has also mentioned the idea of CBMs and a hot line, but has not elaborated on these points.

Fourth, both the KMT and the DPP have supported a peace agreement with China. While Lien Chan has proposed the idea of a confederation, Chen suggests the establishment of permanent representative missions in the two capitals, and Soong has at times proposed "a 30-year non-aggression pact" with China, followed by a 20-year European-style integration. Lien, Soong, and Chen would all reportedly accept a U.S. role as endorser and guarantor in any cross-Strait peace agreement.[50]

---

[49]The desire to acquire those capabilities necessary to keep any conflict with Mainland China away from Taiwan's shores as much as possible has been voiced by Chen Shui-bian in particular.

[50]"Taiwan Presidential Candidates' Perspectives on National Defense," Cheng-yi Lin, Research Fellow, Institute of European and American Studies, Academia Sinica, ROC, at http://www.dsis. org.tw/ peaceforum/papers/2000-02/TP0002002.htm.

Fifth, both parties propose the substantial exchange of military intelligence with countries such as the United States and Japan and the establishment of direct and secure communications with their forces. They also favor improvements in Taiwan's joint air and naval operation capabilities and direct operational links with both U.S. and Japanese forces.

Sixth, both parties also stress the use of certain areas where they presumably enjoy a comparative advantage over the Mainland, such as information warfare. For example, they support the idea of carrying out offensive information operations against the PRC when Taiwan's security is threatened. The DPP in particular stresses the acquisition of command, control, communications, computer, intelligence, surveillance, and reconnaissance (C4ISR) systems to achieve information warfare superiority.

Seventh, under a digital or computerized armed force, both Lien Chan and Chen Shui-bian advocate a more streamlined defense structure and reductions in the total number of armed forces. Lien Chan proposes to reduce the number below 320,000; Chen argues for a further reduction to 250,000.

Finally, the leaders of both major parties also favor the development of early warning and missile defense systems and improvements in Taiwan's passive defenses. The DPP in particular advocates the deployment of long-range early warning radar, space reconnaissance and surveillance assets, and tactical unmanned aerial vehicles in order to reinforce its early warning systems (more on missile defense systems below). James Soong has also stated that he supports any efforts to improve Taiwan's defense force, including a missile defense system.[51]

Regarding ballistic missile defense, we should add that Taiwan political leaders from every segment of the ideological spectrum largely focus on the political aspects of BMD at the expense of the complicated military aspects of the problem. They seek to reassure the Taiwan public that "something" is being done to protect the population from Chinese ballistic missile attack. They also portray missile defense as a means of strengthening U.S.-Taiwan defense cooperation, thereby enhancing the ability of the island to resist coercion from the Mainland. At the same time, Taiwan politicians remain sensitive to possible Chinese perceptions and reactions. Members of the Legislative Yuan regularly question the cost and utility of expensive and vulnerable early warning radars and lower-tier missile defense systems, but few understand the technical and financial aspects of the issue. Moreover, while leading politicians have been publicly

---

[51]Ibid.

supportive of missile defenses, in private they are reportedly more cautious. Many in the elite maintain that missile defense, especially Upper Tier (UT) systems, are not yet proven, too provocative, and too expensive. As a result, government officials and leading political figures studiously seek to avoid giving the impression that they want to press the United States to make a decision on Upper Tier BMD systems in Taiwan. Indeed, although the acquisition of various elements of land- and sea-based Lower Tier (LT) systems are under way, Upper Tier faces significant obstacles. There are fears, for example, that it could provoke a PRC preemptive strike. Moreover, the timeline for the deployment of key systems is very long—as much as 10–20 years for limited coverage systems—and the systems integration requirements are enormous, with reforms of air defense and C3I posing the most vexing challenges.

Despite significant movement by both the KMT and the DPP toward a more moderate and pragmatic center, the elites of both parties continue to hold contrasting positions on the basic issue of national identity, as well as with regard to specific aspects of both foreign and defense policy. While supporting the establishment of the above-mentioned Three Links, the DPP leadership at the same time assiduously avoids the use of any policy formulations or statements that might link Taiwan with the Mainland politically, even over the long term. Unlike most KMT leaders, they resist the idea that eventual unification on the basis of a common foundation of democracy and prosperity is or should be the objective of the ROC government. At most, they will state that it is a possibility, while implying that it is not a priority. Indeed, the DPP leadership rejects KMT notions such as "One China respectively interpreted by each side" (i.e., the so-called 1992 "consensus") or "One China in the future" as part of a misleading "One China" myth. Instead, DPP leaders tend to imply that any future relationship with the Mainland, under even the best of conditions, should in some sense preserve the complete sovereignty of Taiwan as an independent state. Moreover, they assert that Taiwan needs to reach a national consensus on preserving the island's *total* autonomy. Although many of these basic positions have been downplayed by the Chen Shui-bian government since it took office—as indicated by Chen's New Year's Eve reference to "political integration" noted above—they continue to be held by various DPP leaders.

In the foreign policy area, DPP leaders criticize what they see as the KMT's excessive past emphasis on the "One China" issue, the relationship with the Mainland, and hence the past competition with Beijing over sovereignty issues in foreign affairs, especially with regard to Taiwan's diplomatic presence. They assert that ROC foreign policy has been dominated by a passive reaction to international forces, has lacked a proactive ability to identify and analyze future international trends, has overemphasized short-term results and traditional formal diplomatic relations, and has neglected nontraditional diplomatic work. In contrast to these alleged deficiencies, DPP leaders call for a "middle way" in foreign policy, based on a "new internationalism" that more actively promotes Taiwan's participation in a wider range of international activities while placing less emphasis on any short-term gains in Taiwan's diplomatic status.[52] The objective of such activities is to present an image of Taiwan as a committed and loyal supporter of and participant in democracy, human rights, humanitarian relief, economic and trade cooperation and development, people-to-people contacts and cultural exchanges, party and local government diplomacy, and a clean and healthy natural environment. Such actions will thereby confirm that Taiwan ". . . respects the world's mainstream values, actively engages in international interactions, and extensively participates in various levels of international affairs, instead of being a 'trouble maker.'"[53] This, in turn, will presumably increase greatly Taiwan's value to the international community and provide Taipei with greater international support and leverage, thus strengthening Taiwan's security and well-being as a sovereign nation.

In reality, this basic logic (i.e., to increase Taiwan's value to the international community through a variety of interactions outside the diplomatic realm) also underlay many aspects of ROC foreign policy during the Lee Teng-hui era. Indeed, it is the basis of Lee's strategy of "pragmatic diplomacy," as suggested above. Many of the differences between the major parties consist largely of emphasis and tone. For example, the DPP emphasizes the need for ROC foreign policy to promote activity in a variety of NGOs in such areas as environment, education, medical science, human rights, disarmament, technology, economics, trade, military issues, and environmental protection.

The DPP leadership strongly emphasizes "democracy and human rights" as the core principle of international collaboration and foreign aid, in part in order to avoid the impression that Taiwan's foreign policy is centered on "money diplomacy" or "spendthrift diplomacy" and to show that Taiwan stands firmly on the side of democracy and joins the international community's effort to promote the development of democratic institutions and individual rights. The DPP leadership therefore advocates the establishment of a fixed annual budget for international humanitarian assistance. In the view of some DPP members, this emphasis on human rights as a key principle in international relations strengthens Taiwan's global stature by providing an alternative to Beijing's

---

[52]Although such a stance does not imply less attention to such activities as the effort to gain admission to the United Nations.

[53]DPP Foreign Policy White Paper.

unremitting stress on state sovereignty. The DPP elite also emphasizes greater involvement by the ROC government in international environmental protection efforts.

As part of the overall effort to expand Taiwan's people-to-people contacts, the DPP leadership stresses the replacement of the Overseas Chinese Affairs Commission with a special task force designed to organize all overseas Taiwan groups and organizations to help advance Taiwan's international interests. In apparent contrast, the KMT leadership under Lien Chan states that the government of the ROC has a "historical duty" to assist overseas Chinese and thus to improve the links with and services provided to overseas Chinese.

The DPP elite also stresses the development of relationships with selected smaller but nonetheless important powers, such as the Benelux and Scandinavian countries, which might not be global powers but are influential in their regions. Finally, while agreeing with the KMT on the need to diversify Taiwan's international economic contacts and resist excessive dependence on the Mainland, the DPP provides more detailed recommendations on how to realize these objectives.[54]

Taiwan's other political parties in some cases show more significant differences on foreign policy issues. For example, the New Party leadership generally reflects the views of the former conservative, Mainland Chinese KMT leadership prior to the Lee Teng-hui era. They thus continue to support ROC claims to sovereignty over both Taiwan and the Mainland, adopt a basically zero-sum approach to the diplomatic competition with Beijing, and strongly endorse cross-Strait political talks on the issue of reunification. In stark contrast, the Taiwan Independence (or National Construction) Party generally pushes the adoption of policies designed to confirm the total and permanent independence of Taiwan as a sovereign state entirely separate from the Mainland. Unfortunately, James Soong and the PFP have expressed few concrete positions on foreign policy beyond those mentioned above.

As indicated above, the KMT and DPP leaderships generally seem to agree on most essential aspects of defense policy. However, some notable differences exist.

---

[54]For example, the DPP White Paper stresses efforts to concentrate on developing high-tech and innovative industries, to diversify Taiwan's export market, upgrade products so that China would rely on Taiwan for upgrading their technology, and raise the cost of a trade war between the two, to lift the inbound investment ratio restriction of foreign capital in Taiwan, and to strengthen the auditing of inbound Chinese capital into Taiwan.

At the most basic level, the DPP is a strong advocate of tighter civilian control over the military, more strenuous efforts to uproot alleged waste and corruption by military officials, and the creation of a force structure that is less oriented toward the interests of the ground forces.[55] These objectives all derive from the fact that some members of the DPP elite harbor a significant level of suspicion and even hostility toward the ROC military and the professional officer corps in particular. Many DPP leaders reportedly view the ROC military as an excessively secretive and corrupt institution that is hostile to the independence-oriented objectives of the DPP and largely resistant to civilian oversight. These beliefs stem primarily from the above-mentioned fact that the ROC military functioned until very recently as an instrument of KMT rule—possessing few ties to any civilian leaders beyond the ROC president—and that the bulk of the officer corps is still composed of Mainlanders, many of whom allegedly continue to support the values and outlook of more conservative KMT and New Party members. This is viewed as especially the case among the senior officers of the ROC Army. Hence, many DPP leaders insist that the first step to building a more secure Taiwan is to bring the military more fully under civilian control,[56] to remove the dominant influence of conservative KMT elements, and to reduce what is regarded as an excessive emphasis on the maintenance of inappropriate ground force capabilities, as opposed to more appropriate air and naval capabilities.[57] In response to these views, many KMT officers in the Taiwan military—as well as many conservative KMT politicians—believe that the DPP's primary intention in seeking greater legislative oversight of the military is to weaken the overall political strength of the KMT by eliminating KMT influence within the armed forces. They also fear that the DPP's efforts at military reform (including drastic reductions in the size of the ROC Army) will reduce Taiwan's aggregate military capabilities.

---

[55]DPP leaders also strongly support a reduction in the term of compulsory military service, from 2 years to 1.5 years.

[56]DPP leaders also stress the need to strengthen civilian control over both the Ministry of Defense and the National Security Bureau.

[57]The above DPP views have exerted a significant indirect influence by generating greater public support for closer media and LY scrutiny of the military, especially regarding defense strategy and budget/procurement matters, and particularly in the wake of the procurement scandals of the early 1990s. Such closer scrutiny has produced four significant consequences to date. First, and perhaps most notable, it has contributed to broader efforts by the LY to reduce defense spending in certain areas. Such spending is increasingly seen as excessive because of corruption or as unduly benefiting the interests of KMT conservatives in the Army as opposed to the overall interests of the military. Second, it has greatly extended the time required to complete the procurement process, as a result of greatly increased levels of LY involvement in that process. Third, it has led to greater efforts by the Ministry of National Defense (MND) to strengthen its role as an intermediary between the LY and the military. The establishment in recent years of such MND offices as the Military Procurement Bureau was motivated in large part by the increased need to respond to LY involvement in the procurement process. Fourth, it has contributed greatly to the effort to place Taiwan's military leadership directly under MND and LY oversight.

Second, from a narrower perspective, DPP leaders appear to place great stress on enhancing the authority and responsibilities of the National Security Council (NSC) in order to make it into the supreme institution in the national security policy process, providing systematic policy formulation, implementation, and coordination of national-level long-term strategies among civilian and defense policy sectors. Some observers believe that the Chen Shui-bian government has indeed strengthened the role of the NSC in policymaking since taking office.

As in the case of foreign policy, James Soong and the PFP have taken few concrete positions on defense policy. Soong is generally depicted by his party as a peace-loving and responsible leader with cautious views in this area.

In addition to the above views of civilian political elites, the ROC military also obviously holds views on foreign and especially defense policy issues. In most areas relating to defense, military views often reflect the interests and requirements of the individual armed services. Hence, the more forward-oriented defense strategy mentioned above is reportedly supported by the ROC Air Force and the Navy, given the potential benefits such a strategy would presumably present for the force structure and budget allocations of both services. It is unclear, however, to what degree the senior military leadership as a whole supports the acquisition of an offensive precision-strike capability based primarily on ballistic missiles. Our sense is that this particular issue is a controversial one within the officer corps.

Among proponents, two basic schools of thought exist on the sort of specific offensive capabilities Taiwan should acquire.[58] One group argues that the acquisition of an offensive counterforce capability is necessary to deter China from launching a conventional attack against Taiwan, and—if deterrence fails—to significantly degrade China's ability to sustain such an attack against Taiwan. These forces would consist essentially of several hundred short-range ballistic missiles (SRBMs) and air assets capable of striking China's ports, theater C3I nodes, and missile launch sites. The second group argues that Taiwan must focus on acquiring offensive strategic countervalue capabilities to threaten major Chinese cities in Central and Southern China, such as Shanghai, Nanjing, Guangzhou, and Hong Kong. These would consist essentially of a relatively small number of intermediate-range ballistic missiles (IRBMs) or medium-range ballistic missiles (MRBMs) with large conventional or perhaps even nuclear or biological warheads, intended purely as a deterrent against an all-out Chinese assault on Taiwan.

---

[58]This analysis is based on interviews conducted in Taipei in 1998 and 1999.

There are many opponents to the acquisition of either type of offensive capability, however. These individuals point out that Taiwan could not develop a large enough offensive counterforce capability to credibly threaten the extensive number of potential military targets existing on the Mainland. Moreover, it would likely prove extremely difficult to locate and destroy China's large number of mobile SRBMs, while Taiwan's relatively small missile force and infrastructure would be a top priority target for Chinese missile, air, and special forces attacks. In addition, an offensive countervalue capability would be of very limited value, opponents argue, because (a) the Chinese would likely be undeterred if Taiwan were only able to threaten Central and Southern cities and not Beijing, and (b) any type of credible countervalue capability would almost certainly require warheads armed with weapons of mass destruction (WMD), which the United States would oppose. An offensive countervalue capability would thus likely prove to be inadequate and could greatly exacerbate U.S.-Taiwan relations. Moreover, it might also provoke a massive preemptive Chinese strike, or at the very least a massive Chinese counterstrike that would almost certainly devastate Taiwan.

Different service-based viewpoints are especially evident in the case of ballistic missile defense.[59] From a political or psychological perspective, many military officers support the idea of missile defense. On a more concrete military level, however, most are extremely skeptical of the military effectiveness of the proposed systems. First, given the relative size and sophistication of the missile threat posed by China, ballistic missile defense in Taiwan faces greater operational challenges and must meet higher expectations than similar systems in the United States or Japan. In terms of challenges, Taiwan's lack of strategic depth and the vulnerability of its missile defense and early warning infrastructure greatly complicate the operational situation, not to mention the increasingly large inventory of Chinese missiles with widely varying ranges and payloads. Despite these challenges, however, the expectations of the effectiveness of missile defense systems among the domestic population remain unrealistically high, potentially imperiling national morale during a crisis. Second, there is widespread concern that the announcement of the sale of UT systems to Taiwan could provoke Beijing to act preemptively. Third, many military officers are wary of the costs of missile defense, and worry that the systems will decimate their already insufficient procurement budgets.

Among the armed services, the ROC Navy is clearly the most supportive of missile defense, because it potentially has the most to gain. The naval platform of

---

[59]Ibid.

choice for either Navy Area Wide or Navy Theater Wide is a ship equipped with the AEGIS Combat System, the most advanced naval system in the world. Prior to 1996, the ROC Navy had received preliminary approval for a limited form of AEGIS to be transferred to Taiwan under the auspices of the so-called Advanced Combat System (ACS), which would have fitted a downgraded version of AEGIS onto four modified Perry-class frigates. The Navy eventually abandoned this purchase, in order to meet other budgetary demands. Since the 1995–1996 crisis, the Navy has sought to revive this program, initially disguising a request for a full version of AEGIS on four larger ships (likely a 9500-ton platform like the Arleigh Burke–class, or the Spanish F-100) under the name of the Evolved ACS program. More recently, however, the ROC government has openly requested that Washington sell it several AEGIS-equipped destroyers. At the same time, even the strongest supporters in the Navy recognize that the costs of such a purchase, which would likely be more than US$1 billion per ship, would cause too much interservice rivalry and opposition. As a result, supporters of the new ACS program describe it as a "national" system, while the Navy's top priority continues to be the acquisition of 8–12 diesel-powered submarines. The sale of such submarines was approved by the United States in April 2001.

The least supportive service branch is the ROC Army, which views missile defense as outside its primary mission: defending the Taiwan coast from massed PRC attack. The Army does support some aspects of the PAC-3 system, possibly even Theater High-Altitude Air Defense (THAAD), and desires to control the C3I infrastructure associated with the systems, but other services (primarily the Taiwan Air Force) have a stronger claim on the latter. The Army is very concerned about the cost and feasibility of BMD, but is even more concerned that the high costs of AEGIS and the early warning radars will require deep personnel cuts, which would disproportionately affect the Army.

In the middle is the ROC Air Force (ROCAF). The ROCAF exhibits strong support for missile defenses, primarily for political and psychological reasons. It recognizes that the missile defense architecture will directly benefit its air defense effort. More important, the ROCAF will be the primary beneficiary of upgrades to Taiwan's sensor networks, early warning capability, and C3I infrastructure, as well as the expected hardening of airfields around the country.

The above discussion of elite backgrounds and viewpoints poses several basic implications for Taiwan's foreign and defense policies. First, certain common basic values and policy outlooks exist among the vast majority of Taiwan's political leadership. In the specific areas of foreign policy and defense policy, the bulk of Taiwan's political elite apparently agree on a wide range of basic principles and policy positions, reflecting the overall pragmatism and growing moderation of Taiwan's dominant political center. The concept of flexible or pragmatic diplomacy is widely supported among elites, although dollar diplomacy is not. Second, the elites of both parties nonetheless continue to hold contrasting positions on the basic issue of national identity. This difference arguably poses the greatest single danger for a radical—and possibly adverse—shift in Taiwan foreign or defense policy in the future. Third, many of the differences between the KMT and the DPP on foreign and defense policies are largely ones of emphasis and tone, not basic substance. Perhaps the most significant difference among political elites relates more to the two areas of cross-Strait relations and basic attitudes toward the ROC military and military leadership in particular. The KMT under Lien Chan is probably more inclined than Chen Shui-bian's DPP to espouse a version of the "one China" concept that would permit resumption of a cross-Strait dialogue. Moreover, a significant difference apparently exists between political and military elites over the ultimate purpose of Taiwan's defense strategy and armed forces. Fourth, there is growing support among both civilian and military elites for a more forward-oriented (some would say offensive) military strategy, designed to increase deterrence and, if necessary, degrade the ability of the Mainland to prosecute direct military action against Taiwan. Fifth, although both civilian and military elites support the general idea of ballistic missile defense, considerable differences exist between military and civilian elites, and among military leaders, over the desired purpose and architecture of a future BMD system.

Societal Views

Democratization, institutional development, generational change, and economic progress have also brought about major changes in the specific political views expressed and level of influence upon the political system exerted by the Taiwan public. During most of the Chiang Kai-shek and Chiang Ching-kuo eras, views expressed by the general public and interest groups on issues relating to national identity and national security were heavily influenced, if not entirely controlled, by the ROC government. Taiwan's mass media, including its polling organs, were under the complete direction of the KMT party apparatus, and the public expression of unorthodox views on critical issues such as state identity and authority, cross-Strait relations, and foreign and defense policies was strongly discouraged and in some instances explicitly illegal. For example, under the existing emergency war regulations in place at the time (e.g., the Provisional Amendments for the Period of Mobilization of the Suppression of Communist Rebellion), citizens could not express support for the notion that Taiwan should become an independent, sovereign country separate from the Mainland and the

ROC, and few native Taiwan citizens would dare state that they consider themselves to be Taiwanese first and foremost, not Chinese. In addition, the KMT party-state apparatus also supervised or controlled the activities and views of specific interest groups organized by workers, farmers, businessmen, and students, thus ensuring that such groups served as pillars of the government.

Hence, it is no surprise that so-called "public opinion" or the views of key segments of society during this period supported fundamental KMT policies, e.g., that the ROC government was the sole legitimate government of a single China encompassing both Taiwan and the Mainland; that the ROC government should exclusively represent the Chinese nation in the international community; that the communist PRC government was an illegitimate challenger to this claim; that the ROC government should strive to eventually reoccupy the Mainland and displace the communist rebel authorities; and that all Taiwan residents were first and foremost culturally, ethnically, and historically Chinese.

However, in response to the forces of political liberalization and economic development, societal views on a wide range of policy-related issues have become more openly expressed and more accurately reflective of Taiwan's increasingly diverse, politically active, and affluent society. In particular, the views of young and old Chinese nationalists of various stripes now contend with supporters of Taiwan independence, pragmatic individuals most concerned with ensuring continued stability and growth for Taiwan, and representatives of a new middle class and a strong, increasingly influential business community that argues for greater international respect for Taiwan, more expansive contacts with the international economy, and stable cross-Strait relations. Moreover, as national and local leadership posts in the executive and legislative realms became subject to increasingly open, democratic, and competitive electoral processes, public opinion has become more important in domestic politics and the policy proposals of the opposition have been given greater legitimacy.[60] To an increasing degree, political elites and government policy in Taiwan both shape and reflect public and group views, including views relating to important foreign and defense policies.

Since the late eighties, a variety of public and group views have emerged on several basic issues indirectly relevant to Taiwan's foreign and defense policies, e.g., support for independence versus reunification versus maintenance of an ill-defined status quo; an individual's personal identity with Taiwan versus China; support for greater or fewer social, economic, and political contacts with the

---

[60]Cal Clark, p. 12.

Mainland; and whether or not China is hostile toward Taiwan. Moreover, public and interest group views are also increasingly expressed on specific issues directly related to foreign and defense policies and cross-Strait relations, e.g., whether the ROC government should undertake a direct and formal dialogue with Beijing and sign a peace agreement with the Mainland; acceptance or rejection of Beijing's entreaties to Taiwan or its "one country, two systems" formula for long-term association; the level of support for the Three Links between Taiwan and the Mainland, for Taiwan's efforts to enter the United Nations, for revision of the National Unification Guidelines, and for the basic foreign policy of pragmatic diplomacy; the level of public confidence in the ability and willingness of the ROC armed forces to defend Taiwan from a Mainland attack and to support a more independence-oriented government; and public support for the adoption of a more offensive-oriented military strategy, for the development of offensive weapons such as surface-to-surface ballistic missiles.

Efforts to accurately measure and assess public and group views and interests on these and other issues are fraught with problems, however, such as political bias and the use of unscientific methodologies. A significant number of opinion polls are conducted each year by Taiwan's political parties, newspapers, and various politically-oriented private groups or foundations on a wide range of subjects. Many such polls arguably produce inaccurate results, either as a result of sampling errors, biased questions, or a subject's awareness of the highly partisan nature of the polling agency. Yet a comparison of both primary and secondary sources on ROC public and group opinion suggest the existence of certain identifiable trends and features of public and interest group opinion in Taiwan on specific issues relating to foreign and defense policy. These include major shifts in basic public views and perceptions, certain stable areas of continuity over time, and specific, strongly held interest-group views.

Since the late eighties, a major shift has occurred in the views of Taiwan's public on two critical issues relating to foreign policy and cross-Strait relations: independence and national identity. On the former issue, polls conducted largely since the advent of the Lee Teng-hui era (and the lifting of martial law in 1987) suggest a gradual but steady shift in public sentiment regarding the question of whether Taiwan should eventually become an independent state or be unified with the Chinese Mainland. A majority of those polled in the late eighties and early nineties appeared to favor unification, either immediately or at some future date, while only a small percentage backed independence. By the late nineties, however, public sentiment had almost reversed on this issue. Well over 40 percent of the populace favored independence at some point in time whereas only 30 percent or so favored unification.[61]

On the latter issue, polls have also suggested that a similar reversal has occurred over the same period concerning the self-identity of the ROC citizenry. While a clear majority of those polled in the late eighties regarded themselves as exclusively or primarily Chinese and less than 20 percent regarded themselves as Taiwanese, by the early- to mid-nineties, a significant proportion of the populace saw themselves as both Chinese and Taiwanese, and an increasing proportion saw themselves as exclusively Taiwanese. By the late nineties, those citizens who considered themselves to be exclusively Chinese had dropped dramatically, while those who thought of themselves as exclusively Taiwanese had risen sharply, constituting around 35–40 percent of the total adult populace; the percentage of citizens who considered themselves both Chinese and Taiwanese by that time had remained fairly steady for several years at between 45–50 percent. This basic reversal among a significant proportion of the populace, from having a Chinese identity to having a Taiwan identity, has occurred largely regardless of ethnic background, age, educational level, gender, and partisan identity.[62] It suggests a view that the sovereignty of the Taiwan state resides primarily with the population of Taiwan and thus requires a new form of social cohesion distinct from the past divisive ethnic criteria characteristic of Chinese nationalism. This has been described by one observer as a "post-nationalist identity."[63]

Together, these two sets of trends suggest that over time the Taiwan public has become increasingly supportive of government policies designed to advance Taiwan's status and influence in the international community as a sovereign, independent country entirely separate from any existing Mainland Chinese

---

[61]See Mainland Affairs Council (MAC) public opinion surveys, presented by the Information Division, Taipei Economic and Cultural Office in New York, on http://ciccl.taipei.org/Mainland/8804el.htm; Sofia Wu, "Nearly 40% of Local People Support Taiwan Independence: Poll," Central News Agency (Taiwan), August 26, 1998; Sofia Wu, "Poll Finds Mounting Pro-Independence Sentiments Here," Central News Agency (Taiwan), September 21, 1998; "Poll Finds Most People Support 'Special State-to-State' Theory," Central News Agency (Taiwan), August 12, 1999; "Opinion Poll Shows Taiwanese Support Independence Over Unification," Deutsche Presse-Agentur, July 3, 1997; "Highest Percentage Ever Consider Themselves Taiwanese," Central News Agency (Taiwan), September 3, 1999.

[62]Liu I-chou and Ho Szu-yin, "The Taiwanese/Chinese Identity of the Taiwan People," *Issues and Studies*, Vol. 35, No. 3 (May/June 1999), p. 33; "MAC Poll Finds Beijing's 'White Paper' Backfires," Central News Agency (Taiwan), March 3, 2000; "Highest Percentage Ever Consider Themselves Taiwanese," Central News Agency (Taiwan), September 3, 1999. To a considerable extent, this development is reflected in efforts to alter ROC textbooks in ways that tend to loosen the identification of Taiwan as a part of China. See Christopher Hughes and Robert Stone, "Research Note: Nation-Building and Curriculum Reform in Hong Kong and Taiwan," *The China Quarterly*, Number 160, 1999, pp. 977–991.

[63]Hughes, p. 155.

regime. In fact, in recent years, polls have indicated strong public support for a variety of policy initiatives or concepts associated with such an effort, including support for Taiwan's entry into the UN as an independent state; for efforts to expand Taiwan's overall level of diplomatic representation and political presence among nation-states, regardless of the presence or absence of Mainland representation in such states; for revision of the 1991 National Unification Guidelines (which envision eventual reunification with the Mainland); for the basic assertion that Taiwan is a separate sovereign state; and for overall efforts to develop Taiwan's foreign ties, even if this were to occur at the expense of some greater tension with the PRC.[64] One poll even suggests that a majority of the Taiwan public reject the notion of trading eventual independence and permanent separation from the Mainland for a PRC commitment never to employ force against the island.[65] And very high percentages of the Taiwan public consistently reject Beijing's "one country, two systems" formula for reunification.[66]

However, the above views should not lead one to assume that the Taiwan public has become supportive of immediate or near-term efforts by the ROC government to alter radically the cross-Strait situation in the direction of independence and to obtain full acceptance by the international community of Taiwan as a non-Chinese political entity. To the contrary, despite the emergence among Taiwan's citizens of a more distinct and separate identity from the Mainland and a long-term trend toward greater public sympathy for eventual independence, the bulk of the ROC public remain highly pragmatic, flexible, and hence cautious when assessing how Taiwan should relate to China and to the international community. The majority of the public—and in particular the business community and the middle class—strongly support policies designed to ensure continued economic growth and social and political stability. They therefore realize that Taiwan has a strong stake in avoiding conflict with the Mainland, both directly, via actions toward Beijing, and indirectly, via its

---

[64]MAC public opinion surveys; "KMT Poll Finds 76% Support Review of Unification Guidelines," Central News Agency (Taiwan), July 9, 2000; "Poll Finds Widespread Support for 'State-to-State' Theory," Central News Agency (Taiwan), August 1, 1999; Sofia Wu, "Nearly 40% of Local People Support Taiwan Independence: Poll," Central News Agency (Taiwan), August 25, 1998; "MAC Polls Find Majority of Taiwan People Want to Maintain Status Quo," Central News Agency (Taiwan), April 26, 1999; Also see Sofia Wu, "Poll Finds Low Approval Rating for Foreign Ministry Performance," Central News Agency, August 1, 2000. This poll found that nearly half of those polled think the government should work even harder to promote Taiwan's UN bid.

[65]Central News Agency (Taiwan), August 25, 1998.

[66]"Majority Favor Cross-Strait Talks: Poll," China News, May 16, 1998; "MAC Poll Finds Beijing's 'White Paper' Backfires," Central News Agency (Taiwan), March 3, 2000; Elizabeth Hsu, "60 Percent in Poll Disagree With Soong's Mainland Policy," World News Connection, December 5, 1999; "MAC Polls Find Majority of Taiwan People Want to Maintain Status Quo," Central News Agency (Taiwan), April 26, 1999; Sofia Wu, "Nearly 40% of Local People Support Taiwan Independence: Poll," Central News Agency (Taiwan), August 25, 1998; Deborah Kuo, "Most Taiwan Residents Support Dialogue With Beijing: Poll," Central News Agency (Taiwan), April 27, 1998.

behavior in the international arena.[67] In fact, in recent months, declining growth rates and a related increase in Taiwan's dependence on economic links with the Mainland have combined to produce a modest but significant increase in popular support for unification, thus reflecting the flexibility and pragmatism of Taiwan's citizens. Moreover, in general, a significant portion of the Taiwan public continue to identify Taiwan and the ROC with a geographic, historical, and cultural notion of "China," despite the above trends.

These sentiments are reflected in the fact that since at least the early nineties, a significant portion of the Taiwan public has supported the maintenance of the status quo in cross-Strait relations. Although the specific meaning of the status quo is usually left undefined,[68] this viewpoint suggests a strong desire to avoid any sudden or radical movement toward either formal, *de jure* independence or reunification.[69] Moreover, at various times, high percentages of the Taiwan public have supported the signing of a peace treaty with the PRC and an official dialogue between the two sides, albeit one conducted on the basis of equality and, according to some polls, the prior existence of a democratic Mainland regime.[70] In addition, as suggested above, significant numbers of the populace continue to identify Taiwan with various versions of "China." For example, in 1998, nearly 50 percent of those polled agreed with the notion that there is currently "One China, two governments" on the two sides of the Taiwan Strait; 46 percent said that both the ROC and the PRC are "China," and 53 percent disagreed with the statement, "Only the PRC on the Mainland is China, we are Taiwan."[71] Taken together, these views suggest the emergence of a moderate center among the Taiwan populace, thus serving to temper the potentially more destabilizing trends regarding independence and national identity noted above.

---

[67]Hence, rapid economic progress and social prosperity have both stimulated the public's desire for increased international recognition of Taiwan's successes and provided a strong incentive to avoid actions that threaten continued development. See Christopher Hughes, *Taiwan and Chinese Nationalism*, Routledge, London, 1997, pp. 78–79.

[68]However, in one poll, a clear majority of those questioned indicated that the status quo was equivalent to the maintenance of Taiwan's *de facto* independence. Sofia Wu, "Poll Finds Mounting Pro-Independence Sentiments Here," Central News Agency (Taiwan), September 21, 1998.

[69]MAC public opinion surveys; "KMT Poll Finds 76% Support Review of Unification Guidelines," Central News Agency (Taiwan), July 9, 2000; "MAC Polls Find Majority of Taiwan People Want to Maintain Status Quo," Central News Agency (Taiwan), April 26, 1998; Julian Baum, "Talking Heads," *Far Eastern Economic Review*, Hong Kong, October 15, 1998, p. 28; Cal Clark, "The Republic of China's Bid for UN Membership," *American Asian Review*, Vol. 13, No. 2, Summer 1995, p. 14.

[70]"Most Taiwanese back signing cross-Strait peace pact," BBC Monitoring International Reports, February 19, 2000; "MAC Poll Finds Beijing's 'White Paper' Backfires," Central News Agency (Taiwan), March 3, 2000; "Highest Percentage Ever Consider Themselves Taiwanese," Central News Agency (Taiwan), September 3, 1999; Deborah Kuo, "Most Taiwan Residents Support Dialogue With Beijing: Poll," Central News Agency (Taiwan), April 27, 1998; Julian Baum, FEER, October 15, 1998.

[71]Sofia Wu, "Poll Finds Mounting Pro-Independence Sentiments Here," Central News Agency (Taiwan), September 21, 1998.

A less clear pattern of public views exists with respect to defense issues. Far fewer opinion polls are taken in this area, and the questions asked are often highly specific and vary considerably over time, thus making it difficult to ascertain trends. Also, as in other countries, few members of the Taiwan public possess an awareness or understanding of defense issues. Hence, a significant portion of citizens express either "no opinion" or "don't know" on defense-related polls. Nonetheless, a few tentative conclusions about public attitudes on defense issues can be discerned by examining general polling results.

First, at the most general level, although a large majority of the Taiwan public appears to hold a positive view toward servicemen, fewer members of the public express confidence in the military's ability to defend Taiwan's national security.[72] Moreover, the public does not evince strong faith in the political neutrality of the military or in its ability to keep its activities open and transparent to society.[73] This is hardly surprising, given the fact that the senior officer corps is composed largely of Mainlanders and that the ROC military as an institution was structured and operated for decades largely in a secretive manner and as an organ of authoritarian KMT rule. In addition, the Taiwan public apparently does not believe that tensions with China will necessarily lead to a military confrontation in the future.[74] Both the public's apparent distrust of the neutrality and openness of the ROC military and its low public expectation of a cross-Strait military confrontation suggest that there is little public support for major increases in Taiwan defense spending.

Second, on a more specific level, the public has at times expressed a high level of support for closer defense relations with the United States, and in particular for the acquisition of military systems that would presumably serve this purpose. For example, the Taiwan public overwhelmingly supports ROC participation in a U.S.-led ballistic missile defense system.[75] At the same time, the ignorance level is high regarding the technical details of such a system. Some members of the public believe incorrectly that it will provide a leak-proof shield against Chinese ballistic missiles. Yet many do not want missile defense batteries or equipment deployed near their homes, believing the sites will attract Chinese missiles.

---

[72]"Military Gets High Rating in Disaster Relief: Poll," *Central News Agency* (Taiwan), July 11, 1999.

[73]Ibid.

[74]Sofia Wu, "Taiwan People Willing to Fight for Homeland: Poll," *Central News Agency* (Taiwan).

[75]"80.5 per cent Taiwanese support Taipei's joining TMD," *Deutsche Presse-Agentur*, March 14, 1999.

Similarly, the experience of the Israeli population during the Gulf War has sensitized the Taiwan public about possible damage from missile debris.[76]

On other sensitive military issues, the Taiwan public expresses decidedly mixed opinions. For example, although over 40 percent of respondents apparently favor the development of long-range offensive missiles in the face of a growing PRC military threat, 26.2 percent oppose such an action, and nearly 40 percent indicate that they are worried that such missile development might stimulate an arms race.[77] As an example of the variation and distortions in polling, a survey conducted by the Public Opinion Association of the Republic of China earlier in the same month displayed a completely different view, with 82 percent of those interviewed saying that they supported offensive missiles versus 9.8 percent against.[78]

Finally, the views of one specific interest group—the business community—at times exerts significant influence upon the foreign and defense policy perceptions and actions of Taiwan's political elites. Rapid economic growth and prosperity have resulted in a stronger and more politically active business community in Taiwan.[79] The rapid expansion of cross-Strait economic ties—and especially Taiwan's booming trade and investment in the Mainland—have created strong business interests favoring cross-Strait stability and deeper, more extensive links between the two sides. Hence, the business community generally favors ROC policies such as the Three Links,[80] resists efforts to limit Taiwan economic involvement in the Mainland, and generally urges mutual restraint and an avoidance of any potentially "provocative" actions by the ROC government in the foreign policy or defense realms.[81]

The above summary of societal views and interests indicates that a long-term pattern of growing support for independence and a deepening identity with Taiwan coexist in the public's mind with a continued acknowledgment of Taiwan's "Chineseness" and a strongly pragmatic approach to external relations.

---

[76]Interviews, Taiwan, 1999.

[77]"Survey Gives 40% Approval Rating to Lien's Long-Range Missile Plan," *China News*, December 20, 1999.

[78]Lilian Wu, "82 Percent Favor Developing Long-Range Missiles," *CAN*, 12 December 1999.

[79]Hughes, pp. 109, 111. Also see Yu-Shan Wu, "Taiwan in 1994," *Asian Survey*, Vol. 35, January 1995.

[80]In the past, the ROC government, supported by a security lobby led by the ROC military, managed to resist pressure from the business community on issues such as the Three Links. See Jean-Pierre Cabestan, "Taiwan's Mainland Policy: Normalization, Yes; Reunification, Later," *The China Quarterly*, No. 148, December 1996 p. 1277. However, the Chen Shui-bian government now strongly supports the establishment of such connections to the Mainland.

[81]See Hughes, pp. 114–116. See Chapter 4 for a further discussion of cross-Strait economic ties.

In this context, foreign and defense policies are viewed as important means to attain certain valued social ends, such as continued economic expansion and prosperity, U.S. (and international) support, and national stability and security. However, they are apparently not viewed by most citizens as mechanisms for attaining full independence or reunification under existing external conditions. Nonetheless, significant elements of the Taiwan public seem willing to support relatively energetic efforts to greatly increase Taiwan's basic profile, reputation, and influence in the international community as a nation-state.

The Decision-Making System

The specific features of Taiwan's leadership decision-making structures and processes also exert a significant influence on the content and direction of its foreign and defense policies, often in decisive ways. During the Chiang Kai-shek and Chiang Ching-kuo eras, the decision-making process in the foreign policy and defense policy realms was dominated by the supreme leader and directed largely through the KMT party apparatus. The ROC president was also head of the KMT and the general-secretary of the KMT led the party organization, in a position similar to that of the premier on the state side (although the KMT general-secretary was a less important player in the decision-making process than the premier and the top state executive leaders).[82] Chiang Kai-shek and Chiang Ching-kuo initiated and oversaw most major policy actions, usually after consulting official and unofficial advisors. The regime's decisions were formally approved or ratified by the KMT's Central Standing Committee, whose membership normally consisted of top officials in the party, army, and state.[83] The details of policy were then apparently formulated and implemented by state and military organs. Some KMT cadres moved back and forth from party to state posts.[84] In general, Chiang Kai-shek ruled on the basis of his enormous personal prestige and by balancing KMT factions and institutions, whereas Chiang Ching-kuo's personal power was probably greater than that of any institution, including the KMT.[85] The president's strong personal authority during this period was further augmented by the effect of temporary provisions and various emergency decrees that, together with his chairmanship of the KMT, endowed the president with virtually unlimited authority. Under the president, the

---

[82]Moody, p. 105.

[83]The CSC would meet once per week, name persons to major party office, nominate persons to major state offices, and formulate and approve policy recommendations that are then sent to the Executive Council or LY for action. Peter R. Moody, Jr., Political Change on Taiwan, Praeger, New York, 1992.p. 105.

[84]Moody, p. 105.

[85]Moody, pp. 25–26.

premier and his cabinet officials could be stripped of their real policymaking powers and relegated to the status of the president's administrative subordinates.[86]

Under this personalistic, KMT-led system, the Legislative Yuan (LY) exerted little independent influence over national security, foreign affairs, and defense policy. Those legislative committees responsible for policies in these areas were completely under the control of the KMT and supported the needs and interests of the KMT-led military and the KMT-led civilian government. For example, the LY National Defense Committee was controlled by a small clique of pro-military KMT members (*junxi li wei*), who resisted revealing any information about national security or defense matters to the LY.

KMT influence over the decision-making process in national security, foreign policy, and defense policy declined gradually during the Lee Teng-hui era as Lee relied less and less on KMT channels to develop proposals, conduct deliberations, and formulate policy. At the same time, other agencies and institutions became more active and to some degree more influential, especially the Legislative Yuan. A more activist LY has in turn provided an avenue for the exertion of influence over the policy process by the various political parties. In addition, the military became more subject to civilian authority and less politicized overall. And the entire policy process has become more open and transparent. Although the personal authority of the president remained strong on key foreign and defense policy issues during the Lee Teng-hui era, the system became more complex, less coordinated, and often subject to internal wrangling. The latter features have become especially evident since the election of Chen Shui-bian to the presidency in March 2000. As discussed above, Chen's election resulted in a fundamental rift between a DPP-led executive branch and an opposition-dominated LY and revealed the severe limits upon the institutional— as opposed to the personal—authority of the ROC president. This situation has arguably weakened the decision-making capacity of the central government.

At present, Taiwan's national security, foreign policy, and defense policy apparatus centers on ten key institutions and their leaders:

1. Offices of the President and Vice President

2. Office of the Premier of the Executive Yuan (EY)

3. National Security Council (NSC)

---

[86]Hung-mao Tien, *The Great Transition: Political and Social Change in the Republic of China*, Hoover Institution Press, Stanford, California, 1989, p. 136.

4.   Ministry of Foreign Affairs (MoFA)

5.   Economic and Technology Agencies

6.   Ministry of National Defense (MND)

7.   General Staff Headquarters (GSH)

8.   Armed Services General Headquarters (GHQ)

9.   National Security Bureau (NSB)

10.   Legislative Yuan (LY).

The functions and responsibilities of each of these policy actors are described, followed by an overall assessment of the decision-making systems in the foreign policy and defense policy arenas.[87]

Offices of the President and Vice President. The president of the Republic of China exercises supreme authority over national security policy at the level of grand strategy, as well as over the broad contours of foreign and defense policy. As Taiwan's sole nationally elected head of state and as commander-in-chief of the ROC armed forces, the president has the final word on such basic national security issues as the formulation of national strategic objectives, the basic principles and concepts guiding foreign and defense policies, the general diplomatic and political strategy toward the People's Republic of China, and the direction of Taiwan's military in time of war.[88]

Operationally, the president exercises control over senior, subordinate actors of the national security policy apparatus through his direct line authority over the premier (who is appointed by the president without the confirmation of the legislative branch and who possesses formal line authority over the operations of government national security organs such as the Ministry of Foreign Affairs and the Ministry of National Defense[89]), and through his direct administrative supervision over two critical national security organs within the Office of the President: the National Security Council (NSC) and its subordinate National Security Bureau (NSB).[90]

---

[87]This discussion is largely drawn from Michael D. Swaine, *Taiwan's National Security, Defense Policy, and Weapons Procurement Process*, RAND, Santa Monica, MR-1128-OSD, 1999.

[88]Yun-han Chu, "The Challenges of Democratic Consolidation," in Steve Tsang and Hung-mao Tien, eds., *Democratization in Taiwan: Implications for China*, St. Martin's Press, Inc., New York, 1999, p. 151.

[89]The president's influence over these bodies is further reinforced by the fact that he appoints all state ministers, on the recommendation of the premier.

[90]Two other organs within the Office of the President with potential influence over national security policy issues are the National Unification Council (NUC) and the National Unification Research Council (NURC). Founded in 1990, the NUC consists of 30+ leaders in various fields, from both government and private sectors, organized into task groups. According to *The Republic of China*

As part of his broad responsibilities as commander-in-chief of the armed forces and supreme authority regarding national security policy, the president of the Republic of China has the final word on defense policy and force structure issues and possesses the formal authority to oversee and intervene in budgetary and procurement decisions concerning major weapons systems.[91] Theoretically, the ROC president is particularly well placed to play a decisive role in these areas because of a direct "command authority" link regarding operational matters that exists between himself and the chief of the general staff (CGS). Until very recently, this link prevented close scrutiny of the activities of the military by the Executive Yuan and, indirectly, the Legislative Yuan. However, a proposed reform of the ROC National Defense Organization Law currently under consideration by the Legislative Yuan is designed to place the CGS entirely under the Ministry of National Defense and ultimately the premier and hence remove an important channel of presidential control over the uniformed military (while also making the military directly subject to LY supervision).

Within the Office of the President, an array of special advisors and deputy advisors to the president provides expert advice on both foreign and defense policies. However, the actual influence of these individuals depends greatly upon their individual stature and connections within the government and, most importantly, on their personal relationship with the president.

The vice president of the Republic of China does not exercise much power within the ROC political system. Most notably, the vice president does not possess any formal, direct authority over key national security organs. Hence, the position's influence within the national security policy arena is largely informal or ex officio, deriving primarily from the vice president's potential role as a key personal advisor to the president.

Office of the Premier of the Executive Yuan. The premier of the ROC is appointed by the president (without the formal consent of the Legislative Yuan), and is thus highly dependent upon the latter's support and good will. However, the premier exercises a significant level of formal and informal authority over national policy, including national security policy. The latter derives primarily from his potential role as a key advisor to the president. The former, more significant, authority

---

Yearbook, 1997 (p. 77), the NUC recommends national unification policies to the president, helps the government to devise a national unification framework, and builds consensus within society and among Taiwan's political parties concerning the issue of national unification. In reality, however, the NUC has little real policy influence. It rarely meets, and functions primarily to support the president's position on national unification issues. The NURC is an ad hoc organization established by Lee Teng-hui as an informal advisory body on Mainland issues. It provides some genuine, albeit secondary, policy input in areas relating to national security strategy.

[91]On occasion, the president has been known to push particular issues, including procurement issues, largely because of their political or diplomatic importance, according to interviewees.

derives from the premier's position as the highest official of the Executive branch: the premier is president of the Executive Yuan, the supreme executive body in charge of administering all the major organs of government. In the national security arena, the premier's formal power exists largely as a function of (1) his line authority over the Ministry of Foreign Affairs, the Ministry of Defense, and the Mainland Affairs Council (the latter formally established in 1991 to handle the growing contacts with the Chinese Mainland);[92] (2) his direction, under the ultimate authority of the president, of a national government policy deliberation and formulation process centered on the Executive Yuan;[93] and (3) his position as one of two vice-chairmen of the National Security Council within the Office of the President (the ROC vice-president is the other vice-chairman).[94]

Although the premier arguably exerts significant levels of influence within all three areas, his input is by all accounts not absolutely decisive to the formulation of core national security, foreign, or defense policies. Moreover, his authority over line ministries is limited largely to supervisory duties and does not entail substantive policymaking functions, although the premier can certainly influence the specifics of ministerial policy at times. The concrete, operational strategies and concepts guiding Taiwan's foreign and defense policies are developed primarily by the respective ministries and through a wider variety of higher-level interactions between the president and the other senior civilian and military leaders discussed in this section.

On balance, as with many other senior national leaders, the premier's level of individual importance to the national security policy process is largely a function of his overall political clout in the ROC government and his particular personal relationship with the president.

---

[92]The Mainland Affairs Council is directly subordinate to the Executive Yuan and is responsible for overall research, planning, review, and coordination of Mainland policy and affairs, as well as the implementation of specific interministerial programs relating to cross-Strait relations. Although not formally involved in foreign or defense policymaking or policy implementation, the MAC plays an important role in shaping policy toward Mainland China, as well as toward the United States and other nations. It is also a major consumer and interpreter of information and intelligence within the foreign and defense policy arenas. We are indebted to Shelley Rigger for this point. For more details on the MAC, see http://www.mac.gov.tw/english/orafunc/ora02.htm.

[93]This process is largely ad hoc in nature and designed to bring a variety of senior officials and experts together to deliberate over a particular policy issue and to generate policy analyses and recommendations for the president. It is normally most concerned with domestic or particular foreign policy issues, and hence does not play a decisive role in the larger national security or defense policy process. The premier serves primarily as the organizer, supervisor, and facilitator of this Executive Yuan process, on behalf of the president.

[94]However, the premier's membership on the NSC is of no great consequence to national security and defense matters largely because the NSC as a body is not a critical player in these arenas, as discussed in greater detail below.

National Security Council. Originally established in 1967 and subsequently restructured through an amendment of the ROC constitution in April 1991, the NSC (*guojia anquan huiyi*) is an advisory body to the president formally charged with determining the ROC's national security policies and assisting in planning the ROC's security strategy.[95] Within this broad mandate, the NSC plays a policy role in a wide variety of areas, including foreign affairs, relations with the Mainland, military defense, foreign intelligence collection and analysis, and domestic security and counterintelligence.[96] Of these functions, the most important for external national security policy are cross-Strait relations, foreign policy, and national defense policy. Although small in size (with an internal staff of less than 60), the NSC exercises formal supervisory authority over much larger national security–related organizations, including the National Security Bureau (NSB), discussed below.

The NSC consists of a senior membership and is supported by a secretariat. The senior NSC membership includes the president, as NSC chairman, and the vice-president and premier, who serve as NSC vice-chairmen. Other senior members of the NSC include the Ministers of Foreign Affairs, National Defense, and Economic Affairs; the NSC secretary-general; the director of the Mainland Affairs Council; the director of the National Security Bureau; and the general secretary of the Office of the President. The NSC secretariat serves as a ". . . staff office to coordinate inter-agency implementation of NSC policy directives, channel intelligence from the intelligence community to the NSC and prepare the agenda for NSC meetings."[97]

Although impressive on paper, the NSC as a body is not a major actor in the national security policy process and in particular has very little influence over defense-related matters. Under the NSC Organization Law promulgated after the 1991 constitutional amendments, the NSC was designated merely as a consultative agency for the president with no decision-making or inter-agency coordination powers. Given the NSC's relatively weak authority, its senior members rarely meet as a body.[98]

By far the most influential figure within the NSC is the secretary-general. As the most senior national security official within the Office of the President, the NSC secretary-general functions as the president's primary national security advisor,

---

[95]*The Republic of China Yearbook 1997*, p. 77.

[96]David Shambaugh, "Taiwan's Security: Maintaining Deterrence Amid Political Accountability," *The China Quarterly*, Number 148, December 1996, London, p. 1289.

[97]Ibid.

[98]Under the law, the president can convene select subgroups of the senior NSC membership.

although the extent of his influence depends very much on the type and level of his policy expertise and his personal relationship with the president.

Ministry of Foreign Affairs. The Ministry of Foreign Affairs is the supreme national government organ responsible for the foreign relations of the ROC. Its activities are primarily limited to the formulation and implementation of civilian policies associated with diplomatic and political relations with foreign states and international organizations. The MoFA's leading official, the Foreign Minister, has some influence over the setting of national security strategy and defense-related policies through various formal and informal interactions with the president and the premier, including private consultations with the president, his involvement in the Executive Yuan–centered policy process and in the policy deliberations of the KMT Central Committee (discussed below), and through his membership on the NSC. Although usually a critical advisor to the premier and president on foreign policy—and especially regarding policy toward key states such as the United States—the Foreign Minister is not a pivotal actor in the formulation of Taiwan's overall national security strategy and has virtually no influence over defense policies.

Economic and Technology Agencies. A wide variety of government organizations play a role in the economic and technological aspects of Taiwan's foreign policy process. The most important of these agencies include the Ministry of Economic Affairs, the Ministry of Finance, the Central Bank of China, and the Council for Economic Planning and Development. The Ministry of Economic Affairs (MEF) and the Ministry of Finance (MoF) are responsible for developing and implementing Taiwan's economic and technology policies, including its foreign trade and investment activities and related efforts to expand the scope and degree of Taiwan's participation in international economic organizations. Taiwan has no separate ministry for foreign trade. Overall policy in that area is largely administered by a single bureau within the MEF. The MEF also contains the International Economic Cooperation and Development Fund (IECDF), which directs the bulk of Taiwan's aid diplomacy efforts.[99] However, the MEF's activities are supported by a separate China External Trade Development Council (CETDC), which coordinates and promotes Taiwan's global economic activities through a significant number of offices throughout the world. The Council for Economic Planning and Development (CEPD) and its predecessors are mainly responsible for formulating economic plans and supervising public

---

[99] A number of humanitarian, loan grant, and technical assistance programs are also administered by the MoFA, the Ministry of Finance, the Council of Agriculture, the Committee of International Technical Cooperation, and the Export-Import Bank of the ROC. See Tuan Y. Cheng, "Foreign Aid in ROC Diplomacy," in Bih-jaw Lin and James T. Myers, eds., *Contemporary China and the Changing International Community*, University of South Carolina Press, Columbia, 1994, p. 176.

enterprises. Although highly influential in the sixties and seventies, the CEPD has reportedly become less active in economic policy formulation in recent years, although it still conducts economic research and oversees major construction projects.[100] Of the above agencies, the Ministry of Economic Affairs arguably exerts the most influence over basic economic policy decisions in the foreign affairs arena, at least on a formal level. The head of this ministry is the only economic policy official on the NSC.

Ministry of National Defense. The Ministry of National Defense (MND) is the supreme national government organ responsible for the defense of the ROC. The power and influence of the MND over broad national security strategy is greatly dependent on the authority of the minister of national defense. This individual exerts significant potential influence over the setting of both national security strategy and defense policy through his interactions with the president (as commander-in-chief and head of state) and the premier (as head of the executive branch). These include private consultations with the president, his direct involvement in the Executive Yuan–centered policy process, and—to a lesser degree—through his membership on the NSC. The primary institutional role of the MND is limited to exercising administrative oversight of the military and to facilitating and coordinating military interactions with the civilian side of government on critical matters such as the defense budget.

In performing its duties, the MND serves, on the one hand, as the major link between the uniformed military and the executive and legislative branches of the government and, on the other hand, as the primary administrative policy channel between the military and the president regarding defense matters. Despite its significant oversight and bureaucratic coordination responsibilities, however, the MND as an institution does not in fact play the lead role in formulating and revising basic defense policy or in determining Taiwan's force structure. The major elements of Taiwan's defense strategy/doctrine and related force structure are developed by the professional military, and specifically the GSH, as described below. The same is true regarding military budget and procurement decisions.[101]

---

[100]Hung-mao Tien, 1989, pp. 126–127, 129, 137.

[101]The overall limited role of the MND in the defense policy process derives in part from the historically dominant influence over the details of defense strategy, force structure, budget, and procurement decisions enjoyed by the armed services, especially the ROC Army. It also reflects the general historical importance of military leaders within the ROC political system. The MND's capacity to play a leading role in determining core aspects of defense policy is also constrained by the highly limited level of expertise residing within the offices of the MND. Most defense-related policy and operational expertise remains firmly within the GSH and the individual armed services.

The MND's formal authority over the military and its involvement in military planning and operational matters could increase, however, depending on the outcome of current legislative efforts under way to eliminate the current direct link that exists, regarding operational matters, between the CGS and the president. This change would thus place the military and specifically the CGS *entirely* under the institutional authority of the MND and might thereby increase the ability of the MND to direct important aspects of defense policy.[102] Other proposed changes would reportedly place the service headquarters directly under the command of the MND and also greatly increase the number and functional expertise of MND offices. If enacted into law, these changes, combined with the convergence of military authority systems under the MND, could significantly shift control over basic military decisions from the GSH to the MND.

General Staff Headquarters. The GSH is the highest level agency in the ROC government responsible for military affairs. It oversees the armed services and all other components of the professional military. Equally important, the GSH serves as the coordinating body and operational locus for the defense strategy/force structure and budgetary/procurement processes within Taiwan's defense policy arena.

As with the MND, the influence of the GSH is primarily exerted through its head, in this case the chief of the general staff (CGS). As the senior ROC official responsible for military doctrine and readiness, and with a direct channel to the president regarding operational military matters, the CGS has the *potential* to exert significant influence over defense-related national security issues and policies. However, the CGS does not normally participate in those broader national policy fora open to more senior leaders (i.e., the Executive Yuan–centered policy process and the deliberations of the NSC), and his formal responsibilities are limited to the military defense arena. The overall influence of the CGS on broader national security policy issues is thus highly dependent upon the specific nature of his relationship with the president and, to a lesser extent, with the minister of national defense.

The CGS exerts significant influence over defense policy, however. As indicated above, under the current dual military authority system, the CGS acts, in the military command system, as chief of staff to the president for operational matters; in the administrative system, he serves as chief of staff to the minister of

---

[102]The CGS would serve as both the military staff for the defense minister and commander of military operations under the defense minister's supervision. Hence, this revision in the National Defense Law would also expose the CGS to greater legislative oversight, as a leading official of the executive branch solely under the direct authority of the premier.

national defense.[103] The character, personal relations, and service orientation[104] of the CGS exert a significant, sometimes decisive, influence over the operations and outlook of the GSH. Each CGS is generally able to shape the general contours of Taiwan's defense policy and force structure in ways that potentially benefit the interests of his particular service. This is especially the case when an Army officer serves as CGS, given the historically privileged position enjoyed by the Army within the ROC armed forces and the continued high concentration of active and retired senior Army officers within the upper ranks of the GSH and the MND. However, because it does not contain the most senior leaders of each armed service, the GSH cannot effectively and authoritatively coordinate the activities of the individual services. The existence of the GSH as a leading bureaucratic entity separate from the armed services thus presents a potential obstacle to the establishment of true jointness among the three services.[105]

Armed Services General Headquarters. The General Headquarters for the ROC Army, Navy, and Air Force are directly subordinate to the GSH.[106] These offices are in charge of "... planning, force buildup, combat readiness, training, and logistics" for their respective service.[107] Each service headquarters is under the command of a commander-in-chief (CinC). Each service CinC exercises clearly dominant authority over his service headquarters in a manner similar to the dominant role exercised by the CGS within the GSH. Each service headquarters is in charge of developing and overseeing the formulation and implementation of that service's defense plans, force structure, and related budgetary and procurement proposals, within the larger national framework set by Taiwan's overall defense strategy and defense budget, under the supervision of the service CinC, and utilizing the information and analysis provided by the service staff offices. As expected, each service headquarters thus acts as a strong advocate of its service's interests within the larger defense budget and procurement decision-making processes supervised by the GSH.

National Security Bureau. The NSB is the supreme national government organ responsible for collecting and processing both civilian and military intelligence. Under ROC law, the NSB primarily oversees intelligence relevant to external

---

[103]*The Republic of China Yearbook 1997*, pp. 123–124.

[104]The post of CGS rotates among the three services, usually on a two-year basis.

[105]The Zhong Yuan Program of military reform (discussed below) would have greatly strengthened the operational link between the GSH and the combat units of the armed services. However, this element of the program has apparently been eliminated.

[106]Four other service general headquarters are also directly under the GSH, but are not discussed because they do not play a significant role in the defense policy process. For further details, see The Republic of China Yearbook 1997, pp. 124–125 and the *1996 National Defense Report, Republic of China*, pp. 159–166.

[107]*1998 National Defense Report, Republic of China*, p. 165.

national security issues, including intelligence collection and analysis concerning the PRC.[108] Given its primary function, the NSB as an institution exerts little direct influence over the formulation or implementation of national security, foreign, or defense policies. However, the NSB's interpretation of raw intelligence can shape the policymaking process in important ways. Moreover, the Director of the NSB has the potential to significantly influence such policy arenas, as a result of his direct involvement in senior policy organs, his military background, and his relationship with the president. The NSB director is normally a three star general, equivalent in rank to a vice chief of staff and a service commander-in-chief. He is also a member of the NSC. Most significantly, however, the NSB director is also able to report directly to the president, despite the fact that the NSB is administratively supervised by the NSC.

Legislative Yuan. The LY is the most important legislative organ of the ROC government. Its powers include general oversight and approval of the national budget, interpellation of the premier and any cabinet members on policy matters and government administration, and deliberative/compliance authority over a broad range of government policies and bills. Any law, statute, special act, or general principle has to be adopted by the Legislative Yuan and promulgated by the ROC president before it can be implemented. Several LY committees examine government policies and behavior and recommend legislative action in several specific functional areas. For the national security, foreign, and defense policy areas, the most important committees include those responsible for national defense, foreign and overseas affairs, the budget, and economic affairs.

As indicated above, prior to the early eighties, the LY's activities were largely controlled by the dominant KMT and hence served to support the policies of the ROC executive branch. During the Lee Teng-hui era, the Legislative Yuan became a more important, independent actor in the national security arena, largely as a consequence of the increasing strength of non-KMT political parties within the government and the concomitant emergence of popular sentiment critical of the tight hold the KMT had exerted over foreign and defense matters in the past. As a result of these developments, stronger attempts have been made to gain greater legislative oversight over foreign affairs, the military, and defense matters in general. This development has been most clearly reflected in increased levels of LY scrutiny of the defense budget and equipment acquisitions by the LY National Defense and Budget Committees, and more frequent interpellations of

---

[108]The National Security Act of 1993 placed the previous domestic security and counter-intelligence functions of the NSB primarily within the Investigation Bureau of the Ministry of Justice and placed the NSB under the administrative direction of the NSC. See Shambaugh, 1996, p. 1290.

foreign affairs, defense, and military officials before the LY National Defense and Foreign and Overseas Affairs Committees.

At present, no clear, dominant viewpoint on foreign affairs and defense issues has emerged within the LY to replace the conservative, pro-military viewpoints of many KMT legislators. This is partly because the expertise of opposition LY members on both foreign and defense-related issues remains extremely weak and a cadre of professional staffers has not yet appeared in the system. It is also because the membership of the committees normally reflects a variety of views on national security and defense matters. The division between KMT and DPP members is especially notable, with significant levels of mutual distrust in evidence.[109]

While increasing significantly during the mid-nineties, the level of LY influence over defense matters had reportedly declined somewhat by the end of the decade, however.[110] This has resulted primarily from (a) the continued failure of DPP and other opposition political parties to develop significant defense-related expertise, (b) the lowering of concerns among some opposition leaders about the political influence exerted over the military by conservative KMT members, and (c) the gradual convergence of views on defense matters between mainstream KMT and mainstream DPP politicians. Nonetheless, many opposition (and some KMT) LY politicians remain frustrated by what they view as the lack of accountability of the armed forces.[111] As indicated above, the ability of the LY to oversee military affairs, including defense and national security strategies, could increase significantly in the future once a proposed streamlining of Taiwan's military authority system goes into effect.

As the above analysis suggests, the formulation and implementation of ROC national strategic objectives and the major principles guiding both foreign and defense policies are highly concentrated in the hands of a few senior civilian and military leaders, and are strongly influenced at times by the views and personality of the president. However, this process is poorly coordinated, both within the top levels of the senior leadership and between the civilian and military elite. In particular, no formal, institutionalized, and regularized

---

[109]For example, according to observers in Taipei, the DPP still views the LY National Defense Committee as the last bastion of KMT conservatism in the political system.

[110]The LY exerts even less influence over specific acquisition decisions than it does over planning and budget issues. No institutionalized or regularized process of legislative examination or supervision of the procurement process currently exists. In general, scrutiny of procurement proposals by the Legislative Yuan is sporadic and largely non-technical in nature, given its limited expertise on defense matters and its lack of access to the early stages of the procurement decision-making process.

[111]As Yun-han Chu states, both the military and security apparatus continue to evade direct supervision by the LY in the name of presidential prerogative. Yun-han Chu, p. 151.

interagency process or mechanism for national security strategy formulation and implementation exists that spans all the key senior civilian and military agencies and policymakers. Moreover, at lower levels of the policy process, no formal institutions exist to provide ongoing policy coordination and implementation of national-level grand strategies among civilian and defense policy sectors. Most notably, there is no formal, institutionalized structure of policy interaction between MoFA and MND leaders and offices.

This lack of regularized policy interaction between senior civilian and military officials and organizations means that national security strategy is developed either on a fragmentary basis within individual responsible agencies, or by the president alone through largely separate—and often private—interactions with senior civilian and military officials and advisors. In general, the ROC president employs both ad hoc, informal meetings with senior officials and advisors or limited bureaucratic policy mechanisms—such as the NSC and the Executive Yuan policy deliberation and formulation process—to receive analysis and advice, convey directives and instructions, and facilitate policy consultations, deliberations, and coordination in the national security policy arena.

Taiwan's foreign policy process, including relations with the United States, is centered on interactions between the ROC president, his key advisors, the minister of foreign affairs and, when required, the minister of economic affairs. Ideally, concrete policy recommendations and basic policy decisions evolve through a process of regular drafting, deliberation, and consultation, usually led by MoFA experts and officials. However, during the Lee Teng-hui era, the major features of foreign policy were often developed by Lee himself, sometimes with input from trusted advisors in the Office of the President. This in part reflected Lee's growing suspicion of the professional foreign policy bureaucracy, which he thought was excessively wedded to the conservative views of the old KMT leadership. Chen Shui-bian has apparently adopted a more consultative process among the senior executive leadership. However, the broader foreign (and defense) policy processes have been severely disrupted by his ongoing confrontation with the KMT-dominated LY.

Taiwan's defense strategy and force structure are primarily determined by the GSH, within the broad parameters provided by Taiwan's overall national security policy, and with critical inputs provided by the service headquarters. Although civilian agencies such as the MND and the president perform general oversight and coordination functions, neither is terribly substantive.[112]

---

[112]However, the level of influence over defense policy and procurement decisions exerted by individual senior civilian officials can vary significantly, depending upon the personal influence and

Moreover, this military-centered defense policy decision-making process is not well integrated into the civilian side of the national security policy process. In response to this deficiency, a proposal exists to establish a National Military Council (*guofang junshi huiyi*) (NMC) as an authoritative, high-level defense decision-making organization composed of both civilian and military leaders.[113] This body would reportedly act as an ad hoc organization (i.e., with no permanent or fixed offices), and be convened by the president as part of his powers as commander-in-chief largely to make major decisions in the defense realm.[114] However, despite its presumably greater authority, the effectiveness of the NMC would depend almost entirely upon the president's willingness to utilize the forum, and the information and analysis provided by subordinate defense organs. Absent a highly proactive president in the defense arena, the uniformed military would thus likely retain its existing initiative and control over the defense policy process.[115]

Taiwan's defense strategy is based on a relatively narrow set of service missions and force structure requirements keyed primarily to the separate interests and outlooks of the three services and an assumption of U.S. intervention in a future major military crisis with the Mainland. Few organizational, financial, or conceptual incentives exist to promote more comprehensive and integrated approaches to defense planning that systematically and consistently link perceived threats to doctrine, force structure, training, and maintenance needs. Moreover, evidence suggests that advanced weapons systems are sometimes desired and/or acquired from foreign sources without a full consideration of the appropriate operational and maintenance requirements of such systems. Indeed, procurement decisions are at times subject to significant influence by a host of factors other than pure warfighting needs, including the political objectives of the president. This results in considerable confusion over the motives behind Taiwan's individual weapons procurement decisions and resulting foreign purchase requests, and a lack of confidence among many outside observers in the ability of the ROC military to gain the maximum benefit from the more advanced weapons systems it acquires from the United States and elsewhere.

---

political calculations of the individual holding the office. At present, it seems that Chen Shui-bian is not eager to take on the military at this stage of his presidency, particularly given his already significant list of domestic difficulties.

[113]Much of the following discussion of the NMC is based upon Ding and Huang.

[114]Less important or less urgent decisions would presumably be made by the president in private consultations with leading defense officials or possibly in the context of the above-mentioned military discussion meeting (*junshi huitan*), as is currently the case.

[115]Almost all interested legislators reportedly oppose the idea of establishing a NMC. Some argue that the NSC already performs the proposed functions of a NMC, but simply needs to be made more authoritative and more subject to LY oversight.

It is too early to tell whether the above decision-making features will continue under the Chen Shui-bian government. Thus far, the foreign and defense policy processes have been severely disrupted by the Chen administration's ongoing confrontation with the KMT-dominated LY. These difficulties, along with Chen's overall need to pursue a moderate policy stance, might eventually lead to a greater reliance on more regular, consultative interactions with the MoFA and the MND. On the other hand, if Chen is able to consolidate his political base within the government, some of his backers in the DPP might pressure the government to place a greater emphasis on less orthodox elements of the DPP's foreign and defense policy platform (e.g., involvement in NGO and human rights activities), thereby generating resistance from the MoFA bureaucracy and the military.

Conclusions

Taiwan's highly dynamic domestic political and social environments exert a significant influence on the ROC government's foreign and defense policies. At the broadest level, the emergence of a highly competitive multiparty system marked by a rather weak commitment to many of the norms of the democratic process has generated a potential for greater policy volatility and uncertainty than existed under the autocratic KMT regime. Moreover, the victory of Chen Shui-bian has resulted in a sharply divided, sometimes chaotic and undisciplined government that arguably has the effect of undermining rational policy deliberation and innovation, and hence the crafting of effective responses to the enormous political and security challenges posed by Mainland China. Specifically, these developments have slowed the defense reform process and perhaps undermined Taiwan's ability to fashion a more unified and integrated set of foreign and defense policies.

Closely related to such trends, Taiwan's political and economic elites have become highly responsive to the demands of open political competition, regional and global economic forces, and the interests of the domestic public and key social groups. On the one hand, this development has resulted in the emergence of a moderate, pragmatic policy perspective among the majority of the Taiwan leadership, reflecting in large part the pragmatism of the Taiwan public. As a result, a strong consensus has emerged across the bulk of the elite regarding certain basic principles guiding Taiwan's foreign and defense policies. On the other hand, the emergence of a more differentiated and complex leadership has created some intense mutual suspicions and significant variations in approach toward specific policy issues. In particular, personal rifts between the professional military and the DPP leadership and between non-KMT political leaders and the professional foreign policy establishment are especially notable—as are, for example, differences over defense priorities, the ultimate purpose of the military modernization process, and the emphasis placed on various aspects of Taiwan's diplomatic policy.

The emergence of a pro–status quo, pragmatic center among the Taiwan populace serves to inhibit any tendencies among the elite to undertake sudden or radical policy departures. However, indications of growing public support for permanent political separation from the Mainland, combined with occasional expressions of support for more assertive efforts to raise Taiwan's international profile and to acquire specific military systems such as offensive ballistic missiles and missile defense systems, provide a potential public foundation for more assertive policies. Taken together, the existence of these potentially conflicting social views, along with Taiwan's volatile political process, serve to pressure political leaders while also providing them with significant room for maneuver in shaping public sentiment.

Finally, the lack of coordination and integration between Taiwan's foreign and defense policy decision-making structures adds to the above difficulties presented by the domestic political and social environments.

4. The Influence of Chinese Policy and Behavior

China's attitudes and actions toward Taiwan arguably exert a decisive influence over ROC foreign and defense policy. As suggested in Chapter 2, the importance of China is rooted in three key areas: China's basic attitude and strategy toward Taiwan, China's economic influence, and Chinese military power. This chapter examines the major features of each of these three areas of Chinese influence and explores the implications of each for Taiwan's current and future foreign and defense policies.

Chinese Policy Toward Taiwan: Basic Features and Evolution[1]

Beijing considers Taiwan to be an inalienable part of China and regards reunification as a "sacred task" of Chinese nationalism. It completely rejects the possibility of Taiwan becoming a fully independent, sovereign state. However, Beijing fears that Taiwan is moving toward permanent separation from the Mainland, perhaps with U.S. support, and has adopted a complex strategy of pressures and enticements to arrest this trend and at the very least to reestablish a more stable *modus vivendi* across the Taiwan Strait. To grasp the complexities of China's policy stance toward Taiwan today, it is important to understand how and why that policy has evolved over the past 20 years or so.

The key elements of Beijing's current policy toward Taiwan emerged largely beginning in the late seventies, in response to a basic decision to shift the thrust of China's policy from confrontation and liberation by force to peaceful reunification through negotiations. This policy line contains nine basic elements, identified by Ralph Clough:[2]

- There is only one China. Taiwan is a part of China and cannot become an independent state.

---

[1]Much of this section is drawn from Michael D. Swaine, "Chinese Decision-Making Regarding Taiwan, 1979–2000," in David M. Lampton, ed., *The Making of Chinese Foreign and Security Policy in the Era of Reform, 1978–2000*, Stanford University Press, Stanford, California, 2001.

[2]Ralph N. Clough, *Reaching Across the Taiwan Strait: People-to-People Diplomacy*, Westview Press, Boulder, Colorado, 1993, p. 126.

- The reunification of Taiwan with China is necessary and inevitable, and the sooner it is accomplished the better.

- Reunification should occur under a formula of "one country, two systems," in which Taiwan will be permitted to retain its existing political, economic, and military systems in return for Taipei's recognition of the government in Beijing as China's sole national government and the ultimate authority responsible for Taiwan's defense and diplomatic relations.

- Reunification talks should begin as soon as possible.

- Reunification talks can be conducted on an equal basis by representatives of the Nationalist and Communist parties, but not by representatives of Beijing and Taipei as two equal governments, since the Taiwan authorities administer only a provincial government.

- The two sides should promote people-to-people interactions to prepare for a smooth reunification.

- The so-called Three Links (direct mail, trade and shipping, and air services) are required to facilitate people-to-people interactions.

- Although the PRC favors peaceful reunification, it nonetheless reserves the right to use military force against Taiwan if necessary, to prevent the island from permanently separating from the Mainland.

- Only the PRC has the right to represent China internationally, so Taiwan can only have economic and cultural relations with foreign countries, not diplomatic relations.[3]

This policy was the logical consequence of two larger policy initiatives taken in the late seventies: the normalization of Sino-U.S. relations and the adoption of economic reform and open-door policies. The former development led to Washington's acknowledgment of Beijing's "One China" stance toward Taiwan and the abrogation of the U.S.-ROC mutual defense treaty.[4] The latter policy required the development of a peaceful and stable external environment conducive to economic growth, including amicable ties with the major powers and with China's Asian neighbors, including Taiwan.

These developments made it possible for Beijing to adopt a nonconfrontational policy toward Taiwan and increased the likelihood that such a policy would be accepted by Taipei. The Chinese leadership—Deng Xiaoping in particular—

---

[3]Some elements of this policy (e.g., the notion of "One China") have existed since at least 1949, but were never explicitly included prior to the nineties as part of a larger reunification talks initiative.

[4]The latter event was soon followed by the August 1982 Sino-U.S. Communiqué in which Washington pledged to reduce the level of U.S. arms sales to Taiwan.

apparently reasoned that Taiwan's loss of U.S. political and military support and the development of closer ties between Beijing and the rest of Asia, combined with an offer to permit the continuation of Taiwan's existing political and economic order under the "one country, two systems" formula, would eventually force Taipei to drop its confrontational stance (marked by a nearly complete refusal to interact with Beijing) and enter into reunification negotiations. The Chinese leadership further believed that China's open door policy and ensuing rapid economic development would increase Taiwan's dependence on the Mainland and thus create even greater reasons for Taiwan to move toward reunification.[5] Therefore, from 1978 to 1992, various noncoercive, cross-Strait elements of Beijing's peaceful reunification policy line were uniformly emphasized and accepted by the senior Chinese leadership.

China's strategy of peaceful reunification underwent a significant adjustment in the early nineties. The first shift dealt with the issue of the "One China" principle, which the PRC had long insisted was a core precondition for discussions. For most of its post-1949 history, the ROC had shared Beijing's view that there was "One China," though Chiang Kai-Shek and his supporters believed that the majority of the territory of this "China" was being held by "Communist bandits" [gongfei]. After the Taipei government renounced its claim to the Mainland, however, officials in Beijing began to doubt the Taiwan government's commitment to the notion of eventual reunification. From Beijing's perspective, a significant breakthrough occurred in 1992 with the talks between the representatives of two quasi-official organizations, the Straits Exchange Foundation (SEF) led by Koo Chen-fu and the Association for Relations Across the Taiwan Strait (ARATS) led by Wang Daohan. These talks resulted in what Beijing continues to believe was an agreement by both sides to accept the notion of "One China," though both sides were free to define "One China" in a way of their own choosing.[6]

Despite this early progress, both sides were not able to build successfully on the foundation of the 1992 meeting. Indeed, from Beijing's perspective, Taiwan appeared to be drifting away the reunification path in 1993–1994. As a result, Beijing promulgated a major policy initiative toward Taiwan in January 1995— the so-called Jiang Zemin Eight Point Initiative (known as the Jiang Eight Points—Jiang Ba Dian):

---

[5]Interviews, Beijing, September 1998.

[6]As indicated above, in recent years, a debate has erupted in Taiwan about the exact details of the agreement reached between Koo and Wang, with some seeking to deny that such an accommodation was ever made by the Taiwan side.

1. Adherence to the principle of "One China" is the basis and premise for peaceful reunification. China's sovereignty and territory must never be allowed to suffer split [sic]. We must firmly oppose any words or actions aimed at creating an "independent Taiwan" and the propositions "split the country and rule under separate regimes," "two Chinas over a certain period of time," etc., which are in contravention of the principle of "One China."

2. We do not challenge the development of non-governmental economic and cultural ties by Taiwan with other countries. Under the principle of "One China" and in accordance with the charters of the relevant international organizations, Taiwan has become a member of the Asian Development Bank, the Asia-Pacific Economic Cooperation forum and other international economic organizations in the name of "Chinese Taipei." However, we oppose Taiwan's activities in "expanding its living space internationally" which are aimed at creating "two Chinas" or "One China, one Taiwan." All patriotic compatriots in Taiwan and other people of insight understand that instead of solving the problems, such activities can only help the forces working for the "independence of Taiwan" undermine the process of peaceful reunification more scrupulously. Only after the peaceful reunification is accomplished can the Taiwan compatriots and other Chinese people of all ethnic groups truly and fully share the dignity and honor attained by our great motherland internationally.

3. It has been our consistent stand to hold negotiations with the Taiwan authorities on the peaceful reunification of the motherland. Representatives from the various political parties and mass organizations on both sides of the Taiwan Strait can be invited to participate in such talks. I said in my report at the Fourteenth National Congress of the Communist Party of China held in October 1992, "On the premise that there is only 'One China,' we are prepared to talk with the Taiwan authorities about any matter, including the form that official negotiations should take, a form that is acceptable to both sides." By "on the premise that there is only 'One China,' we are prepared to talk with the Taiwan authorities about any matter," we mean naturally that all matters of concern to the Taiwan authorities are included. We have proposed time and time again that negotiations should be held on officially ending the state of hostility between the two sides and accomplishing peaceful reunification step by step. Here again I solemnly propose that such negotiations be held. I suggest that, as the first step, negotiations should be held and an agreement reached on officially ending the state of hostility between the two sides in accordance with the principle that there is only "One China." On this basis, the two sides should undertake jointly to safeguard China's sovereignty and territorial integrity and map out plans for the future development of their relations. As regards the name, place and form of these political talks, a solution acceptable to both sides can certainly be found so long as consultations on an equal footing can be held at an early date.

4. We should strive for the peaceful reunification of the motherland since Chinese should not fight fellow Chinese. Our not undertaking to give up the use of force is not directed against our compatriots in Taiwan but against the

schemes of foreign forces to interfere with China's reunification and to bring about the "independence of Taiwan." We are fully confident that our compatriots in Taiwan, Hong Kong and Macao and those residing overseas would understand our principled position.

5. In face of the development of the world economy in the twenty-first century, great efforts should be made to expand the economic exchanges and cooperation between the two sides of the Taiwan Strait so as to achieve prosperity on both sides to the benefit of the entire Chinese nation. We hold that political differences should not affect or interfere with the economic cooperation between the two sides. We shall continue to implement over a long period of time the policy of encouraging industrialists and businessmen from Taiwan to invest in the Mainland and enforce the Law of the People's Republic of China for Protecting the Investment of the Compatriots of Taiwan. Whatever the circumstances may be, we shall safeguard the legitimate rights and interests of industrialists and businessmen from Taiwan. We should continue to expand contacts and exchanges between our compatriots on both sides so as to increase mutual understanding and trust. Since the direct links for postal, air and shipping services and trade between the two sides are the objective requirements for their economic development and contacts in various fields, and since they are in the interests of the people on both sides, it is absolutely necessary to adopt practical measures to speed up the establishment of such direct links. Efforts should be made to promote negotiations on certain specific issues between the two sides. We are in favor of conducting this kind of negotiations on the basis on reciprocity and mutual benefit and signing non-governmental agreements on the protection of the rights and interests of industrialists and businessmen from Taiwan.

6. The splendid culture of five thousand years created by the sons and daughters of all ethnic groups in China has become ties keeping the entire Chinese people close at heart and constitutes an important basis for the peaceful reunification of the motherland. People on both sides of the Taiwan Strait should inherit and carry forward the fine traditions of the China culture.

7. The 21 million compatriots in Taiwan, whether born there or in other provinces, are all Chinese and our own flesh and blood. We should fully respect their life style and their wish to be the masters of our country and protect all their legitimate rights and interests. The relevant departments of our party and the government including the agencies stationed abroad should strengthen close ties with compatriots from Taiwan, listen to their views and demands, be concerned with and take into account their interests and make every effort to help them solve their problems. We hope that Taiwan Island enjoys social stability, economic growth and affluence. We also hope that all political parties in Taiwan will adopt a sensible, forward-looking and constructive attitude and promote the expansion of relations between the two sides. All parties and personages of all circles in Taiwan are welcome to exchange views with us on relations between the two sides and on peaceful reunification and are also welcome to pay a visit and tour places. All

personages from various circles who have contributed to the reunification of China will go down in history for their deeds.

8. Leaders of the Taiwan authorities are welcome to pay visits in appropriate capacities. We are also ready to accept invitations from the Taiwan side to visit Taiwan. We can discuss state affairs, or exchange ideas on certain questions first. Even a simple visit to the other side will be useful. The affairs of the Chinese people should be handled by ourselves, something that does not take an international occasion to accomplish. Separated across the Strait, our people eagerly look forward to meeting each other. They should be able to exchange visits, instead of being kept from seeing each other all their lives.[7]

Although based on the core principles laid out in the late seventies and early eighties, the Jiang Eight Points focused primarily on the modalities of cross-Strait discussions leading to reunification. It listed various specific proposals, such as the convening of a cross-Strait dialogue between equal representatives and an agreement to end hostilities, and emphasized the need for a phased process of rapprochement and negotiations leading to reunification. Unlike the policy shift of 1978–1982, which reflected Deng's desire to resolve the Taiwan issue during the eighties, the Jiang Eight Points did not anticipate such "speedy" reunification; rather it sought only an agreement on a transitional framework that would stabilize the status quo, facilitate economic exchanges, and generally preempt any permanent separation of Taiwan from the Mainland.[8] Moreover, the proposal suggested that as long as Taiwan would negotiate under the principle that there is only one China and Taiwan is a part of China, Beijing would consider all of Taiwan's concerns.[9]

The Jiang Eight Points were formulated in response to various new domestic and external developments confronting the Chinese leadership in the early nineties. These included, first and foremost, Lee Teng-hui's apparent efforts to legitimate, both domestically and internationally, a "One China, One Taiwan" arrangement that Chinese leaders feared would likely result in the permanent separation of the two; second, apparent adverse shifts in the U.S. stance toward the island such as Washington's 1992 decision to sell F-16 aircraft to Taiwan and the September

---

[7]Jiang Zemin, "Continue to Promote the Reunification of the Motherland," Xinhua, 30 January 1995.

[8]Chu Yun-han, p. 15.

[9]Of course, what specifically is meant by "One China" was and remains unclear to many Taiwan residents. If the concept implies recognition of the ultimate sovereign authority of the People's Republic of China over Taiwan—as is sometimes stated or implied by Chinese sources-—then it is almost certainly unacceptable. If, however, it means a single Chinese nation or political entity whose specific form must be determined through joint negotiations between the two sides—as is also sometimes implied by Chinese sources—then it might prove acceptable to many Taiwan citizens.

1994 limited "upgrade" in relations with Taipei,[10] and, third, various structural and personal opportunities for policy change resulting from the Chinese leadership succession process and in particular the rise of Jiang Zemin's influence. Jiang undoubtedly believed that a peaceful breakthrough on Taiwan would serve to confirm the continuity of his policies with Deng Xiaoping's, boost his stature among the public, strengthen his position among his colleagues and rivals for power, and defuse concerns among the military over an increasingly independence-minded Taiwan.[11]

China's basic policy toward Taiwan underwent a further modification in the latter half of the nineties, as a result of the Taiwan Strait "mini-crisis" of 1995–1996. That event significantly increased Chinese fears that Washington was supportive of Lee's strategy of "creeping independence" and was reversing its policy on "One China." After the crisis, the Jiang Eight Points became part of a larger political-military-diplomatic strategy, designed

- to constrain Taiwan's freedom of action internationally

- to weaken Lee Teng-hui's influence within Taiwan

- to increase the political and military incentives for a post-Lee Teng-hui government to begin a genuine process of political negotiation, based on the Jiang Eight Points and the nine basic elements of Taiwan policy outlined above

- to achieve China's objectives by force, if the above efforts fail and Taiwan moves unambiguously toward independence

- to deter Washington from intervening militarily in the event of a future Taiwan-Mainland confrontation.

To attain these objectives, China undertook initiatives in three areas throughout 1997–2001: First, Beijing intensified efforts both to establish a political dialogue with Taipei[12] and to increase leverage on the ROC government by strengthening Taiwan's economic links with and presumably its dependence on the Mainland.[13] This initiative was accompanied by broader diplomatic interactions

---

[10]Many Chinese leaders saw the U.S. sale as a violation of the 1982 Sino-U.S. Communiqué in which Washington had pledged to gradually reduce arms sales to Taipei. Moreover, for many, the U.S. action confirmed that Washington was modifying its past "One China" stance to encourage pro-independence sentiment on Taiwan.

[11]As Chu Yun-han states (p. 12), "formulating a new policy guideline on the Taiwan issue was a strong political statement about the coming of Jiang's era."

[12]Overall, this peace initiative was intended to pressure Taipei to begin political talks with Beijing by presenting Taiwan as the more rigid, unreasonable party in the continued stalemate.

[13]The latter element of Beijing's approach has probably existed since the early nineties, but became much more important at the end of the decade.

across Asia, Russia, and Europe, intended to improve ties and thereby reduce U.S. diplomatic leverage regarding Taiwan among third countries and to assure observers that the Taiwan issue was *sui generis* and that Beijing's more muscular approach did not portend an overall aggressive Chinese foreign policy line.

Second, Beijing made renewed efforts to improve relations with Washington and in particular to obtain a formal pledge that the United States was unambiguously opposed to Taiwan's political independence, would not support a "One Taiwan–One China" solution, and would not back Taiwan's efforts to enter international bodies that required statehood for entrance.[14] The Chinese also sought assurances from Washington that it would reduce its level of military assistance to Taiwan and attempted to increase Washington's incentives to maintain good relations with Beijing by strengthening America's economic involvement in China.[15] Chinese leaders and strategists are especially concerned that U.S. leaders deliberately seek to provide an effective theater ballistic missile defense system (including both LT and UT capabilities) to Taiwan, and to U.S. forces in Japan. Many Chinese believe that such BMD systems would greatly strengthen the U.S.-Taiwan defense relationship, embolden Taiwan's leaders to move toward more formal independence, and counter the overall deterrent effect of those Chinese IRBMs capable of striking U.S. forces in Asia.

Third, the Chinese intensified their efforts to enhance China's military capabilities vis-à-vis both Taiwan and the United States. These efforts were designed to raise the credibility of a use of force against Taiwan, and thus to deter the U.S. from providing direct military assistance to Taiwan in the event of a future military confrontation across the Strait, or at the very least to delay the deployment of such assistance. Since 1996, China has increased its production of short-range ballistic missiles; reached agreements to obtain from Russia additional sophisticated naval, air, and air defense assets of possible use against Taiwan; and increased its attempts to acquire the capability to detect, track, target, and attack U.S. carrier battle groups. It has also repeatedly expressed strong opposition to the acquisition by Taiwan of a dedicated ballistic missile defense system.

Beijing provided an authoritative explanation of this overall carrot-and-stick approach in February 2000, with the publication of a second White Paper on Taiwan. This document offered the most complete explanation to date of

---

[14]Washington ultimately agreed to a public affirmation of what became known as the "Three Nos" during the second Clinton-Jiang summit in mid-1998.

[15]Beijing's ultimate objective was to persuade Washington to encourage Taipei to begin talks under the "One China" principle.

Beijing's position on Taiwan's status, Lee Teng-hui's allegedly "splittist" behavior, and future cross-Strait talks. While providing an extensive set of intended incentives to resume the stalled cross-Strait dialogue, the White Paper nonetheless also stated for the first time in an authoritative policy document what Chinese officials had been saying less formally for years—that Beijing would consider using force if Taipei indefinitely avoids entering into meaningful talks with the Mainland.[16] The document was an effort to repudiate Lee's July 1999 characterization of Mainland-Taiwan relations as a "special state-to-state relationship"[17] and an attempt to both pressure and entice a post-Lee leader to resume the cross-Strait dialogue.

The above basic policy and three-pronged supporting strategy have remained in place to the present. The election of DPP candidate Chen Shui-bian to the ROC presidency in March 2000 did not appreciably alter this strategy, although it has produced some tactical modifications and certain new emphases. Beijing was initially very alarmed by Chen's election, and sought, both before and immediately after the event, to intimidate Taiwan's citizens and the new ROC government by drawing attention to the grave dangers to cross-Strait peace presented by the DPP's ascension to power, and by demanding that the Chen government explicitly renounce the pro-independence platform of the DPP. However, it has since adopted a more sophisticated approach, reflecting (a) a consideration of the enormous difficulties Chen has faced in governing Taiwan since his election, (b) the obvious dangers of a backlash in both Taiwan and the United States presented by taking too aggressive a stance, and (c) the support and leverage Chen has received by adopting a conciliatory, cautious, and pragmatic public position on cross-Strait relations, the independence issue, and constitutional revision, as indicated in Chapter 2. The most important initiatives include the following:

First, Beijing has sought to improve ties with a wide range of Taiwan politicians, businesspersons, and cultural figures by inviting them to China and encouraging them to make statements supportive of the "One China" concept, the opening of a political dialogue with Beijing, and other seemingly moderate, anti-DPP positions. The goal of this "united front" tactic is to isolate and presumably weaken support among the Taiwan public for the Chen Shui-bian government. This campaign has arguably been strengthened considerably by the continued

---

[16]For the full text of the White Paper, entitled *The One-China Principle and the Taiwan Issue*, see http://taiwansecurity.org/IS/White-Paper-022100.htm.

[17]Lee's statement was taken by Beijing as a deliberate attempt to strengthen both domestic and international acceptance of Taiwan as a sovereign nation entirely separate from and equal to Beijing, and to prevent Lee's successor from pursuing a more accommodating policy toward the Mainland. For a full transcript of Lee's remarks, see http://www.gio.gov.tw/info/99html/99lee/0709.htm.

decline of the Taiwan economy and the accompanying increase in cross-Strait economic links that have occurred in recent years (both are discussed below). These developments have contributed to an increase in public and business support for greater cooperation with the Mainland, as well as an apparent increase in popular support for eventual unification, as indicated above.

Second, Beijing has gone even further than during the 1997–2000 period to present a stance of moderation and flexibility regarding cross-Strait dialogue. Although Chinese officials continue to insist that the Chen government must explicitly affirm its commitment to the notion of "One China" before any official talks can begin (or before the Three Links can be established), they have also given more explicit indications that they do not equate a future "One China" with the government of the People's Republic of China and that they are willing to consider a range of formulas for future reunification. In particular, Chinese officials have indicated their willingness to accept the 1992 "agreement" reached between Taipei and Beijing, in which both sides affirmed the notion of "One China," but reserved their own definition of what the concept means.

Beijing apparently calculates that the Chen government can be pressured by domestic political opposition, a divided and seemingly paralyzed central government, domestic economic problems, and a more moderate PRC approach to cross-Strait relations to affirm some version of a "One China" concept. Failing that, the PRC leadership apparently believes that Chen Shui-bian will prove unable to govern effectively through his term of office and will likely be replaced by a more flexible government, led perhaps by a KMT leader less associated with the more objectionable policies of the Lee Teng-hui government, by James Soong, or by some type of "moderate" coalition of parties. However, Chinese leaders are undoubtedly concerned that the recent return of Lee Teng-hui to politics and the closely related establishment of the Taiwan Solidarity Union will result in the emergence of a viable Chen-Lee coalition that could successfully resist any return to more "flexible" policies.

Many Taiwan observers of China's policy believe that the above mixed strategy of incentives and pressures reflects an internal power struggle between hardliners and moderates in the leadership. Such an interpretation, however, significantly distorts the nature of the Taiwan policy process and leadership relations on this issue. The Chinese leadership as a whole is in agreement on the basic assumptions underlying Taiwan policy. Although political and bureaucratic interests serve as a basis for debate in a consensus-oriented policy process, such differences have largely arisen over timing and emphasis, not fundamental direction. Moreover, Jiang Zemin is able to decisively influence, if not control, grand strategy toward Taiwan. At the same time, he cannot simply dictate any particular policy course to the senior leadership. He has to balance the interests and preferences of the major leaders and organizations involved in Taiwan security issues, in particular those of the People's Liberation Army (PLA) on the one hand and the Foreign Ministry and other civilian officials on the other.[18]

Indeed, the serious confrontation with Washington that resulted from Beijing's military displays in 1995–1996 served to exacerbate the natural contrast in policy preferences between these two groups. Following the crisis, Foreign Ministry and other civilian entities reportedly stressed the feasibility of containing Taiwan and moving toward attainment of the Jiang Eight Points through political and diplomatic means, particularly the improvement of relations with the United States. While in agreement on the ultimate objectives, the military and some hardliners within the Party stressed the need to continue developing China's military capabilities vis-a-vis Taiwan. However, these were not mutually exclusive views, and the above strategy clearly reflects elements of both sets of preferences.[19] In other words, the Chinese military does not dictate PRC policy regarding Taiwan, even though military leaders have generally been very attentive to Taiwan policy because of their obvious institutional responsibilities. This attentiveness has only increased in the nineties, as a result of the growing capabilities and pro-independence orientation of the Taiwan leadership.[20]

The above presents several implications for Taiwan's foreign and defense policies, including cross-Strait relations:

China is placing significant political pressure on the Chen Shui-bian government through the "united front" strategy. Some political leaders and businesspersons are directly or indirectly urging the Chen government to agree to some version of the "One China" principle in order to begin official talks or to establish the Three Links. Yet Chen's political base in the DPP and the strong suspicions of the

---

[18]Military leaders have at times apparently expressed criticism of what they have viewed as overly conciliatory approaches adopted by the Foreign Ministry. Yet the standing PLA leadership does not formally develop and present "positions" on overall grand strategy toward Taiwan. Moreover, as head of the Party's Central Military Commission, Jiang Zemin serves as the primary channel for the expression of the military's views to the senior Party and state leadership.

[19]Interviews, Beijing, September 1998. Some outside observers believe that the military leadership (and perhaps many Party figures as well) concluded during the 1995–1996 crisis that China will eventually be required to use force to resolve the Taiwan situation. The authors have been unable to confirm this assertion. If true, it would tend to suggest that a significant gap exists between the military and civilian organs such as the Foreign Ministry and the Taiwan Affairs Office over the possibility of a peaceful solution emerging.

[20]In general, the PLA's most active role in the policy process is limited to (a) providing intelligence and assessments on the domestic situation on Taiwan, the U.S.-Taiwan and U.S.-Japan-Taiwan security relationships, and the military balance across the Strait; (b) pressing for support from the civilian leadership for the acquisition of weapons and equipment to more effectively deal with Taiwan-related security contingencies; and (c) applying various types of military pressure on Taiwan.

Taiwan populace toward the Mainland government continue to prevent him from acceding to this pressure. As frequently suggested above, the so-called "One China" principle has now become associated, in the minds of many Taiwan residents, with Beijing's version of "One China," i.e., "One country, two systems." Moreover, it is not currently clear what Beijing means by the concept— i.e., does "One China" mean the People's Republic of China or does "One China" mean "one Chinese nation," or something else?[21] However, the future emergence of a Chen Shui-bian–Lee Teng-hui coalition government might strengthen Chen's political position and increase his policy flexibility. This, in turn, could prompt Beijing to alter its current high-pressure stance.

China has not altered its long-standing stance opposing Taiwan's entrance into the UN or any other international organization that requires statehood for membership. Thus, on this issue, the impasse remains. Yet China does not appear to be actively resisting efforts by the Chen government to more energetically pursue ROC involvement in a variety of nondiplomatic international efforts, including humanitarian, environmental, democratic, and NGO affairs. However, Beijing will likely oppose such activities if they are perceived as leading to greater support among various states for Taiwan's entrance into statehood-based international organizations.

China's renewed effort, after the 1995–1996 crisis and again after the Kosovo War, to improve relations with Washington increased ROC anxieties that Beijing and Washington might in some sense "collude" to constrain Taiwan's options or to place pressure on Taiwan to enter into meaningful cross-Strait talks. The Bush Administration has probably allayed such concerns in recent months as a result of its arms sales decisions and tough rhetoric in support of Taiwan's security (see below). However, if the Taiwan government determines that the U.S. Executive Branch is acting to undermine its interests, it could attempt to use the Congress to restrain or alter such actions, as the Lee Teng-hui government did repeatedly during the Clinton presidency. And such pro-Taiwan congressional initiatives could in turn prompt the Chinese government to intensify its pressure on Taipei.

China's increasing emphasis on strengthening the credibility of its military options against Taiwan is of growing concern to Taipei (and Washington). This element of Beijing's policy, and the resulting threat it poses to Taiwan and Asian stability, are understandably being used by the ROC government to obtain quantitatively and qualitatively greater levels of weaponry and related military assistance from the United States, and to develop closer military and political relations between

---

[21]The authors would like to thank one of the reviewers for making this point.

Taipei and Washington. Significant steps in this direction were in fact taken by the U.S. government in April 2001, when Washington agreed to provide Taiwan with (or to assist Taiwan in obtaining) more-advanced early warning and reconnaissance aircraft, surface naval combatants, submarines, and various types of technical assistance and support.[22] The possible acquisition from the United States of BMD systems and their related support infrastructure or platforms provides an increasingly important means for Taiwan to advance its political and security objectives. However, China's strong opposition to Taiwan's acquisition of a ballistic missile defense system—especially a UT system that would likely require close U.S.-Taiwan defense cooperation—presents a serious consideration for Taipei.

Chinese Economic Forces: Taiwan Trade and Investment on the Mainland

During the nineties, trends in Taiwan's trade and investment with China have shown the increasing importance of China to the economic vitality and even perhaps the survival of critical ROC economic sectors. Cross-Strait trade officially began in 1987, when the ROC government lifted the ban on indirect economic interaction with the Mainland. Over the next ten years, economic relations between the two sides developed from sporadic trading activities by Taiwan's small and medium-sized enterprises to large-scale investments involving millions or even billions of U.S. dollars by Taiwan conglomerates. According to the ROC's Mainland Affairs Council, the value of two-way trade between Taiwan and the Chinese Mainland grew to US$23.95 billion in 1998. Over 82 percent of the indirect trade was exports from Taiwan, which totaled US$19.84 billion, down 11.67 percent from 1997. Major export items to the Mainland included industrial machinery and equipment, electronic parts, plastics, man-made fibers and industrial textiles (See Table 1). Imports from the Chinese Mainland soared 4.85 percent to US$4.11 billion in 1998. The bulk of the imports were agricultural and industrial raw materials. In 1992, investment in the Mainland by Taiwan businesses was legalized, quickly pushing the Chinese Mainland to the top of the list of major recipients of Taiwan's foreign investment. By 2000, the level of Taiwan's foreign direct investment (FDI) in the PRC was officially estimated at US$40 billion, but a more accurate estimate places

---

[22]These decisions are discussed in greater detail below.

Table 1

**Approved Mainland Investments by Sector,
1991–1998**

Sector	Percentage
Electronics and electrical products	26.72
Food and beverage	11.27
Metal products	10.85
Plastics products	10.10
Chemicals	8.25
Others	32.81

Source: ROC Ministry of Economic Affairs.

the number between US$70–$100 billion.[23] Similarly, the trade figures are likely too conservative, because of indirect trade through Hong Kong. Perhaps the most telling indicator is the rise of "China fever" or "Shanghai fever" among young Taiwan citizens.[24] While the government estimates the number of Taiwan expatriates living on the Mainland at 40,000, there are reportedly 200,000 Taiwan expatriates living around Shanghai alone.

The growth of cross-Strait trade and investment has led to some serious macroeconomic distortions. First, the trade flows themselves are imbalanced. From 1987 to 1998, Taiwan's trade surplus with the Chinese Mainland increased from just over US$1 billion to US$15.7 billion. As a consequence of these trends, Taiwan's concerns about trade dependence on the Mainland are rising. While approximately 11.13 percent of Taiwan's 1998 trade was with the Mainland, export dependency stood at 17.94 percent, and import dependency at 3.93 percent. Second, these China-linked economic ties have also distorted the structure of the Taiwan economy. Largely labor-intensive sunset industries, such as clothing and toy production, have been pushed off-shore by rising labor and production costs on the island, as well as increasingly strict environmental regulation. Recent years have witnessed the transfer of low-end information technology (IT) production, including assembly of components, and the 1999 earthquake has even led some to contemplate the transfer of more advanced aspects of Taiwan's IT sector, such as sophisticated semiconductor foundries.

Apart from economic considerations, the growing dependence on economic ties with the Mainland for Taiwan's continued prosperity has important political implications. For some in Taiwan, this dependence represents a strong potential point of leverage for Beijing in its efforts to convince Taiwan to begin political

---

[23]Chu Yun-han.

[24]Annie Huang, "China Attracts Taiwan's Best Talents to High-Tech Industries," Associated Press, 16 February 2001.

talks. As indicated above, Beijing has in fact attempted to use economic ties with Taiwan to influence or pressure Taiwan businesspersons to exert pressure on ROC government to be moderate or to accept Beijing's stance. Aware of the dangers presented by this situation, the ROC government has attempted to limit or shape the size or contours of economic interactions with the Mainland. In 1996, the Lee Teng-hui government presented a new policy that called for "patience over haste," restricting Taiwan investments initially to less than US$30 million and subsequently to less than US$50 million. This policy was opposed by both business and academic circles within the ROC, though it is widely believed to have been subverted by the use of offshore front companies. In the aftermath of the Asian financial crisis of 1998–2000, the ROC government reiterated that it would continue the policy in the future as the region's financial situation remained unstable. More recently, however, the Chen Shui-bian government has shown some signs of relaxing the policy in the face of Taiwan's worsening economic situation and intensifying opposition from business.[25]

Juxtaposing the government's caution in cross-Strait trade against the business community's support for expanded interaction grossly oversimplifies the situation, however. In reality, a complicated debate exists over whether growing cross-Strait economic ties will lead to greater Taiwan dependence or to interdependence and even perhaps to greater PRC restraint, especially regarding the use of force. On the one side, there are many strong and growing business constituencies on Taiwan that favor stable cross-Strait political relations and expanding cross-Strait economic ties. In terms of specific policies, many businesspersons agree with the decision to approve the three mini-links, which allows trade, transportation and postal services between the islands of Kinmen and Matsu and the Mainland, and support future approval of the three regular links. Some members of the business community have even made direct contact with the PRC government in Beijing, and their economic power influences the actions of the Legislative Yuan and the political parties. Yet business interests are as likely to urge restraint by both Taipei and Beijing as to encourage Taiwan to become more integrated with and dependent upon the Mainland. Similarly, government officials recognize the potential strategic benefits—such as reduced incentives for PRC use of force—offered by trade and investment with the Mainland, while remaining cognizant of the reduced flexibility and maneuverability imposed by the growing level of intercourse.

---

[25]"Officials Clarify Status of 'No Haste, Be Patient,'" Central News Agency, Taipei, August 14, 2001.

However, the seductive logic of the economic interdependence argument is potentially undermined by the two trenchant criticisms offered by Christensen and Betts in their Winter 2000 *National Interest* article.[26] The first argument centers on the dynamic of the strategic interaction itself:

> . . . both sides in a political dispute have a stake in not overturning profitable economic integration. The PRC might not want to kill the golden goose, but neither would Taiwan or the United States. Why, then, should Beijing be any more anxious to back down in a crisis than Taipei or Washington? Mutual dependence makes a political conflict a game of chicken, in which each side expects the other to bow to the stakes, and in which collision may result rather than concession.

The evidence provided in the previous chapters of this report clearly support this line of analysis, though the authors perhaps could have laid even more emphasis on the exacerbating role of the strategic *triangle* rather than any of the individual dyads. The second argument deals with the sensitive and unpredictable issue of Chinese nationalism:

> There is little reason to assume that sober economic interest will necessarily override national honor in a crisis. A tough stand by Beijing may be viewed from the inside as essential for regime survival, even if it is not seen by detached observers as being in China's "national interest." In an imbroglio over Taiwan, which capitals will feel the strongest emotional inhibitions against backing down? Beijing and Taipei both have a greater material, moral and historical stake in the outcome than does the United States.

Both of these arguments raise serious questions about the efficacy of economic interdependence in reducing China's incentives to use force.

Yet the impact of growing economic interactions with the Mainland, the resulting increasing level of support for such interactions among Taiwan business elites, and recent economic difficulties have converged to spur the government to place greater emphasis on expanding and diversifying its international economic activities outside the Mainland. Even so, most interlocutors in Taiwan recognize that this effort had some inherent limitations. First and foremost, there are few attractive alternatives. The transfer of sunset industries to the low-labor-cost environment of the PRC is eminently rational in an economic sense, while the expansion of trade relations with other countries cannot simply be achieved through government policy and regulation. The irresistible forces of the market therefore make it difficult for Taiwan to reduce its level of involvement with the PRC economy, and any government strategy predicated on using this trade and

---

[26]Richard K. Betts and Thomas J. Christensen, "China: Getting the Questions Right," *The National Interest*, No. 62, Winter 2000/2001, pp. 17–30.

investment as a bargaining chip lacks credibility. This circumstance has presented the Taiwan leadership with a dilemma: either increase economic interaction with the Mainland and strengthen the economy of its potential conqueror, or continue to implement an unenforceable and possibly counterproductive policy of restricted economic interaction with the Mainland.

Recent events, however, suggest that Taipei's policies of restraint and caution have been overtaken by Taiwan's economic downturn. In little over a year, from April 2000 to July 2001, the stock market dropped from over 10,000 to under 5,000.[27] By the second quarter of 2001, Taiwan's economy had contracted by 2.35 percent and was forecast to contract by an unprecedented 0.37 percent for the year.[28] The flight of capital to the Mainland in search of cheap labor had only been exacerbated by political gridlock and the pro-environment policies of the DPP. DPP efforts to shut down Taiwan's fourth nuclear power plant, for example, have called into question the government's pro-business attitude.[29] According to ROC government statistics, approved investments in the Mainland by Taiwan-based companies increased 33 percent to US$1.06 billion for the first five months of 2001.[30] This has prompted one Taiwan economist to predict that if the trend continues Taiwan's economy could be "destroyed."[31] However, despite these warnings and faced with the realization that controlling capital flows to the Mainland was impossible, the DPP opted to increase economic integration with the Mainland. On 14 August 2001, Chen Shui-bian announced that the "no haste, be patient" policy would be replaced by a policy of "proactive openness and effective management" that would replace the investment limits on individual companies with a limit on the total amount of Taiwan capital invested in the Mainland.[32]

Accompanying the capital flight is an increasing number of Taiwan professionals in industries such as high technology, banking, securities, and insurance who are moving with their families to the Mainland for employment. Estimates of the number of Taiwan residents living in Shanghai range as high as 200,000. Media outlets in Taiwan have declared that the island is overcome with "Shanghai fever," and bookstores in Taipei are filled with books outlining how to work and

---

[27]"Second Quarter Growth Unlikely to Top One Percent; CEPD," *Taiwan Economic News*, 5 July 2001.

[28]"Taiwan's Economy Goes Into Recession," *Taipei Times*, 18 August 2001.

[29]Allen T. Cheng, "The United States of China," *Asiaweek.com*, 6 July 2001.

[30]"Investment in Mainland Surges; Investment in Taiwan Falls," *Taiwan Economic News*, 18 June 2001.

[31]"Mainland Investment Could Wipe Out Taiwan: Expert," *Liberty Times*, 5 July 2001.

[32]"Officials Clarify Status of 'No Haste, Be Patient,'" Central News Agency, 14 August 2001, and "Chen Affirms End to 'No Haste' Policy," *Taiwan Headlines*, 15 August 2001.

live in the PRC. In some cases these professionals are bringing their entire families to the Mainland, yet the incidence of Taiwan businessmen maintaining mistresses or second families in the PRC has become a national-level debate in Taiwan. These China-based businessmen have created an increasing demand for familiar food and institutions, including such things as Taiwan schools, and the signs and sights in some sections of Shanghai reportedly have begun to resemble parts of Taipei.

These economic and social trends have profound domestic political implications in Taiwan, as well as for cross-Strait relations. As more Taiwanese live and even grow up in places like Shanghai, the possibility exists for many of them to remain citizens of the ROC, but also develop a strong sense of identity with the Mainland. Observers in Taipei assert that the gradual reduction of a Taiwan identity and the rise of a Chinese identity among the Taiwan populace could generate less support for pro-independence political parties and more support for accommodation with the Mainland.[33] Perhaps sensing a change in attitude, the KMT unveiled a draft of its policy platform recommending "confederation" with the Mainland. The draft also proposed lifting the ban on direct trade, transportation, and postal links between the Mainland and Taiwan. While the confederation proposal was ultimately rejected by the KMT for fear of alienating voters, the fact that it proposed such a policy may indicate the beginning of a gradual shift in public attitudes toward relations with the Mainland. While the vast majority of Taiwan's citizens do not support reunification, the growing economic dependence on the Mainland may influence many of them to accept an accommodation with China, especially if public confidence in the cohesiveness and effectiveness of Taiwan's government wanes.

Chinese Military Modernization and Taiwan's Foreign and Defense Policies

The military dimension of the complex cross-Strait relationship has arguably increased in importance since the early nineties, in response to growing political and diplomatic tensions between Beijing and Taipei. China's military capabilities and intentions—both generally and with respect to Taiwan in particular—thus constitute a key factor influencing Taiwan's foreign and defense policies.

---

[33]Chu Yun-han.

Chinese Military Modernization of Relevance to Taiwan

From the broadest perspective, China has been engaged since at least the mid-eighties in a multipronged effort to reduce China's existing vulnerabilities while increasing the utility of its military forces for purposes of securing diplomatic and political leverage issue in four core areas:

- To defend Chinese sovereignty and national territory (especially critical coastal facilities) against attacks from highly sophisticated military forces

- To employ military power as a more potent and versatile instrument of a more extensive regional and global set of foreign diplomatic policies

- To better cope with a range of potential security threats or concerns along China's periphery, especially in maritime areas[34]

- Ultimately, to attain power projection and extended territorial defense capabilities commensurate with great power status in the 21st century.[35]

These requirements have led to a significant transformation in China's strategic outlook and resulting force requirements—from that of a continental power requiring a minimal nuclear deterrent capability and large land forces for "in-depth" defense against threats to its northern and western borders, to that of a combined continental and maritime power requiring a more sophisticated conventional and unconventional force structure with medium- and long-range force projection, mobility, rapid reaction, and off-shore maneuverability capabilities and a more versatile and accurate nuclear weapons inventory.

In the area of conventional weapons systems, key modernization programs of relevance to Taiwan focus on the eventual creation of the following:[36]

---

[34]These threats or concerns include a militarily powerful United States, an economically powerful and increasingly independent Japan, a more militarily capable and economically emergent India, a host of rising second and third tier Asian powers (including South Korea and most of the ASEAN countries), and the emergence of relatively unstable Islamic states on China's Central Asian borders.

[35]To achieve such ambitious ends, however, it is important to note that Chinese rulers also recognized that the military modernization efforts of the Chinese state must be built on a prior foundation of indigenous scientific, technological, and economic capabilities. Hence, the strategy demanded that military modernization proceed at a pace that does not undermine the attainment of essential civilian development priorities; nor should it be allowed to proceed at a pace that unduly alarms periphery states or major powers, and thus erodes China's generally benign threat environment.

[36]This list is derived from David Shambaugh, "China's Military: Real or Paper Tiger?" *The Washington Quarterly*, Volume 19, No. 2, Spring 1996, pp. 26–27; Michael D. Swaine, "China," in Zalmay Khalilzad (ed.) *Strategic Appraisal 1996*, RAND, Santa Monica, California, 1996, pp. 203–205; and James Mulvenon, "Appendix One: Chinese Unconventional and Conventional Capabilities and Doctrine,""in Swaine, "China and Arms Control," paper prepared for the Council on Foreign Relations Workshop on Constructive Engagement with China, New York City, April 1995.

- A smaller, more flexible, better motivated, highly trained and well-equipped ground force, centered on rapid reaction combat units with a limited airborne drop and amphibious power-projection capability[37]

- A modest (by great power standards) green- or blue-water naval capability centered on a new generation of frigates and destroyers with improved air defense and fire control, more modern nuclear and non-nuclear submarines, a more capable naval air arm, improved submarine warfare and anti-submarine warfare capabilities, and possibly one carrier battle group[38]

- A more versatile, advanced air force, with longer-range interceptor/strike aircraft, improved air defense (with airborne early warning (AEW) aircraft); extended and close air support; and overall improved power projection capabilities, including long-range transport and lift and in-flight refueling capabilities

- A combined arms tactical operations doctrine utilizing more sophisticated C3I, early warning, and battle management systems, and both airborne and satellite-based assets, as well as information warfare capabilities

- A diverse and relatively large number of accurate, solid-fueled, conventionally armed short- and medium-range ballistic and cruise missiles with both fixed and mobile capabilities.

During the past decade, and especially within the past five years, China's military modernization program has witnessed significant progress in several of the above areas. The most notable advances in indigenous weapons and support systems have occurred in the areas of ballistic and cruise missiles, the mobility and response time of selected units, logistics, C2, and air and naval support of ground forces associated with combined arms operations, and some surface and subsurface naval combatants. At present, priority areas for the future include serial production of an indigenous fourth-generation fighter-bomber; submarine-launched anti-ship cruise missiles and intermediate-range ballistic missiles; long-range, land-attack cruise missiles; long-range, over-the-horizon radars and downlink capabilities; space-based, real-time surveillance capabilities; and more accurate guidance systems for short- and medium-range ballistic missiles. It should be noted that the most significant advances in sophisticated systems and

---

[37]Rapid reaction units (RRUs) are ""specially trained for different geographical and climatic conditions, [and are] geared to strengthen mobility and operational coordination in preparation for small-scale warfare on and around China's border areas." Bates Gill and Taeho Kim, *China's Arms Acquisitions from Abroad: A Quest for 'Superb and Secret Weapons,'* SIPRI Research Report No. 11, Oxford University Press, Oxford, England, 1995, p. 64.

[38]Such a naval force would be capable of engaging in what the Chinese term "offshore active defense" (*jinyangfangyu*).

high-tech subsystems have largely taken place as a result of expensive acquisitions from foreign, primarily Russian, sources.[39] Moreover, all of the above advances occurred from a relatively low baseline, and are still far from the capabilities required by China's overall modernization program.

Assuming that Beijing is able to sustain or even accelerate somewhat the current tempo of its modernization program and overcome a fairly wide range of persistent development problems, one might expect that, at best, China could attain the following general military capabilities by 2010–2015:[40]

- The ability to conduct limited[41] air and sea denial (as opposed to sea control) operations up to 250 miles from China's continental coastline

- The ability to strike a wide range of civilian and military targets in East, Southeast, and South Asia[42] with a large number (perhaps 1,000+) of nuclear or conventionally armed short- and medium-range ballistic missiles

- The ability to transport and deploy 1–2 divisions (i.e., approximately 15,000–30,000 fully equipped soldiers) within 100 miles of China's continental borders, via land, sea, and air transport

- The ability to overwhelm any likely space-based or air-breathing missile defense system deployed in Asia.

If one projects the above trends for another ten years or so to the year 2025, one might expect the following general military capabilities:

- The ability to routinely patrol a single, non-carrier surface and sub-surface battle group within 1,000 nautical miles of China's continental coastline

- The ability to conduct both sea and air denial operations within 500 nautical miles of China's continental coastline

---

[39]One source estimates that the total cost of China's purchase of Russian weapons and equipment during 1991–1994 was US$4.5–US$6 billion. One should add to this the cost of the more recent Su-27 co-production agreement, which is estimated at US$3 billion. The same source estimates that China has purchased US$2–US$3 billion worth of military equipment and technology from Israel since the early 1980s. See Bates Gill and Taeho Kim, *China's Arms Acquisitions from Abroad: A Quest for 'Superb and Secret Weapons,'* SIPRI Research Report No. 11, Oxford University Press, Oxford, England, 1995, pp. 55, 99.

[40]These estimates are speculative and derive from the authors 'own analysis. They do not represent conclusions reached by RAND or the U.S.government. Moreover, these estimates do not assume that China will necessarily succeed in any effort to attain the capabilities listed.

[41]The word "limited" here denotes the ability to carry out sea denial activities primarily against a small number of surface and sub-surface assets in selected, limited areas over short periods of time.

[42]Such targets would include all major metropolitan areas in Japan, Korea, Taiwan, the Philippines, Southeast Asia, and India and most major U.S. military installations in Asia.

- The ability to attempt a naval blockade, with air support, of islands within 200 nautical miles of China's continental coastline
- The ability to transport and deploy 3–4 divisions (i.e., approximately 45,000–60,000 fully equipped soldiers) within 200 miles of China's continental borders, via land, sea, and air transport.

Implications for Taiwan's Security

As the above indicates, China's weapons programs place an increased emphasis on acquiring both air and naval medium- and long-range detection, surveillance and power projection capabilities. Such capabilities are designed in large part to strengthen the credibility of Beijing's military options against Taiwan, and to deter the U.S. from deploying military force (and in particular aircraft carriers) in an effort to counter such options. The acquisition of even rough approximations of the above capabilities thus poses several significant implications for Taiwan's security and defense policy over the short, medium, and long term.

China's growing military capabilities could pose a potential threat of armed coercion or actual assault on Taiwan in four major ways: (1) via low-level intimidation (military exercises, weapons displays, confrontations at sea or in the air, and various kinds of covert subversion); (2) via naval blockade or interdiction efforts; (3) via a limited missile and/or air attack again Taiwan territory or strategic targets; and (4) via a full-scale attack. The specific type of danger presented by each type of military action, and the likelihood of each action, vary significantly.[43]

Low-Level Intimidation. The specific danger presented by low-level acts of intimidation is primarily psychological, not material. That is, the PRC cannot materially damage or destroy Taiwan's military capabilities or economic infrastructure through such actions. However, the will of Taiwan's populace to resist Mainland pressures and the willingness of Taiwan's leadership to concede to Mainland demands could nonetheless be significantly eroded if the PRC is perceived as being able to harass Taiwan with relative impunity. China currently possesses (and has demonstrated) the ability to harass Taiwan through military exercises and missile firings in the vicinity of the island. At present, Taiwan has no credible capability to prevent or interdict such actions. It does not possess a

---

[43]Much of the following discussion of possible Chinese military actions against Taiwan is taken from Michael D. Swaine, "The Modernization of the People's Liberation Army: Implications for Asia-Pacific Security and Chinese Politics," in Hung-mao Tien and Yun-han Chu, eds., *China Under Jiang Zemin,* Lynne Rienner Publishers, Boulder, Colorado, 2000.

missile defense system capable of intercepting Chinese ballistic missiles. Moreover, even if capable, it would probably not want to obstruct or militarily prevent Chinese exercises or missiles operating outside Taiwan territory or territorial waters, for fear of Chinese retaliation and escalation. However, Taiwan at present possesses the capability to deter or counter confrontations at sea or in the air, given its relatively superior air and naval forces.[44] The threat currently posed to Taiwan by low-level covert acts of subversion is extremely difficult to measure. This is because estimates vary enormously, even within the Taiwan military, of the size and capability of any Mainland Chinese "fifth column" forces operating on Taiwan and the likely impact *limited* subversive actions by such forces would have upon strategic targets and popular morale.[45]

Over the long term, the ability of Chinese forces to conduct low-level harassment of Taiwan via ballistic missiles, military exercises, and sea and air confrontations will likely increase significantly, largely because of relative improvements in PLA air and naval forces, and the likelihood of significant increases in the number and accuracy of short- and medium-range ballistic missiles. These greater capabilities will thus likely increase Mainland China's potential ability to weaken popular morale on Taiwan. Taiwan's vulnerability to such an outcome will arguably be reduced by expected significant improvements in Taiwan's early-warning system, the hardening of critical facilities such as air bases and command and control centers, and the likely existence, within 10–15 years, of a rudimentary ballistic missile defense system. Such capabilities could significantly alleviate the psychological impact of PRC low-level intimidation efforts. Ultimately, however, the ability of the PRC to threaten Taiwan through such efforts alone will depend essentially on such specific considerations as popular assumptions regarding the level of U.S. and international support for Taiwan, and popular confidence in the ability of Taiwan's leadership to maintain order while under attack and to avoid an escalation of any confrontation to higher levels of conflict. Taiwan's military leaders are acutely aware of the greater relevance of such issues to this type of threat, and many express concerns that Taiwan's civilian leadership is not taking appropriate steps to deal with such issues.

In addition to such concerns, Taiwan's confidence in U.S. support for the island in the face of low-level intimidation efforts could be affected, over the medium

---

[44]As examples of low-level intimidation, our definition of such confrontations is limited largely to tense, cat-and-mouse jostling between individual air and naval platforms of the type frequently witnessed between Soviet and American forces during the Cold War. They do not include deliberate attempts at blockade or interdiction.

[45]It is highly unlikely that Mainland China would undertake provocative efforts at covert subversion (such as attacks on critical infrastructure) merely to intimidate Taiwan. Such actions would more likely occur in the context of larger scenarios involving blockades, attacks, or a direct invasion of Taiwan (see below).

and long term, by perceptions of China's ability to threaten U.S. naval forces. As suggested above, the Chinese are undertaking efforts to acquire the capability to locate, track, target, and strike sophisticated blue-water naval combat formations such as carrier battle groups. The acquisition (or perceived acquisition) of such capabilities could significantly complicate any U.S. decision to deploy naval forces in support of Taiwan and hence could erode Taiwan's confidence in U.S. support for the island.

Naval Blockade or Interdiction. The specific danger posed by Chinese efforts at naval blockade or interdiction is both material and psychological. Even extremely limited interdiction efforts (e.g., a Chinese declaration of intent to selectively halt or in effect harass individual freighters passing into or out of a Taiwan port) could exert a major adverse psychological impact on Taiwan's maritime commerce, both at present and in the future. Indeed, this specific type of threat is currently the most likely for this category, given the fact that China is arguably unable, at present or in the near term, to establish even a partial blockade of Taiwan intended, for example, to seal off maritime commerce into a specific port or ports. The ability of Taiwan to withstand such limited interdiction efforts would largely depend on the type of psychological factors mentioned above.

However, within a decade, China will almost certainly acquire the capability to undertake a partial or complete blockade of Taiwan. Specifically, as indicated above, by 2007–2010, China would probably be able to attempt sea denial capabilities in the vicinity of Taiwan sufficient to sustain a partial blockade; by 2020, China would likely have the ability to attempt a more complete blockade. But the critical question from a military perspective is whether or not China could successfully *enforce* such blockade attempts. Over the medium term (i.e., until roughly 2010) it seems unlikely that China will be able to enforce a blockade against determined Taiwan resistance. Despite a likely Chinese numerical advantage in destroyers, guided-missile frigates, and submarines, Taiwan will almost certainly possess a naval force with markedly superior maritime surveillance and detection, antisubmarine warfare (ASW), and antisurface warfare (ASUW) capabilities; hence it could arguably break a Chinese blockade attempt without U.S. assistance. Some analysts (and many Taiwan military officers) insist that the current absence of advanced diesel attack submarines, combined with limited airborne ASW platforms (i.e., the current absence of P-3 aircraft), will place Taiwan at a major disadvantage in countering a growing naval blockade threat from China. In response to these and other considerations, the U.S. government in spring 2000 reversed its long-standing stance against providing submarines to Taiwan and indicated that it would assist Taipei in acquiring such vessels.

However, it remains unclear as to how Taiwan might acquire diesel submarines, since no nation is currently able and/or willing to provide them.[46] Moreover, some American analysts believe that a relatively small number of diesel submarines (e.g., 10–15) would not significantly augment Taiwan's ASW and ASUW capabilities in the waters around Taiwan, for a variety of reasons.[47] It thus seems that the primary purpose of such submarines would be psychological, i.e., to deter or complicate a Chinese decision to attempt a blockade. Although possibly useful, the cost of producing such a psychological effect would likely be extremely high for Taiwan financially, and would arguably force cutbacks in other more vital areas. And it might not have the desired deterrence effect. An absence of P-3 ASW aircraft would present a more significant, yet not lethal, vulnerability, given likely acquisitions by Taiwan of other capable airborne ASW platforms, such as Hughes and Sikorsky ASW helicopters. Nonetheless, P-3 aircraft have been approved for sale to Taiwan.[48]

Overall, the most significant vulnerability to a possible Chinese blockade or interdiction effort derives from so-called "software" factors. In particular, the ROC Navy is severely constrained, in handling any attempted blockade, by an absence of skilled personnel able to operate its increasingly sophisticated platforms and a lack of rigorous and sufficient training in ASW and ASUW tactics. For both political and financial reasons, the Taiwan military persists in a two-year conscription system that prevents the development of adequate skill levels.[49] In addition, Taiwan's ability to develop effective countermeasures to Chinese naval blockade and interdiction efforts might be undermined by an absence of agreement within the Taiwan military over the seriousness of the blockade/interdiction threat. The ROC Army believes that the greatest military danger to Taiwan over the medium term is presented by a combination of

---

[46]The United States no longer manufactures diesel submarines and those countries that do are unwilling to sell them to Taiwan, largely because of Chinese pressure.

[47]For example, diesel submarines are far slower than surface combatants; hence it would take many submarines to significantly threaten blockading patrol craft. Also, many of the waters on the west, north, and south sides of Taiwan present significant difficulties for submarine operations against enemy submarines.

[48]Another point to keep in mind is that a naval blockade would almost certainly require a significant period of time to be effective; moreover, a Chinese blockade would likely be considered an act of war and would constitute an attempt to obstruct maritime commerce. All of these factors would greatly increase the likelihood that the United States would be both willing and able to assist in deterring or defeating a Chinese blockade attempt.

[49]The Taiwan military is also arguably weakened by a host of internal personal, political, and cultural obstacles, such as an excessive reliance on officers instead of a professional corps of non-commissioned officers (NCOs), little lower-level problem-solving and initiative, and a poor level of officer recognition of the need for sophisticated information warfare and battle management systems.

sudden attacks on Taiwan territory by Chinese commando and rapid reaction forces, supported by coordinated "fifth column" attacks on critical strategic targets on Taiwan, followed by a large-scale amphibious invasion using an armada of small boats. The ROC Navy believes that the greatest threat to Taiwan is posed by a combination of ballistic missiles attacks and a naval blockade, aimed at pressuring Taiwan to sue for peace. Debates between the ROC Army and Navy over the most urgent threat to Taiwan could significantly affect funding priorities over the medium term and long term, given the fact that such priorities are greatly influenced by whichever service is in control of the military command structure.[50] Finally, over the long term, Taiwan's confidence in handling a significantly improved PRC capability to blockade the island will likely depend greatly on the ability and willingness of the United States to provide assistance.

Air and/or Missile Attack. The PRC's missile tests during the Taiwan Strait crises of 1995 and 1996 highlighted the growing strategic importance of China's short-range ballistic missile force for the conduct of Taiwan's foreign and defense policies. The perceived threat posed by these missiles has largely driven the debate in Taiwan about the merits of acquiring theater ballistic missile defense systems. In order to understand the range of Taiwan institutional responses to these developments, however, it is first necessary to evaluate the threat to Taiwan in greater detail, although the threat assessment process itself should be considered part of the Taiwan policy dynamic.

The specific danger presented by direct missile and/or air attacks against Taiwan is both psychological and material. Taiwan will probably possess a very capable technical defense against limited attacks by aircraft, especially over the medium term. Within a decade, Taiwan will probably have a sizable and advanced air-defense network, comprising an airborne early-warning system, an automatic command-and-control network, a relatively large, modern air force equipped with stand-off air-to-air missiles, and several new surface-to-air missiles. Such a system will likely provide an adequate defense against PLA air strikes against Taiwan and surrounding waters, even by relatively high numbers of aircraft.[51]

---

[50]Military budget allocations are greatly influenced by the chief of staff of the Taiwan military. This position revolves every three years among the three services.

[51]As Harlan Jencks notes, "The PLAAF still lacks precision air-to-surface munitions, particularly long-range ones; long-range navigation gear; capable strike aircraft; and electronic warfare (EW) gear, particularly electronic counter-countermeasures (ECCM). Moreover, there is little evidence that PLA training is adequate, or that it is improving. There is little prospect for breakthroughs in any of the equipment areas, barring massive infusions of expensive foreign assistance; and it does not appear that the PLA is even shopping for foreign precision-strike gear. Instead, it appears to be concentrating on air-superiority weapons like the Su-27 and F-10." See Harlan Jencks, "Wild Speculations on the Military Balance in the Taiwan Strait," in James R. Lilley and Chuck Downs, eds., *Crisis in the Taiwan Strait,* National Defense University Press, Washington, D.C., September 1997, p. 148.

This assessment of course assumes that Taiwan provides the necessary personnel and infrastructure to support such a system. For example, in the ROC Air Force, there is a major concern about maintaining veteran pilots: with a steady reduction in the number of slots available for senior officers, and uncompetitive pay, many pilots are now leaving the military to work for commercial airlines. Moreover, future possible limited air attacks against strategic targets on eastern Taiwan (e.g., by long-range Su-27s) could seriously demoralize the population. The Mainland's ability to conduct such heretofore impossible attacks could lead many Taiwan citizens to believe that Chinese forces can launch attacks on Taiwan from any direction. The ultimate impact of such attacks will thus again depend greatly on political and psychological factors.

China's growing missile capability presents a more complicated—and almost certainly a more significant—threat to Taiwan. A small number of ballistic missile attacks (e.g., a strike against unpopulated parts of Taiwan) would obviously present no significant direct military threat to the island, but could provoke significant panic. Over the short term, Taiwan will possess no credible military defense against such terror attacks. Even over the medium term (i.e., before 2010), and despite the acquisition of significantly improved air defense systems, Taiwan will probably remain highly vulnerable to a ballistic missile attack.[52] This will be especially true if Mainland China succeeds in significantly increasing the number and accuracy of its short and medium-range ballistic missiles, as is likely.[53] The ability of Taiwan to withstand such missile attacks will again depend very much on the steadfastness of Taiwan's leadership and populace.

In a passive sense, the missile forces opposite Taiwan act as a deterrent to unwanted behavior by the government in Taipei, especially, e.g., any major movement towards independence. Indeed, the missile exercises in 1995 and 1996 highlight the very real possibility that China may, as a result of actual or perceived Taiwan provocations, use its missile forces as part of an "active" compellence campaign, in which it seeks to persuade Taiwan to retreat from a stated position or action. In July 1995 and March 1996, China fired DF-15 SRBMs into the waters surrounding Taiwan to express its displeasure over Taiwan President Lee Teng-hui's visit to the United States. Some members of the Chinese

---

[52]Improvements in Taiwan's air defense system will be almost entirely relevant to defense against attacks from various types of aircraft, not ballistic missiles, as discussed below.

[53]It is very probable that the PRC will have deployed many hundreds of such missiles by 2010, including the Dongfeng-15 (DF-15) missile (known more commonly in the West by its export designation, M-9, or in the Pentagon as the CSS-6), the shorter-range Dongfeng-11 (DF-11), (also known as the M-11 or CSS-7), and a smaller number of other systems such as the longer-range DF-21 (CSS-5). The DF-21s could be located well within Chinese territory, safe from retaliation even by U.S. forces.

leadership have reportedly concluded that this effort was a success, since it compelled Taiwan to tone down its "pragmatic diplomacy" campaign, which had been making inroads among Caribbean, South Pacific, and Southeast Asian countries, and led to the overwhelming defeat of the DPP candidate in the presidential election. In the future, China might seek to use its SRBMs to reverse policies aimed at building and deploying a BMD system in Taiwan, either by firing more missiles in the waters surrounding the island, overflying the island with a missile, or significantly upping the ante by landing missiles on unpopulated areas of Taiwan.

Once a certain inviolable "red line" (defined by China) has been crossed, however, the SRBM force arrayed against Taiwan quickly becomes the spearpoint of an offensive Chinese campaign against it. The most obvious red line would be an open declaration of independence by Taiwan. However, several other less obvious actions (e.g., a national referendum on Taiwan's status, the replacement of the Republic of China with the term "Republic of Taiwan" in the constitution, etc.) could also constitute such red lines. At the same time, even in the absence of such provocative initiatives by Taipei, it cannot be ruled out that China might attack preemptively if the PRC leadership perceived that a calculated "window of opportunity" were closing. The source of this change could be either technological (e.g., the arrival of ballistic missile defense systems) or political (e.g., an impending change in the constitution, or an increase in the power and influence of pro-independence forces), and would likely be viewed by Beijing as requiring decisive action. China's SRBM force would likely constitute the opening salvo of any military action, possibly striking airfields, ports, and critical command and control centers throughout the country.

This possibility was confirmed in a 1999 Pentagon study, which highlighted the serious threat China's short-range missiles pose for non-hardened military targets, command and control nodes, and Taiwan's military infrastructure.[54] The goal of these opening thrusts would likely be to eliminate Taiwan's qualitative advantages in air and naval superiority, as well as to prevent Taiwan's military and civilian leadership from accurately perceiving the strategic, operational, and tactical dimensions of the conflict. For the Chinese, attacks against civilian population centers would serve little purpose. Instead, such attacks would likely be extremely counterproductive, uniting the citizenry in angry opposition to Beijing's intentions.

---

[54]U.S. Department of Defense, *Report to Congress Pursuant to the FY99 Appropriations Bill.*

Despite the clear operational uses of China's SRBM force, however, Beijing's reliance on these potent weapons ironically serves to highlight the PLA's failings and weaknesses in many of its conventional military capabilities. As indicated below, most foreign and Chinese observers readily admit that the Chinese do not currently have the capability to successfully invade Taiwan with conventional forces. They do not have enough amphibious craft or marines for a coastal invasion, nor do they appear to be engaged in a crash program to rectify these shortcomings. Small numbers of advanced fighter aircraft and the logistical and communications limitations of ground control intercept (GCI) tactics mean that the PLA could not sustain large numbers of sorties over the Strait against more numerous and advanced Taiwan air forces, thus sacrificing air superiority. China's naval forces, while modernizing, could not provide significant amounts of naval fire support, and do not have the logistics system to sustain operations for more than a few weeks. Moreover, proven PLA capabilities in heliborne assault and other small unit operations would not be decisive. A comparison with D-Day in 1944 is instructive. Allied forces enjoyed virtual air supremacy, massive naval fire support, large numbers of amphibious craft and soldiers, and almost complete strategic surprise over the Germans. China would enjoy none of these advantages in a conventional invasion of Taiwan.

Because of these weaknesses and China's resulting reliance on SRBMs, Beijing naturally views the introduction of theater ballistic missile defenses to Taiwan as fundamentally destabilizing to the strategic, operational, and tactical status quo, and a significant barrier to its eventual goal of reunification of Taiwan with the Mainland. Not surprisingly, China has been extremely critical of U.S. transfers of PAC-2 systems to Taiwan, and has issued warnings about the transfer of future systems. Some of the Chinese criticisms, such as the accusation that the transfer of BMD systems to Taiwan violates the Anti-Ballistic Missile (ABM) Treaty and U.S. commitments to the Missile Technology Control Regime (MTCR)—an international export control arrangement designed to hinder the proliferation of missiles capable of delivering weapons of mass destruction—are specious on their face. From official statements, however, it appears that China is far more concerned about the political implications of the introduction of BMD systems in Taiwan than the military-technical implications of the defensive systems, which it could likely overwhelm with some confidence.

The main political concern for Beijing is that BMD will provide a forum for enhanced defense cooperation between Taipei and Washington, including cooperative R&D on the systems themselves, assistance in associated deployment and training, and, most troubling, the enmeshing of Taiwan into an integrated intelligence and early warning system. The net result, according to one senior

Chinese military commentator, would be a "quasi-military alliance relationship."[55] Secondary concerns center on the implications of BMD deployment for Taiwan's foreign and defense policies. According to Zhu Chenghu, deputy director of China's National Defense University Institute for National Strategic Studies:

> With US connivance and support, splittest elements on Taiwan may say that they not only have US backing but also have reliable ABMs that can effectively intercept a missile counterattack from the Mainland. In this way they may go further and further along the path of splitting the motherland and even openly desire independence.[56]

It is the combination of these various political implications for theater ballistic missile defense that vexes the Chinese, resulting in something akin to a strategic frustration-aggression complex.

Of course, the offense-defense dynamic of missiles and BMD is interactive, and China has an array of responses to the possible introduction of missile defense systems in Taiwan. While it is true that China is already modernizing its missiles *without* BMD systems in place, the introduction of effective BMD systems will likely accelerate the production of SRBMs on the Mainland, and encourage the development of much more accurate guidance systems and countermeasures meant to overcome BMD. Moreover, at least one interlocutor has made an implicit threat that the transfer of BMD to Taiwan removes China's responsibility to adhere to its various commitments on transfers of missiles and missile-related technologies. Quoting Zhu Chenghu again, "Since the United States can take the lead in violating this system, other countries are perfectly justified in refusing to carry out its provisions and cooperating with other countries in missiles and missiles technology."[57] Such transfers would have implications far beyond the Taiwan Strait, affecting the threat posed by so-called rogue states to U.S. force and allies around the world.

We should note that the Taiwan military has consistently maintained a robust assessment of the Chinese missile threat, though the politicization of these estimates is often driven by intelligence revelations from the United States. Taiwan's Ministry of National Defense in February 1999 claimed that the PRC possessed more than 100 M-class missiles in storage capable of targeting

---

[55]Zhu Chenghu, "What is the Purpose of the US Theater Missile Defense Scheme?" *Liaowang*, No. 7–8, 15 February 1999, pp. 38–39.

[56]Ibid.

[57]Ibid.

Taiwan.[58] This announcement came on the heels of a leak of an alleged classified Pentagon report that China had increased its SRBM deployments in the areas across from Taiwan.[59] In January 2000, one of former President Lee Teng-hui's advisors predicted that the PRC would have 900 short-range ballistic missiles aimed at Taiwan by 2010.[60]

Apart from estimates of the numbers of missiles, Taiwan leaders have also made numerous public statements about the origins as well as the perceived strategic, political, and economic costs of the PRC missile threat. First, Taiwan officials have been clear in their contention that ROC consideration of theater ballistic missile defenses is a response to China's missile buildup. Former Foreign Minister Jason Hu denounced Chinese criticisms of BMD as "magistrates who are free to burn down houses while the common people are forbidden to even light lamps," and asserted that Taiwan would not have considered joining BMD had the Chinese communists not deployed so many missiles along the coast facing Taiwan.[61] His comments were echoed by General Tang Fei, who argued in March 1999 that Taiwan was "forced" to consider the feasibility of joining the BMD program by Chinese missile deployments.[62] Second, Taiwan officials have made sober calculations of the possible costs of Chinese missile attack. According to Su Chi, former chairman of the Mainland Affairs Council, Chinese missiles "may not constitute much of a threat, because each missile can only cause a hole about the size of half a basketball court."[63] But he also pointed out that the psychological impact of a missile attack could be more extensive than the physical damage they would cause.[64] Moreover, the economic costs of missile attacks could be prohibitively high. The Chunghua Institute for Economic Research estimated that the official efforts to prop up both the local stock market and the Taiwan dollar in the aftermath of the 1995–1996 tests cost US$18 billion.[65]

Over the long term, Mainland China's technical ability to threaten Taiwan with limited ballistic missile and air strikes will likely increase significantly, if China is

---

[58]"Citing Threat of Chinese Missiles, Taipei Calls Defenses Inadequate," Reuters, 11 February 1999. See also Sofia Wu, "Ministry Reiterates Warning on Mainland Missile Threat," Central News Agency, 23 March 1999.

[59]Tony Walker and Stephen Fidler, "China Builds Up Taiwan Missiles," *Financial Times*, 10 February 1999; Bill Gertz, "China Moves Missiles in Direction of Taiwan," *Washington Times*, 11 February 1999.

[60]"Taiwan Official Says U.S. to Sell It 4 AEGIS Warships," Taiwan Central News Agency, 9 January 2000, FBIS-CHI-2000-0109, 23 January 2000.

[61]Luo Ju-lan, "Foreign Minister Defends Joining TMD," *Zhongguo shibao*, 9 March 1999, p. 2.

[62]Sofia Wu, "Defense Minister Meets General Shalikashvili, Discusses TMD," Central News Agency, 9 March 1999.

[63]Oxford Analytica, "Taiwan Missile Defenses," 18 February 1999.

[64]Ibid.

[65]Ibid.

able to overcome many of the above-mentioned shortcomings in the deployment of its airpower offshore and assuming that the United States does not develop and provide a relatively effective BMD system for Taiwan. Yet even over the long term, the ultimate impact of such an improved strike capability will depend primarily on nontechnical factors. Among these factors, the most important variable will be the reaction of the United States. Even a large number of ballistic missile and air attacks alone, barring a rather quick collapse of Taiwan's will to resist, would take a considerable period of time to destroy strategic targets and seriously weaken Taiwan's morale. This would provide the United States with adequate time to respond with appropriate political and military countermeasures. This is not to deny, however, that such a situation would pose a significant danger of escalation. Nor is it to deny that, despite the above deficiencies, China might nonetheless feel compelled to undertake sustained air and/or missiles attacks, or even a full-scale assault on Taiwan.

Full-Scale Attack. Such an attack might consist of either a sudden, surprise onslaught involving an all-out air, missile, and naval strike against Taiwan followed immediately by attempted landings on at least some offshore islands, and possibly on the main island; or a direct and massive assault on Taiwan that passes the offshore islands entirely. The specific dangers presented by a full-scale attack on Taiwan for the purpose of defeating and occupying the island are obvious. Fortunately, however, Mainland China will likely remain unable to undertake such a massive attack over the medium term, and perhaps over the long term as well. The PLA would need to establish both air and sea superiority over the Taiwan Strait to launch and sustain an effective attack against Taiwan. It would then need to possess a sufficient number of transport vessels to convey its forces across the Strait and an ability to unload those forces on Taiwan's shores in sufficient numbers to overcome local resistance, defend against counterattacks, and secure strategic targets.

As indicated above, the PLA currently lacks the capability to undertake any of these tasks (except, perhaps, to convey forces across the Strait—it could utilize non-military cargo and container ships, commercial aircraft, and fishing boats; but such an effort would prove disastrous without the other elements required for an attack).[66] Moreover, the PLA is not currently acquiring many of the essential elements for a major attack on Taiwan, including a sizable amphibious force capable of placing significant numbers of troops on shore, and a significant combat air transport capability. As indicated above, barring a major acceleration

---

[66]At the same time, such a chaotic assault could conceivably be used to distract Taiwan and the United States from a more focused and limited effort to seize Taiwan's ports and airfields.

of efforts in this area, the PLA might be able, at best, to transport, via air and sea vessels, approximately 15,000–30,000 combat troops across the Strait by 2010. This would be entirely inadequate to subdue Taiwan, unless such an effort proved so psychologically damaging to Taiwan's populace and military, even in the absence of a clear Chinese victory, that Taiwan simply collapsed. Again, Taiwan's susceptibility to such pressure is largely a function of the political and psychological factors discussed in the above threat scenarios. In addition, because of logistical, C3I, and transport/infrastructure weaknesses in Eastern China, the PLA could not concentrate the necessary men and materiel within striking range of Taiwan without being detected well in advance by American and Taiwan intelligence. Such early detection would presumably provide sufficient time to undertake political and military countermeasures designed to reassure the populace and deter the Chinese.[67]

Over the long term, Mainland China's technical ability to launch a major attack against Taiwan will likely increase. Yet the PLA's ability to prevail in such a scenario would still remain in doubt, as many of the same considerations that come into play over the medium term would still be in effect. For example, an ability to transport 45,000–60,000 troops by the year 2020 (noted above) would likely prove insufficient, and in any event could not be attempted without significantly telegraphing Chinese intentions well in advance.

However, one important point should be kept in mind: If the Chinese were to undertake such a desperate action, they would probably also be prepared to attempt to deter the United States from deploying major forces in support of Taiwan, using conventional and perhaps even nonconventional means. This might result in a major conflict between China and the United States, including the danger of a nuclear confrontation. The willingness of China to run such an enormous risk would depend in large part on Chinese perceptions of the basic stakes involved at the time,[68] of America's resolve to assist Taiwan, of Taiwan's willingness to permanently separate itself from the Mainland, and of the willingness of the United States and the international community to support such an effort. In other words, under such a scenario, Taiwan's "vulnerability" is again largely a function of particular political and psychological factors, given China's likely limited technical capabilities.

---

[67]Even PLA attempts to prevent such detection by carrying out massive preparations under the guise of "exercises" would likely prove extremely difficult to accomplish.

[68]It is certainly not inconceivable for China's leaders to conclude that it is preferable to undertake a dangerous course of military action than not to act and thereby lose Taiwan permanently and in the process fatally undermine their regime.

A Nuclear Threat? As Harlan Jencks points out,[69] the possible use of nuclear weapons against Taiwan has generally been ignored, largely because most analysts assume that Mainland China would not employ such weapons against fellow Chinese and would not do so not in response to anything other than a clear threat of nuclear attack. However, it is not inconceivable that China might employ nuclear weapons against Taiwan in one of three ways: (1) as a display of resolve, against an uninhabited, small island or reef near Taiwan; (2) in the form of a massive air-burst, resulting in an electro-magnetic pulse (EMP) designed to paralyze Taiwan's civilian and military electronics grids; and (3) as an attack on a U.S. carrier battle group. Each of these actions would be extremely risky for Beijing to undertake, particularly the latter two options. They could result in a rapid escalation of the confrontation to a major conflict between China and the United States, possibly involving nuclear war. The likelihood of the first scenario seems relatively low, given the existence of less risky alternative means of achieving a similar objective. The second and third scenarios also seem unlikely, unless they were undertaken in the context of a major attack against Taiwan. Under such circumstances, Beijing might calculate that its chances of success were made marginally greater by the use of both an EMP and a nuclear attack against a carrier. But such acts would greatly increase the already significant dangers presented by a massive attack, and present many of the same vulnerabilities and dangers discussed above.

Conclusions

In its strategy towards Taiwan, Beijing considers Taiwan to be an inalienable part of China and regards reunification as a "sacred task" of Chinese nationalism. It completely rejects the possibility of Taiwan becoming a fully independent, sovereign state. However, Beijing fears that Taiwan is moving ineluctably toward greater independence, perhaps with U.S. support, and has adopted a complex strategy of pressures and enticements to arrest this trend and at the very least to reestablish a more stable *modus vivendi* across the Taiwan Strait. Among these pressures are a "united front" strategy with the KMT opposition in the Legislative Yuan, a zero tolerance policy for Taiwan's attempts to increase its international space, a renewed effort to reinforce its strategic relationship with Washington, and an increasing emphasis on strengthening the credibility of its military options against Taiwan.

---

[69]Jencks, September 1997, p. 160.

In terms of economic influence, cross-Strait trade and investment statistics clearly highlight the extent to which the two sides enjoy greater and greater levels of economic interaction. For some in Taiwan, this dependence represents a strong potential point of leverage to Beijing in its efforts to convince Taiwan to begin political talks. As indicated above, Beijing has in fact attempted to use economic ties with Taiwan to influence or pressure Taiwan businesspersons to exert pressure on the ROC government to be moderate or to accept Beijing's stance. Aware of the dangers presented by this situation, previous ROC governments have attempted to limit or shape the size or contours of economic interactions with the Mainland. Under the Chen Shui-bian government, however, Taiwan's growing economic interactions with the Mainland, the resulting increasing level of support for such interactions among Taiwan business elites, and Taiwan's recent domestic economic difficulties (induced in large part by the prolonged domestic political confrontation between the Chen government and the opposition) have combined to make such an effort virtually impossible.

The last and perhaps most important area of Chinese influence over Taiwan's foreign and defense policymaking is Chinese military power. As a result of the 1995–1996 tensions over Taiwan, China's weapons programs now place an increased emphasis on acquiring capabilities designed to strengthen the credibility of Beijing's military options against the island, and to deter the U.S. from deploying aircraft carriers in an effort to counter such options. Even by 2010, the type of increased Chinese capabilities summarized above could lead China's leaders to attempt a variety of military actions against Taiwan, including another, more intensive round of military intimidation through various exercises and missile "tests," a naval blockade, a limited direct missile or air attack, and even perhaps limited ground incursions in an attempt to establish a fait accompli in Beijing's favor that the United States would find difficult to counter.

It is unlikely that the Chinese leadership would attempt such actions unless they believed that Taiwan were about to achieve a permanent independence status. Moreover, it should be stressed that the ability of China to prevail in any attempt to employ military force against Taiwan, even by the year 2020, is by no means certain. Yet these preparations themselves contribute to an arms race across the Strait, driving Taiwan's foreign and defense policymaking apparatus to seek deeper defense commitments from the United States and greater numbers of advanced military systems, including theater ballistic missile defenses.

5. The Influence of the United States and Japan

Introduction

The United States and Japan currently wield substantial influence over Taiwan's foreign and defense policymaking. This influence is partly a function of history but also reflects the realities of Taiwan's geographic, economic, political, and military circumstances. Not surprisingly, these two countries also feature prominently in both the theater ballistic missile defense and pragmatic diplomacy issue. This chapter will explore these linkages in greater detail, evaluating the dynamics of past and present trends, and extrapolating those findings for the future.

Historical Progressions

The influence of Japan and the United States upon Taiwan government policy has deep historical roots. For Taipei, the United States has always been its most critical backer, providing political, military, economic and ideological guidance and material assistance of various forms for more than 100 years.[1] Japan, by contrast, was a military opponent of the KMT on the Mainland and a colonial oppressor of the island for fifty years.[2] Like most post-colonial entities, however, Taiwan still enjoys deep ties to its former master, mainly cultural but also deeply economic and political in nature.[3]

As such long-standing ties would suggest, Taiwan's relationships with the United States in particular have been extremely complex over the years, marked by significant periods of both cooperation and conflict. In order to understand the dynamic, it is necessary to view the interaction from both directions. For Taiwan, the relationship with the United States has been both a blessing and a curse. On the positive side of the ledger, America has provided political,

---

[1]Hung-mao Tien, *The Great Transition: Political and Social Change in the Republic of Taiwan*, Hoover Institution Press, Stanford, California, 1989, p. 227.

[2]John King Fairbank, *The United States and China*, 4th edition, Harvard University Press, Cambridge, Massachusetts, 1976, p. 354.

[3]For a recent discussion of the fascination of young Taiwan citizens with Japanese popular culture, see Philip Pan, "Taiwan's Teens Take Style Cues From Tokyo," *Washington Post*, 27 November 2000, p. A16.

economic, and military support at critical times in Taiwan's history, arguably preventing the island numerous times (1950, 1954, 1958) from being coerced into premature unification with the Mainland. Although less formal than before, various spoken and unspoken commitments continue to this day in the form of the Taiwan Relations Act and annual U.S. arms sales to Taipei. At the same time, U.S. support has not always been consistent, and at key junctures in history (1972, 1978) Taiwan has witnessed dramatic reversals of U.S. policy in the furtherance of such global strategic interests as balancing the Soviet threat. As a result of these perceived "betrayals," Taiwan is understandably paranoid about even the slightest change in U.S. attitudes toward the island, demanding a never-ending series of symbolic and material restatements of support. The situation also leads Taipei to spend an inordinate amount of time trying to divine U.S. strategy, assess the state of Sino-U.S. relations, probe the relative strength of Washington's commitment to Taiwan, and deftly manipulate the American political system to ensure a continued coalition of supporters.

For the United States, diplomatic relations with Taiwan at different times have been shaped by American domestic politics, U.S. ideological currents, changing strategic calculations, and other considerations of U.S. national interest. Psychologically, American attitudes toward Taiwan have been characterized by emotions ranging from sympathy, perhaps even empathy, to frustration. These two poles have resulted in a continuous set of debates within the United States about the utility and risks involved in deep ties between Washington and Taipei. On the positive side, Taiwan has often been portrayed, first by the so-called "China Lobby" and later by Taipei's U.S. government and congressional allies, as an attractive and useful strategic partner for the United States. The Kuomintang government, both on the Mainland and later on the island, was depicted as sharing core American values, including being nominally democratic, Christian, and virulent in its opposition to Washington's enemies (be they the Japanese, Chinese Communists, or others). The press coverage surrounding Madame Chiang Kai-Shek's address to a joint session of Congress was perhaps the most extreme expression of this view, though the capitalist miracle on the island since the 1960s and the process of genuine democratization begun in 1988 have only served to bolster the argument and give it new relevance in the post–Cold War world.

On the negative side, the perceived inadequacies of the various ROC governments and their sometimes desperate and destabilizing actions on behalf of their own perceived security needs have been a source of frustration for some in the United States. This view draws its lineage from General "Vinegar Joe" Stilwell's criticisms of General Chiang Kai-Shek's political, economic, and military policies, particularly his prosecution of the war (or lack thereof) against the Japanese and the Chinese Communists in the late 1930s and 1940s.[4] Truman's administration became "disenchanted" with the Chiang regime after the failure of the Marshall Mission in 1947, resulting in the exclusion of Taiwan from the U.S. pre–Korean War "defense perimeter."[5] During the martial law period, the more unseemly aspects of Kuomintang authoritarianism, such as the suppression of dissent and the government-sponsored murder of Henry Liu in the United States, were criticized but ultimately subordinated to the overall anti-communist effort. More recently, former President Lee Teng-hui's efforts at expanding Taiwan's "international space," often at the direct zero-sum expense of Beijing, and his articulation of controversial formulations for cross-Strait relations were seen by some observers as being overly provocative and endangering to stability in the region.

Thus, both sides are beset by competing visions of the other, with the balance often tipped by outside events, such as the Korean War, the Sino-Soviet split, the end of the Cold War, Tiananmen Square, or the PRC's 1995–1996 missile exercises. The remainder of this section will explore the historical phases of the relationship in more detail, drawing links between the events of each particular period and the dynamics of Taiwan's foreign and defense policymaking.

Pre-1972 Relations with Taiwan

Taiwan's relationship with the United States prior to 1972 was marked by the "overwhelming dependence" of the former upon the latter.[6] This reliance predated even the founding of the Kuomintang as a formal party—the KMT's founder, Sun Yat-sen, was raising money in Denver when the 1911 Revolution broke out in China. While the Kuomintang in its early years drew inspiration and organizational direction from the Soviet Comintern,[7] the onset of World War Two witnessed unprecedented levels of official U.S. material support to the Kuomingtang and its new leader, Chiang Kai-Shek, epitomized in the aircraft supply of Chiang's forces over the Burma "hump" by General Chennault's "Flying Tigers," and the U.S. logistical sealift and airlift of half a million Nationalist soldiers to Manchuria in 1945.[8] Despite a brief lull in U.S. support following the humiliating defeat of KMT forces on the Mainland and their retreat

---

[4]See Barbara Tuchman, *Stillwell and the American Experience in China, 1911–1945,* Bantam, New York, 1972.

[5]Tien, p. 229.

[6]Tien, p. 228.

[7]Fairbank, pp. 238–239.

[8]This support is discussed in Fairbank, pp. 340–344; and Tuchman.

to Taiwan, the outbreak of the Korean War solidified the U.S. defense commitment to the island, and this political, diplomatic, economic, and military assistance grew to "massive" proportions as the Cold War deepened.[9]

In terms of Taiwan's foreign and defense policymaking, the regime's clear dependence on Washington resulted in predictable policy distortions, driven by the perception among the Taiwan leadership and general public that the ROC's survival depended on continued U.S. support. During World War II, the Nationalist government was frustratingly resistant to U.S. advice, ignoring the policy prescriptions of a series of American officials (Stilwell, Hurley, Marshall), while wasting Washington's generous material support in its eventual failed campaign against the Communist Red Army.[10] After the outbreak of the Korean War and the signing of the 1954 Mutual Defense Treaty, U.S. influence upon Taiwan decision-making was profound, though the relationship reportedly was more cooperative than before, involving some explicit coordination of some diplomatic, intelligence, and military policies.

U.S. Strategic Reorientation Toward China

At the apex of Taiwan's diplomatic success in 1971, Taipei had formal diplomatic ties with 68 nations, while only 53 recognized Beijing's primacy. Of the former, the most important was the United States. Between Nixon's visit to China and normalization of Sino-U.S. relations in 1978, however, U.S.-Taiwan relations could be best characterized as enduring a gradual "strategic and diplomatic disengagement."[11] The reason for this disengagement was the belief that official Sino-U.S. and U.S.-Taiwan bilateral relations were zero-sum in nature. While the United States and China could not agree on the terms of American troop withdrawal from Taiwan in the 1972 Shanghai Communiqué, the language in the text that reaffirmed the "ultimate objective of the withdrawal of all U.S. forces and military installations from Taiwan" marked the beginning of the end for the Washington-Taipei alliance. Accordingly, the United States began gradually to cut back its military presence on Taiwan, while simultaneously softening its public stance towards the PRC.[12] Japan, by contrast, broke quickly from Taiwan, shifting diplomatic recognition from Taipei to Beijing in September 1972.

---

[9] Tien, p. 228.

[10] Between 1941 and 1949, American aid to the Nationalist government totaled US$6 billion in credits, goods, and equipment. See Fairbank, p. 345.

[11] Tien, p. 228.

[12] Tien, p. 234.

Taiwan's foreign and defense policymaking during this period was deeply affected by America's disengagement. After the shock of "betrayal" wore off, it is likely that senior Taiwan officials began to see the island's extreme levels of dependence on the United States as a liability rather than an asset. Though the 1970s were marked by a series of inconclusive negotiations between China and the United States over establishing full diplomatic relations, the Taipei government began to hedge against the possibility of a complete break of official relations with Washington. Analysts of Taiwan's later political and economic reform policies point to this period as the beginning of the transition to market liberalization and pragmatic diplomacy, both of which were seen as substitutes for American security guarantees. Taiwan's defense policies, by contrast, seem relatively unchanged during this period, reflecting a bureaucratic inertia that has really only been addressed since the PRC's missile exercises in 1995–1996.

De-Recognition and the Taiwan Relations Act

After President Carter's announcement on 15 December 1978 of his decision to establish formal diplomatic relations with the PRC and de-recognize Taiwan, U.S.-Taiwan relations could be characterized as "non-diplomatic but substantive."[13] They were non-diplomatic in a formal sense, following the closure of the American Embassy, the abrogation of the 1954 U.S.-ROC Mutual Defense Treat, and the withdrawal of all U.S. military personnel. Yet substantive relations survived, thanks in no small part to the passage of the Taiwan Relations Act (TRA) by Congress in 1979, which Congressman Clement Zablocki, chairman of the House Foreign Affairs Committee, described as "absolutely necessary . . . for continuing, without interruption, our commercial, cultural, and other non-diplomatic relations with Taiwan."[14] Indeed, some senior American politicians asserted that the TRA might actually "enhance" relations, since Taiwan had been removed as a "diplomatic issue between China and the United States."[15]

In fact, the TRA immediately became a critical variable in Taiwan's foreign and defense policymaking, since it defined the limits of the possible for U.S.-Taiwan political and security relations. First and foremost, the TRA sought to maintain some semblance of the American security commitment to the island as enshrined in the now defunct Mutual Defense Treaty, though formal relations with the PRC meant that this commitment had to be couched in more ambiguous terms than a

---

[13]Tien, p. 228.

[14]Wolff and Simon, p. 8.

[15]Wolff and Simon, p. 1.

direct promise of U.S. intervention.[16] As a result, probing the strength of the U.S. resolve to defend Taiwan at any given time became a key and abiding feature of Taipei's foreign and defense policies.

One principal measure of this commitment was the level of "defensive arms sales" sanctioned by the TRA. The Reagan administration immediately ran into conflict with the PRC over the sale of new fighter aircraft or upgraded aircraft to Taiwan. While the resulting August 17, 1982 Communiqué expressed a desire to gradually reduce arms sales to Taiwan over time, the ROC also received the above-mentioned Six Assurances from Washington that included an assurance that Washington would not consult with Beijing prior to making specific arms sales decisions. Thus, the annual arms sales process became a periodic litmus test of congressional and Executive Branch support for Taiwan. This could change somewhat in the future, however, as a result of the Bush administration's decision in April 2001 to replace the regular annual arms sale deliberation/decision process with a less regularized, "as-needed" approach to arms sales.

In other areas of foreign and defense policymaking, the post–de-recognition period was also fruitful. As Tien Hung-mao writes, the "warming of U.S.-PRC relations enabled the Reagan Administration to help Taiwan with little risk of rupturing its ties with Peking."[17] In the area of foreign policymaking, the number of Taiwan representative offices in the United States, known as the Coordination Council for North American Affairs (CCNAA) and later as the Taipei Economic and Cultural Representative Office (TECRO), continued to expand in numbers from the original ten to twelve in 1987.[18] More important, Taiwan officials found it easier to gain access to U.S. government officials during the Reagan administration than during the Carter years, provided that the meetings did not take place in government offices. These contacts, as well as continuing support from congressional allies, sustained the level of arms sales to the island, though limits on purchases and inability to seek alternative suppliers constrained the procurement aspect of Taiwan's defense policymaking.

From a strategic perspective, the abrogation of ties between Taiwan and the United States and Japan forced the island to change the approach of its campaign

---

[16]In fact, some observers (most notably Doak Barnett) argued that the unilateral defense pledge from the United States ("the United States will make available to Taiwan such defense articles and defense services in such quantity as may be necessary to enable Taiwan to maintain a sufficient self-defense capability") went further than the terms of the Mutual Defense Treaty. See Barnett, 1981, p. 5.

[17]Tien, p. 239.

[18]In Japan, the counterparts to these organizations are the ROC's East Asia Association and Japan's Interchange Association.

for greater international standing, refocusing its attention from the pursuit of formal diplomatic relations to what the ROC called "substantive relations," including "non-diplomatic links with foreign countries through trade, cultural exchanges, athletic competitions, commercial and economic ties, KMT party-to-party connections, and military cooperation."[19] The central feature of this strategy was economic relations, and Taiwan's miraculous economic performance since the late 1970s has formed the basis for a new form of international legitimacy and recognition. These trade ties have allowed Taipei to "offset its diplomatic isolation" and "survive as a political entity in the community of nations."[20]

While security relations still make up a significant percentage of U.S. relations with Taiwan, economic ties form the overwhelming share of relations with Japan. Indeed, these relations were solidified long before de-recognition, although they have grown steadily since the breaking of formal ties. Between 1952 and 1986, U.S. investment in Taiwan totaled US$1.85 billion, compared with US$1.38 billion from Japan. In the middle 1980s, however, Japanese investment overtook funding from the United States. In 1986 alone, Japan invested US$253.6 million compared with US$138.4 million from the United States. By 1999, U.S. investments had reached US$570 million, compared with US$525 million from Japan (16.4 percent of the total).[21]

A similar situation exists in trade volume between the countries. By the mid-1980s, the United States and Japan combined for more than half of Taiwan's trade volume, with Japan exports outpacing U.S. exports by a significant margin (34.2 percent, or US$8.3 billion, versus 22.4 percent, or US$5.4 billion). This ranking was still in place in 1999, when Japanese imports accounted for 27.6 percent of the total compared with 18 percent from the United States, but the absolute volume of imports from both countries had increased a dramatic 900 percent in the intervening fifteen years. In terms of markets for Taiwan goods, exports to the United States still make up a dominant share, though this dependence has decreased dramatically from 47.7 percent in 1986 to 25.4 percent in 1999. Exports to Japan are a distant third following Hong Kong, receiving less than 10 percent of the total.[22]

[19]Tien, p. 250.
[20]Tien, p. 250.
[21]*Republic of China Yearbook 2001,* Government Information Office, Taipei, May 2001.
[22]Ibid.

Tiananmen Square and the End of the Cold War

At the close of the 1980s, Taiwan still had limited official contact with the international community, with little hope of overcoming the global strategic logic of the superpower triangle.[23] However, two trends, one domestic and one international, were poised to upset this equilibrium. Domestically, Taiwan had at long last begun to democratize its political system, initiating the process that would eventually discard its authoritarian system and its martial law decree. When combined with its disproportionately impressive economic power, this liberalization of its political system had significant normative reputational effects, particularly with respect to democratic countries like the United States. Internationally, the communist states were beset by a series of rolling internal crises, resulting in the collapse of the Berlin Wall and the Tiananmen Square massacre. For Taiwan, these two events fundamentally changed the internal dynamic of policymaking and the milieu in which those policies were developed and implemented. Overall, they had a mixed effect upon the achievement of Taiwan's security goals, perhaps reflecting the new uncertainties of the times.

As indicated in previous chapters, domestically driven changes increasingly forced Taiwan's foreign and defense policymaking into the open light of nascent democratic oversight, though the continued dominance of the KMT in the government meant that the intrusiveness of this oversight was limited. The lifting of martial law also unleashed an actively free press, whose investigations of corruption surrounding foreign arms purchases and money lobbying in the United States exposed parts of a previously secretive and unaccountable system. International changes increased the uncertainties of Taiwan's position, but the breakup of the Soviet bloc and the concomitant faltering of the superpower triangle also afforded new room for maneuver on the international scene. Lee Teng-hui's policy of "pragmatic diplomacy" explicitly exploited these cleavages, though there is heated debate about whether these measures ultimately enhanced or undermined Taiwan's security.

The 1995–1996 Missile Crisis and the DPP Presidential Victory

The Chinese missile exercises and the election of Chen Shui-bian have had profound effects upon the style and content of Taiwan's foreign and defense policymaking. Beijing's displays of force and the new escalation of bellicosity towards Taiwan and its leaders infused the cross-Strait situation and Taiwan's

---

[23]In 1988, Taiwan was a member of only eight international institutions and was recognized by only 22 of 160 nations in the world.

corresponding policies with a sense of urgency and danger not seen since the 1954 and 1958 crises. While pragmatic diplomacy's gains were largely undone by Beijing's new aggressive pressure on the few remaining diplomatic supporters of Taiwan, the self-evident threat from the PRC allowed Taiwan to make dramatic strides in defense relations with the United States.

Specifically, the missile tests energized advocates of increased arms sales and military exchanges on both sides, politicizing the process in a public fashion and greatly enhancing the role of Congress. As a result, open fissures appeared in the Executive Branch of the U.S. government between the Defense Department, which favored greater sales and interaction, and the State Department and National Security Council, which generally did not want to upset the political and diplomatic dynamic of the U.S.-China-Taiwan triangle. These fissures were particularly visible in the controversial area of BMD systems, which were seen by some as precisely the type of defensive systems mandated by the TRA and by others as unproven systems likely to escalate an arms race between China and Taiwan. Taiwan's foreign and defense policies generally sought to exploit these conflicts without openly appearing to encourage divisions in the U.S. government bureaucracy. This was achieved by rallying public congressional support and legislative assistance to those bureaucracies, particularly the Pentagon, that were more favorable towards the sale of BMD systems to Taiwan.[24]

The election of the DPP's Chen Shui-bian to the presidency in March 2000 and the retention of control of the Legislative Yuan by the KMT were greeted with a measure of anxiety by the U.S. government, particularly given the DPP's open advocacy of independence in the past. Immediately after the election, the DPP sent a small delegation of well-chosen envoys to Washington to rally its supporters and reassure key elements of the government. Washington's concerns turned out to be unwarranted, since Chen's government has pursued a relatively moderate course in cross-Strait relations. Moreover, the transition of government in the United States has precluded any new initiatives or policies on this topic. In the absence of a formal U.S. policy review, there continues to be reluctance to insert the U.S. government between the two parties as mediator. Instead, Washington is likely to continue with a policy that American Institute on Taiwan (AIT) Director Richard Bush calls "rhetorical even-handedness, creation of a positive context, and focus on process."[25] The elements of this approach include the U.S.-Taiwan security relationship, especially arms sales, and encouraging

---

[24]Information in this paragraph is derived from interviews conducted in Washington and Taipei with former U.S. and ROC officials in May 2001.

[25]Speech by Richard Bush, "Cross-Strait State of Play," February 2001.

both sides to resume dialogue. It also includes what Bush terms "intellectual facilitation"—i.e., clarifying for each side the views of the other, but not passing messages. This approach rests on the twin assumptions that the two sides are actually willing to engage each other after a few more signals or concessions and that there is some hope of reconciling the serious substantive differences between the two sides. The advantage of this approach is that it allows both sides to play for time, but PLA modernization and economic growth may make it unsustainable over the long-term.

The United States, Japan, and Pragmatic Diplomacy

While Taiwan's pragmatic diplomacy policy is aimed at the world, Taipei pays particular attention to the reception of the policy in Washington and Tokyo, since their support for Taiwan's efforts to enlarge its international space is a key determinant of the policy's overall success.

The United States and Pragmatic Diplomacy

In its efforts to maximize all possible political and diplomatic assistance and recognition provided by the international community, Taiwan views the United States as the critical anchor, since Washington is best equipped to provide Taipei with sufficient defense commitments and foreign policy support necessary to press the island's case around the world. Yet the United States has consistently sought to interject ambiguity into these issues, maintaining informal ties with Taiwan and narrowly circumscribing security guarantees in order to achieve an appropriate balance between competing national interests. With respect to former President Lee Teng-hui and current President Chen Shui-bian's specific policies of pragmatic diplomacy, Washington never actively encouraged Taiwan's various efforts but did periodically seek to refine certain bilateral arrangements related to transits, meetings, and declaratory policies about Taiwan's status, especially after the crises surrounding Lee's transit through Hawaii in 1994 and his visit to Cornell University in 1995.

While many of the restrictions on Taiwan's activities remained constant during the first Bush administration, the Clinton team during its first term achieved some early success in securing Taiwan's entry into the ADB and APEC. The new administration sought to address the issue more fully in a Taiwan policy review that was initiated in mid-1993, dropped it to deal with higher-profile China issues, and then re-addressed it with greater vigor in mid-1994. One important impetus for renewal of the discussion was the diplomatic row surrounding Lee Teng-hui's proposed transit en route to meetings in Central America. After first being told to transit through Mexico, Lee was permitted to stop over in Hawaii, but he reportedly objected to his reception and refused to disembark his aircraft. Spurred by this embarrassing incident and the resulting congressional pressure, the participants in the Taiwan policy review sought to resolve some of the more onerous aspects of the bilateral relationship, including Taiwan's objections to the name of its quasi-embassy, the Coordinating Council for North American Affairs, and the restrictions on meetings between Taiwan officials and their American counterparts.

The review resulted in a number of specific measures. Both the Chinese and the Taiwan governments reacted badly to the changes, which some in the U.S. government paradoxically took as a sign of a policy success. First, the name of Taiwan's representative office was changed to the Taipei Economic and Cultural Representative Office (TECRO). Second, transits were permitted, though under ad hoc arrangements, and "transits" were explicitly differentiated from "private visits."[26] Third, some U.S. officials were allowed to meet with their Taiwan counterparts in their offices, though officials from the State Department and the Executive Office of the President were exempted. Fourth, the Clinton administration declared its intention to support Taiwan's participation in international organizations that did not require statehood for membership, though Washington maintained its opposition to Taiwan's quest for UN membership. Agencies and departments within the U.S. government were tasked with drawing up lists of international organizations that met these criteria. After Taiwan pushed its case too hard by protesting at the World Health Organization (WHO), however, European support for the U.S. policy was significantly reduced, and Beijing began vigorously opposing Taiwan's membership in any international organizations, regardless of entrance requirements.

Despite these changes and clarifications, however, the relative fragility of Washington's policy towards pragmatic diplomacy was exposed by President Lee Teng-hui's request in 1995 to visit his alma mater, Cornell University. At first, the U.S. government turned down the request, and Secretary Christopher communicated this decision to the Chinese government. Under intense congressional pressure, however, the administration reversed itself and issued a visa for Lee to conduct a private visit to the university. This action set off a sequence of escalatory events aimed at affecting Taiwan's presidential election in March 1996, culminating in Chinese missile tests and the U.S. dispatch of two carrier battle groups to the waters near Taiwan.

---

[26]As an example of a private visit, Taiwan officials were allowed to visit their children who were studying at U.S. universities.

In the wake of the Lee visit and the resulting crisis, the Clinton administration again addressed the substance of its Taiwan policy, in particular the administration's attitude toward pragmatic diplomacy and the state of U.S.-China relations. The most direct consequence of this internal review appeared in 1998 during President Clinton's summit in China. At a meeting in Shanghai, Clinton publicly articulated the so-called "Three Nos": no support for Taiwan independence, no recognition for a separate Taiwan government, and no backing of Taiwan's entry into international organizations.[27] Outside observers interpreted his statement as a concession to his Chinese hosts, though White House officials said Clinton was simply repeating a long-standing informal policy and not signaling a substantive shift in U.S.-Taiwan relations. Interviews with a former administration official confirm that the Three Nos were indeed a public statement of an unofficial policy, but also highlight a subtle change in government policy. Whereas the 1994 policy review concluded that the United States would support Taiwan's efforts to join international organizations that did not require statehood, the later review concluded that the United States would not support Taiwan's efforts to join organizations that did require statehood. To some this may appear to be a semantic distinction only, but in the semantically charged atmosphere of cross-Strait relations the distinction was an important and significant change.

Opposition to the Three Nos in Washington policy circles was immediate, though the criticisms generally took two forms. To one side, the main objection was the lack of a fourth "no," highlighting U.S. opposition to the use of force to settle the conflict. Pro-Taiwan advocates, by contrast, objected to the entire package as an unnecessary tilt towards Beijing's view of the cross-Strait problem. The debate continued through 1999 and became a minor policy feature of the 2000 presidential campaign. Unlike the 1996 platform, which did not mention Taiwan, the 2000 Democratic policy platform promised to continue to engage China and to investigate ways to cooperate across a broad range of issues, while insisting on adherence to international standards on matters including "bellicose threats directed at Taiwan."[28] In particular, the Democratic policy statement supported a resolution of cross-Strait issues that is both "peaceful and consistent with the wishes of the people of Taiwan." Moving even closer to the Republican platform in 1996, the Democratic platform asserts America's "responsibilities" under the Taiwan Relations Act, though it remains committed to a "one-China" policy.

---

[27]"Clinton's China Policy Dropped," Associated Press, 19 March 2001.
[28]Nat Bellocchi, "US Parties' Platforms on Taiwan," *Taipei Times,* 24 August 2000.

The 2000 Republican platform, by contrast, was marked by a serious dispute over core policies toward China and Taiwan.[29] According to press reports, an early draft of the party's platform asserted that "America's commitment to a one-China policy is based on the principle that there must be no use of force by China against Taiwan." One group of Republicans fought during the drafting of the platform to remove any reference to the one-China policy, a formulation from the 1970s under which the United States severed formal diplomatic ties with Taiwan and established them with Beijing. Former representative Bob Livingston (La.), a member of the platform committee, led a push to change the first draft of the Republican platform. "There is a sloppy tendency in policy to say that our policy in Asia is based on the one-China policy," said Bruce Jackson, chairman of the Republican platform subcommittee on foreign policy and a delegate at the Republican convention.[30] "Nonsense. Our policy in Asia is based on freedom, democracy and the peaceful resolution of disputes." But aides close to then-Governor Bush backed a more moderate view. "The United States has a very big interest in continuing the policy that has served everyone well: No one changes the status quo," said Condoleezza Rice, Bush's foreign policy advisor during the campaign and now national security advisor in the Bush administration.[31]

Led by Rice and Robert D. Blackwill, a lecturer at Harvard University and former State Department official, the Republican candidate's campaign forged a compromise that acknowledged the existence of the one-China policy without endorsing it. The final version read: "America has acknowledged the view that there is one China. Our policy is based on the principle that there must be no use of force by China against Taiwan." The platform went even further, arguing that the United States would "honor our promises" and that Taiwan "deserves our support including sale of defensive weapons . . . deserves our support for membership in the WTO, WHO . . . and other multilateral institutions." Moreover, it argued that "all issues regarding Taiwan's future must be resolved peacefully and must be agreeable to the people of Taiwan." If China violates these principles, then the platform concluded that the United States will respond appropriately under the Taiwan Relations Act. Yet criticism continued after the compromise. According to Jackson, "What we wrote is that America acknowledges that there is a view that there is one China. That is China's view."[32]

---

[29]Steven Mufson, "In GOP, a Simmering Struggle on China Policy," *Washington Post,* 22 August 2000.

[30]Ibid.

[31]Ibid.

[32]Ibid.

After Bush's delayed victory in the presidential race, the Taiwan government immediately asserted the need for reassessment of U.S. policy regarding transits and meetings. In early December, President Chen Shui-bian told a group of visiting U.S. scholars—many of them former officials—that Washington should review what he called unreasonable restrictions on visits by senior Taiwan officials to the United States and vice versa.[33] "We hope U.S. officials responsible for foreign and security affairs don't have to wait until they retire to visit Taipei," Chen told his guests, including former U.S. assistant secretary for East Asian and Pacific Affairs Winston Lord and President Bill Clinton's former Senior Director for Asia Kenneth Lieberthal. Chen also declared his opposition to the Three Nos.[34] "I hope the new U.S. government can avoid mentioning the so-called 'three nos' policy," said Chen, who was especially critical of attempts to block Taiwan's entry into international organizations. "If it really needs to have 'three nos,' we suggest that it add a fourth no stating that it opposes Communist China using military force to resolve the Taiwan issue," Chen said.

By March 2001, key foreign policy officials had begun to reveal features of the Bush administration's Taiwan policy.[35] In testimony, Secretary of State Colin Powell confirmed that the "Six Assurances," first outlined by the Reagan Administration in 1982, remain part of U.S. policy toward Taiwan. As indicated above, the "Six Assurances" made clear that Washington had not agreed to set a date to end arms sales to Taiwan; had not agreed to consult the PRC government before selling weapons to the ROC; had not agreed to revise the Taiwan Relations Act; had not altered its position regarding sovereignty over Taiwan; would not mediate between Taiwan and the Mainland; and would not exert pressure on Taipei to enter into negotiations with Beijing. Moreover, Powell declared his support to Taiwan's participation in the WHO but stopped short of a pledge to push for an observer role for the country in the upcoming meeting of the World Health Assembly. According to Powell, "we believe there are ways— and I have to review this—but the government's position over the years has been

---

[33]"U.S. Told Not To Sacrifice Taiwan's Interest," Reuters, 6 December 2000. At the time of his statement, U.S. Public Law 103-416, sec. 221, states that whenever the president of Taiwan or any other high-level official of Taiwan shall apply to visit the United States for the purpose of holding discussions with U.S. federal or state government officials concerning trade or business with Taiwan that will reduce the U.S.-Taiwan trade deficit, prevention of nuclear proliferation, threats to the national security of the United States, the protection of the global environment, the protection of endangered species or regional humanitarian disasters, the official shall be admitted to the United States, unless the official is otherwise excludable under the immigration laws of the United States. The "otherwise excludable" phrase refers to illegal conduct or contagious health problems and also includes the phrase, "unless the Secretary of State personally determines that the alien's admission would compromise a compelling United States foreign policy interest."

[34]"U.S. Told Not To Sacrifice Taiwan's Interest," Reuters, 6 December 2000.

[35]"'Six Assurances' Remain US Policy: Powell," Taiwan Headlines, 9 March 2001, in http://th.gio.gov.tw/show.cfm?news_id=7883.

there should be ways for Taiwan to enjoy full benefits of participation without being a member," noting that U.S. policy has been that membership in international organizations that require statehood be reserved for Mainland China.[36] However, he said, "the past policy has been, which seems to have served the nation well, to find ways for Taiwan to participate without belonging to these international organizations."[37]

Less than two weeks later, the State Department made an even more significant change, abandoning Clinton's controversial "Three Nos" declaration. Asked about a report in a Japanese newspaper account that said the Bush administration had dropped the "Three Nos" policy, State Department spokesman Richard Boucher said, "We adhere to the one-China policy. It's a policy that we have told the Chinese government directly."[38] To outside observers, Boucher's deflection of the question strongly implied that the "Three Nos" were no longer an operative feature of U.S. policy, and other officials have done nothing to repudiate this notion. Secretary Powell's comments and Boucher's clarifications suggest that the Bush administration might be committed to expanding Taiwan's international space, in spite of Chinese objections. At the same time, the retention of the one-China principle indicates that there are still limits to possible movement in this area, particularly Taiwan's efforts at pragmatic diplomacy that are perceived to be unnecessarily provocative.

Japan and Pragmatic Diplomacy

For Taiwan's efforts to implement pragmatic diplomacy and expand its international space, Japan is perhaps second only to the United States in importance. Because of its own internal legal and political constraints, Japan cannot offer substantial defense commitments or foreign policy support to Taiwan, though its key role in the U.S.-Japan defense alliance does offer indirect defense support. Japan is also an important advocate for Taiwan's efforts to expand its international economic space, given the fact that Taiwan is one of Japan's most significant economic partners. Yet for the same reasons as the United States, Japan's relationship with Taiwan is informal and marked by considerable ambiguity. Like Washington, Tokyo has never actively encouraged Taiwan's pragmatic diplomacy but has periodically modified its bilateral arrangements to fit changing circumstances and has rebuffed significant efforts by Beijing to further restrict those arrangements.

---

[36]Ibid.

[37]Ibid.

[38]"Clinton's China Policy Dropped," Associated Press, 19 March 2001.

Since 1972, Japan has maintained its relations with Taiwan as an exchange of a private and regional nature, retaining non-governmental, unofficial ties in line with the 1972 Japan-China Joint Communique.[39] Unlike the United States, Japan has not enacted domestic law to institutionalize its relationship with Taiwan, and has studiously avoided official contact with Taiwan since 1972 to avoid annoying Beijing.[40] At the same time, Taiwan enjoys powerful support in Japan. Three hundred and twenty Japanese lawmakers are members of a "Japan-Taiwan discussion group" in parliament, according to Taipei's economic and cultural representative office, the island's unofficial mission in Japan.[41]

Much of this support in Japan is a historical holdover from Japan's colonization of Taiwan from 1895 to 1945, which forged deep political, economic, and even linguistic ties that have survived de-colonization. Taiwan's former President Lee Teng-hui, who was a graduate of the University of Kyoto and speaks fluent Japanese, was emblematic of a significant "Japanese-language speaking generation" in Taiwan that reciprocated these ties. Lee in particular cultivated a strong relationship with Japan by alluring many Japanese with his ability to communicate on a wide range of topics in fluent Japanese. While this older cohort of Japanese-speaking officials completely withdrew from the political front-line after Lee lost his presidency, common economic interest continues to solidify the connection. Bilateral Taiwan-Japan trade totaled US$41 billion in 1997, compared to US$65.2 billion between Japan and China. Japanese investment in Taiwan totaled US$550 million in 1997.[42] For many Japanese businesses, Taiwan was a foothold for the region that largely withstood the Asian financial storm, although its economy has since declined considerably.

In the latter part of Lee's tenure as president, particularly following the 1995–1996 missile crisis, China placed increasingly greater pressure on Japan to limit its relations with Taiwan, but Japan has consistently rebuffed their entreaties. Upon his ascension to office, former Prime Minister Keizo Obuchi struck Japan's traditional middle ground on cross-Strait relations, calling on China and Taiwan to settle their sovereignty dispute peacefully. "The problem is one which should be handled by Chinese people," Obuchi told parliament. "I fervently hope that parties concerned will hold a dialogue over the Taiwan issue and that they will reach a peaceful resolution."[43] In July 1998, Taiwan had officially welcomed the

---

[39]Kazuo Kodama, "Why Japan Must Shed Its 'One-Nation Pacifism Skin,'" Asia-Pacific Media Network, 21 June 2000. Kodama is Minister of Information for the Government of Japan.

[40]"China, Japan Clash Over 'Three Nos,'" Agence France Presse, 2 November 1998.

[41]Ibid.

[42]*Republic of China Yearbook 1998*, Government Information Office, Taipei, 1998.

[43]"Japanese Premier Calls for Peaceful Resolution of Taiwan Issue," Agence France-Presse, 10 August 1998.

election of Obuchi, saying it hoped he would promote ties between Taipei and Tokyo. "It is hoped that with Mr. Obuchi as the new prime minister, the ties between the Republic of China (Taiwan) and Japan will improve on the present basis," Foreign Ministry spokesman Roy Wu said.[44] During the parliamentary session, Obuchi declined to specify areas to be covered under new Japan-U.S. defense guidelines signed in April. The guidelines expand military cooperation to cope with conflicts in the region. The revision of the 1978 guidelines has been intensely criticized by China, which fears it could lead to interference in its affairs with Taiwan. "Regional conflicts mean events which can affect Japan's peace and security seriously and the guidelines do not include a purely geographical definition of the conflicts," Obuchi said.[45] Under the guidelines Tokyo can provide support, including the supply of fuel and the transport of soldiers, for U.S. forces in "areas surrounding Japan" when the country's peace and security is threatened.[46]

For China, however, Obuchi's comments were inadequate. As both sides began their preparations for Jiang Zemin's visit to Japan in November 1998, the level of rhetoric about Japan-Taiwan relations increased markedly. In the run-up to the meetings, Chinese Foreign Minister Tang Jiaxuan laid down markers on the question of an apology for Japanese wartime atrocities in China and Japan's relations with Taiwan, warning: "We believe if both sides . . . deal appropriately with some issues existing, especially the two principle issues of history and Taiwan, the relationship between China and Japan will develop continuously, stably and soundly," he said.[47] Tang's remarks were seconded by Chinese Premier Zhu Rongji, who expressed concern that Taiwan is gaining encouragement from conservative Japanese politicians who want closer ties between Japan and Taiwan. In a press conference, Zhu pointed out that Japan agreed in two pacts—1972 and 1978—to recognize China's claim to sovereignty over Taiwan. As a result, he argued that "the Japanese side should adhere to such principles, honor their commitments and do some real deeds to safeguard the friendly relationship," he said.[48]

By "real deeds," Zhu referred to China's pre-summit demands that Japan publicly state its own version of the U.S. "Three Nos," declaring that Tokyo does not support Taiwan independence, recognition of two Chinas or Taiwan

---

[44]Ibid.

[45]Ibid.

[46]Interview with Japanese defense attaché to the United States.

[47]"China Says Taiwan Central to Sino-Japanese Ties," Agence France-Presse, 10 November 1998.

[48]"Jiang Wants 'Real Deeds' on Taiwan Issue," South China Morning Post, 6 November 1998.

membership as a sovereign nation in any international organization.[49] Beijing sought to enshrine this declaration in a joint statement with Tokyo at the conclusion of the Obuchi-Jiang summit. To spur Japan, Chinese interlocutors reportedly reminded their Japanese counterparts of the fact that U.S. President Bill Clinton declared the same "Three Nos" policy during a speech in Shanghai in June 1998. One press report even suggested that Beijing might be willing to "reciprocate" yen loans by agreeing to commit investments in Japan in exchange for greater Japanese concessions on Taiwan.[50] Much to the chagrin of Beijing and delight of Taipei, however, Japanese interlocutors reportedly countered that Clinton's Shanghai speech did not carry the same weight as a written document, and therefore Japan refused to place such a declaration in a joint statement. If Japan did agree to mention Taiwan in the joint statement, officials reportedly told the Chinese that Tokyo would not go beyond the language of the 1972 Sino-Japanese Communiqué, in which Japan offered that it "understands and respects" the Chinese position over the Taiwan issue.

Japan steadfastly maintained this position through the course of the summit, which was widely regarded by outside observers as a disaster for Sino-Japanese relations.[51] According to a Japanese official speaking on background, Prime Minister Keizo Obuchi reiterated Japan's policy of recognizing Beijing while maintaining only unofficial relations with Taiwan.[52] Obuchi then reportedly told Jiang that Japan's stance over Taiwan remained unchanged from a previous joint statement with China in 1992.[53] According to a Foreign Ministry official, Obuchi confirmed to Jiang that Tokyo was still opposed to independence for Taiwan, asserting "our stance of not supporting Taiwan's independence remains unchanged."[54] Yet the Japanese government refused to publicly declare this or any other principle governing its relations with Taiwan in the form of "Three Nos," much less put them in writing in a Sino-Japanese joint statement.

Predictably, Taiwan was heartened by Japan's refusal to accede to additional Chinese demands. According to Sheu Ke-sheng, then–deputy chairman of the Mainland Affairs Council, Taiwan was "happy to see Japan pragmatically deal

---

[49]"China, Japan Clash Over 'Three Nos,'" *Agence France Presse*, 2 November 1998.

[50]Willy Wo-Lap Lam, "Jiang to Warn US, Japan over Taiwan," *South China Morning Post*, 24 November 1998.

[51]Interviews with Japanese officials and China experts, Tokyo, January 2001.

[52]"Obuchi: Japan Still Opposed to Taiwan Independence," *Agence France-Presse*, 27 November 1998.

[53]Ibid.

[54]Ibid.

with reality" in not altering its position toward Taiwan.[55] Taipei also seized on the discord to attack China's strategy of pressuring the United States, Japan, and other powers to support its diplomatic embargo against Taiwan, warning that Beijing was using "big-power diplomacy" to get its way in Asia and attempting to draw overseas Chinese community groups away from supporting the island. According to then–Taiwan Foreign Minister Jason Hu, referring to Clinton's June summit in Beijing, "the Chinese communists evidently feel their international image has improved since the visit by U.S. President Clinton."[56] "They are wooing influential countries with the aim of establishing superpower status and becoming the region's next overlord," Hu said, adding that Taipei was forming a task force to study Beijing's big-power diplomacy.[57] In particular, he argued that Taipei was on guard against attempts by Beijing to engineer a worldwide boycott of Taiwan's Double Tenth celebration on next year's 50th anniversary of the founding of the People's Republic of China on the Mainland.[58]

Other analysts in Taiwan also expressed satisfaction with Japan's response to China's demands. "I think Taiwan must be relieved about the outcome," said Andrew Yang, an expert on Taiwan-China military strategies.[59] "Tokyo is very much in line with current U.S. policy—no support for Taiwan's independence but no real support either for its reunification with the Mainland," Yang said. "But China will try again and again. They won't give up."[60] Taiwan media cautiously hailed Japan's refusal to let Beijing dictate the terms of its Taiwan policy. "The unwillingness of Tokyo to officially state the 'three noes' . . . can be read as the Japanese government's reluctance to go along with Beijing in its intensified efforts to isolate Taiwan internationally," the *China Post* said in a commentary.[61] But Taipei political analyst Tim Ting said Beijing's unrelenting squeeze nonetheless was wearing down support for Taiwan, with major powers gradually accepting its view that Taiwan must bow to the Beijing's government's sovereignty. "This will give Taiwanese diplomatic policy a very difficult environment to continue to struggle against Chinese pressure," Ting said.[62]

The same issues were revived again during Obuchi's trip to China in July 1999. The May 1999 passage of the revised U.S.-Japan Defense Guidelines in the

---

[55]Jeffrey Parker, "Wary Taiwan Tight-Lipped on Japan-China Discord," Reuters, 27 November 1998.

[56]Ibid.

[57]Ibid.

[58]Ibid.

[59]Ibid.

[60]Ibid.

[61]Cited in ibid.

[62]Ibid.

Japanese Diet intensified the discussion, since China fears these military arrangements are designed to protect Taiwan in the event of Chinese military action against the island.[63] The pact allows Japan for the first time to provide logistical support for U.S. forces, including use of civilian airports and seaports, as well as transporting food, fuel, and other nonmilitary items in the event of an Asian crisis. During his visit, Obuchi reportedly told the Chinese leadership that the new defense pact will by no means pave the way for a revival of Japan's wartime militarism.[64] Again, Obuchi faced demands from Beijing to issue an explicit "Three Nos" statement denying support for Taiwan. Obuchi, however, stuck firmly to Japan's stance of adhering to the 1972 joint declaration stipulating that Japan recognizes only "One China."

While Tokyo's policies have not changed with the transition from Obuchi to Mori to Koizumi, there are concerns that the election of Chen Shui-bian to the presidency of Taiwan could eventually inject new tension into the Taiwan-Japan relationship. Some DPP members believe that, despite its strong economic presence in Asia—which until the 1997 Asian financial crisis rivaled or surpassed that of China—Japan has hesitated to support Taiwan, fearing a troubled relationship with China. With the election of Chen, the criticism is coming from those in charge of the government administration. While the Japanese private sector shows general support for Taiwan's democratic achievement, some Taiwan officials criticize the Japanese government for continuing to act with excessive caution. Yet Taiwan's pragmatic diplomacy cannot push too hard on Japan, given the general weakness of the Japanese government, the nearly-decade-long stagnation of the Japanese economy, and the danger that too much pressure might reduce Japan's willingness to provide logistics support to the United States in the event of a Taiwan conflict.

The United States, Japan, and Taiwan Theater Missile Defense

The United States and Japan have a profound, perhaps even predominant influence over Taiwan's decision-making for theater ballistic missile defense, shaping the pace, trajectory, and ultimate composition of Taiwan's BMD programs. Before discussing the relative influence of these two countries, it is necessary to explore the historical background of Taiwan's interest in BMD.

Taiwan's interest in missile defenses predate the 1995–1996 missile tests. Instead, Taiwan was impressed by the touted performance of the Patriot batteries during

---

[63]"Japan PM to Sidestep Sticky Issues In China," Reuters, 7 July 1999.
[64]Ibid.

the Gulf War. At first, carefully controlled Pentagon reports about the effectiveness of the Patriot strongly suggested that the systems had achieved a high level of success against the Scud-based missiles of Iraq. Over time, however, the analyses of Ted Postel at MIT and the internal assessments of the Israeli military began to chip away at the official story. Eventually, it was revealed that the Patriot batteries had not actually been as successful as advertised, but in fact had achieved a very low rate of success against Baghdad's attacks.[65]

Despite these concerns, however, Taiwan purchased three batteries of the PAC-2 missile system in 1993, with an initial order of 200 missiles at the cost of US$706 million,[66] US$385 million,[67] and US$1.3 billion. The 1995 and 1996 Chinese missile tests, however, dramatically increased the salience of BMD for Taiwan's political and military leadership. Before the crisis, BMD had been dismissed by some because of the unproven and expensive nature of the technologies, as well skepticism about their military effectiveness against a differentiated ballistic missile attack by the Mainland. Instead, emphasis seemed to be placed on the acquisition of advanced conventional weapons systems, such as submarines, to blunt a potential invasion of Taiwan, as well as the strengthening of political ties with the United States, to ensure ready defense of Taiwan in a future conflict with China. After the crisis, however, BMD systems became more attractive in some quarters in Taiwan, as they were increasingly seen as potent political symbols of enhanced U.S.-Taiwan defense cooperation.

The PAC-2 systems first arrived in Taiwan in 1997, and the three units, comprising missiles, wheeled vehicles, and multifunctional radar, were deployed in and around the capital city of Taipei. Two of the sites were designated as operational units and a third site was reserved for training, though it could be made operational in a crisis.[68] For a variety of political and commercial reasons, these missile batteries were called Modified Air Defense Systems (MADS) instead of PAC-2 Plus. The actual capability level of the systems on the ground in Taiwan is somewhat under dispute, with different messages coming from the lead contractor Raytheon and U.S. government representatives overseeing the project. Some reports claim that Taiwan's systems are in fact equal to the best Patriot systems fielded by the U.S. Army, including the PAC-3 Configuration 2 Guidance Enhanced Missile (GEM) and upgraded battle management (BM)/C3I support systems. Other informed sources dispute this claim, asserting that the contractor has overstated the capabilities of the delivered equipment. At an

---

[65]GAO reports.

[66]"Taiwan to Expand Anti-Missile Capabilities," Agence France Presse, 2 February 1999.

[67]"Taiwan Developing Missile Defense Alternative," Associated Press, 7 February 1999.

[68]Interviews, Taiwan, 1998.

annual news conference in August 2000, for example, Defense Minister Wu admitted that the Hankuang #16 exercise exposed the low interception rate of the MADS against the DF-15.[69] Since the delivery of the initial MADS batteries, however, Taiwan has continued to request additional systems. In 1999, the United States agreed to sell three more MADS batteries to Taiwan. Moreover, Taiwan has reportedly requested follow-on systems to protect other cities, including Taichung and Kaohsiung.

After the 1995–1996 crisis, some in Taiwan began to examine some of the other, more advanced theater ballistic missile defense systems under development, such as Navy Area Wide (NAW), Theater High-Altitude Air Defense (THAAD), Navy Theater Wide (NTW), and Airborne Laser (ABL). Unlike with MADS, however, Taiwan interlocutors inquired not only about the possibility of purchasing the systems, but also about participating in their research and development. Taiwan did not publicly express its interest until 1998, when then–Chief of the General Staff Tang Fei clearly suggested that Taiwan would be interested in selectively joining some of the programs currently under way.

At first, the BMD programs were not attractive to Taiwan, primarily because of the extremely high cost of developing the various proposed systems, which were expected to be borne largely by Japan and other participants, possibly Taiwan. Faced with prospect of spending billions of procurement dollars on unproven systems of dubious utility, the Taiwan government initially balked at entering the program, choosing instead to mirror the slow, gradualist, "wait-and-see" approach adopted by Japan. The Ministry of National Defense reportedly wanted to conduct a comprehensive review and careful evaluation of the cost and effectiveness of BMD. Moreover, the top leadership knew there were political costs to discussing interest in BMD without the protection of the systems themselves, including pressure from both the Mainland and the U.S. government. Under pressure from Washington, President Lee Teng-hui reportedly instructed government leaders in 1998 to restrict themselves to brief policy statements about BMD, designating the Ministry of National Defense as the only institution allowed to address the issue in any detail.[70]

More recently, however, the Taiwan government's noncommittal attitude appears to have been replaced with a greater desire to pursue a variety of BMD options, ranging from indigenous systems to purchase of foreign systems. This

---

[69]Fang Wen-hung, "DefMin Wu Shih-wen Says Taiwan to Continue to Try to Obtain Early Warning System," Central News Agency, 31 August 2000; Brian Hsu, "Cash Crunch Halts Anti-Missile Plan," Taipei Times, 31 August 2000.

[70]Lu Te-yun, "Li Teng-hui Limits Officials' Comments on TMD Issue," Lianhebao, 29 March 1999, p. 4.

change of heart is directly linked to trends on the Mainland. Even before Chen Shui-bian's victory, senior Taiwan officials pointed to increases in Chinese missile deployments as justification for the deployment of BMD. Former Defense Minister Tang Fei testified before the Legislative Yuan in February 1999 that "how to counter China's missile threat has been given top priority among the military's ongoing arms buildup plans."[71] Around the same time, the Ministry of National Defense issued a statement asserting that "Beijing's past actions showed that countermeasures to missiles were vital."[72] As a result, General Tang and others asserted that Taiwan was interested in any defensive system available on the international market, though they were unwilling to commit any specific system, either foreign or domestic.[73]

Instead of locking the ROC military into any particular future system, Taipei has gradually revealed the outlines of a general development plan for BMD. In the first stage, the island seeks to procure a low-altitude defense and interception system, in conjunction with long-range early warning radar to minimize damage from PRC missiles.[74] At the heart of this strategy is a desire to keep Taiwan's options open by not confusing questions about U.S. arms sales of BMD components with the plan to build a missile defense system, which could be done indigenously. The government maintains that it is inclined to join a U.S.-led BMD effort, and will continue to make a serious study and appraisal of the progress of system programs in the United States. Until the technology is available, however, Taiwan will probably continue to take a wait-and-see attitude with regard to PAC-3, NAW, or NTW.[75] Meanwhile, research institutions like Chungshan have moved forward with basic projects that can be incorporated with the traditional weaponry systems.[76]

Japanese Influence on Taiwan and BMD

Japan enjoys indirect influence over Taiwan's decision-making about theater ballistic missile defenses. This influence is felt in mainly two areas: political/security affairs and military affairs. In the political/security arena,

---

[71]"Taiwan to Expand Anti-Missile Capabilities," *Agence France Presse,* 2 February 1999.

[72]Mure Dickie and Stephen Fidler, "Taiwan Voices Fears Over Arms Buildup," *Financial Times,* 11 February 1999.

[73]Taiwan to Expand Anti-Missile Capabilities," *Agence France Presse,* 2 February 1999.

[74]Yang Hsiu-feng, "Defense Minister Tang Fei on Missile Pre-Warning System," *Zhongyang ribao,* 3 March 1999, p. 3.

[75]Lu Te-yun, "Li Teng-hui Limits Officials' Comments on TMD Issue," *Lianhebao,* 29 March 1999, p. 4.

[76]Luo Hsiao-he, "Defense Minister Tang on Starting 'Basic' TMD Projects," *Lianhebao,* 10 March 1999, p. 2.

Japan has an active defense treaty and security alliance with the United States. In terms of status, therefore, Japan occupies a position in a ring much closer to the United States than Taiwan, though both countries could be said to be actively engaged in various forms of alliance building and alliance maintenance with Washington. As a result, Taiwan closely analyzes Tokyo's policies towards Washington. This is especially true in the context of theater ballistic missile defenses, where Japan is assumed to be have right of refusal on BMD whereas Taiwan is still an aspirant. Although the Department of Defense is correct to deny the existence of an "Asian BMD network," Taiwan nonetheless views inclusion in BMD cooperation with the United States as "joining" an effort in parallel with the Japanese. Thus, Taiwan carefully observes Japanese moves in the BMD area for signals about American commitment to regional deployment, regional assessments of the Chinese missile threat, and regional calculations of PRC reactions to potentially destabilizing modernization programs. Evidence of increased American commitment to deployment in Japan, explicit identification of the Chinese missile threat by Japanese analysts, and willingness on the part of Japan to pursue BMD programs despite the expected PRC objections all would tend to encourage Taiwan's enthusiasm for BMD cooperation with the United States, whereas trends in the opposite direction might serve as disincentives for participation.

On the military side of the equation, particularly questions of BMD procurement and operations, Japan also offers some guidance and lessons for Taiwan, though players in Taipei appear to understand that U.S.-Japan BMD cooperation is not a realistic road map for Taiwan's theater ballistic missile defense efforts. At the level of military strategy, for instance, it is notable that both Japan and Taiwan share a similar mission (island defense) and similar constraints (procurement within a defensive orientation), while facing a similar threat (stand-off weapons—principally ground-to-ground ballistic missiles—with little credible fear of triphibious assault). Additional links are possible at the operational level. Since Tokyo is already actively engaged in the beginning of joint research and development of some BMD systems, Taiwan might view Japan as a testbed for systems that the ROC military might want to acquire.[77] Japan already possesses some of the requisite conventional platforms for BMD, particularly in the naval realm. For example, Japan's Kongo-class destroyers with the AEGIS combat system are readily upgradable for either the proposed NAW or NTW systems. It should come as no surprise, therefore, to hear persistent rumors in Taipei about a group of retired Japanese admirals visiting then-President Lee Teng-hui and

---

[77]Unfortunately, the timelines for these systems mean that decisions often need to be made years in advance with little foreknowledge of eventual technological successes or failures.

extolling the virtues of the AEGIS system, and subsequent official Taiwan interest in acquiring Arleigh Burke–class destroyers armed with AEGIS.[78] Finally, the Japanese experience presents Taiwan with a foreshadowing of some of the difficult military, bureaucratic, and operational challenges that BMD will present, such as the need for enhanced C3I and joint operations reform.[79]

U.S. Influence on Taiwan and BMD

Of the external influences on Taiwan's decision-making about theater ballistic missile defenses, the United States is clearly dominant. This suasion is exercised informally through advice and support from pro-Taiwan elements inside and outside of the U.S. government, including former officials, think tankers, industry representatives, and congressional members and staffers. Since the informal channels of influence are largely opaque by design, this analysis will focus on formal channels of influence, including unofficial government-to-government contacts through the AIT, the BMD-related arms sales process, the military-to-military exchange process, and formal congressional legislation. It is important to note that Taiwan does not receive a consistent set of messages from this wide-ranging set of interlocutors, which includes opponents, advocates, and agnostics on the issue of missile defenses. Moreover, Taiwan authorities, both military and civilian, occasionally express resentment of American influence, due to what they perceive as arrogance, smugness, inattention to Taiwan's needs, and lack of understanding of Taiwan's complexity.

Unofficial Government-to-Government Relations

The designated U.S. organ for unofficial commercial, diplomatic, and military relations between the United States and Taiwan is the AIT. In the area of theater ballistic missile defense, AIT officials do not see their role as actively shaping the Taiwan policy community's attitudes about BMD, given the general reluctance of the State Department and its related institutions to destabilize the cross-Strait situation by forcing Taiwan to make a premature decision about an unproven system.[80] Instead, AIT provides BMD information and source documents to the relevant Taiwan military offices, sometimes even attempting to provide classified information via the ENDP (Exception to National Defense Policy) process.

---

[78]This rumor was ubiquitous in Taipei during field interviews in May 1999.

[79]Some Japanese have already begun to work through these problems. As an illustration, see Masahiro Matsumura, "Redesigning Japan's Command and Control System for Theater Missile Defense," *Defense Analysis,* Vol. 16, No. 2, 2000, pp. 151–164.

[80]This analysis is based on interviews with AIT officials from 1998 to 2001.

According to AIT officials, the purpose of this information dissemination is to point the relevant Taiwan officials in the "right direction," and prevent them from making ill-informed decisions. Of course, this process involves far more than simply the dissemination of technical information, since the information itself is the product of U.S. policy decisions and therefore likely helps shape Taiwan thinking about BMD in ways consonant with U.S. interests and goals.

A second major source of influence over Taiwan's foreign and defense policymaking is the military-to-military exchanges between the two countries. The abrogation of the 1954 Mutual Defense Treaty and the transfer of diplomatic recognition to Beijing effectively ended the close military coordination between the United States and Taiwan. The Taiwan Relations Act mandated that military-to-military exchanges should continue, legislating that "determination of Taiwan's defense needs shall include review by United States military authorities in connection with recommendations to the President and the Congress."[81] Military-to-military contacts continued through the 1980s and early 1990s, but never again reached the same level of closeness, despite repeated complaints that the lack of contact had hurt the ability of Taiwan's military to defend the island. Specifically, advocates for reenergized ties argued that Taiwan's military was becoming extremely insular in the absence of fuller exchanges, and was having difficulty upgrading its strategy, tactics, and training without coordination with the U.S. military.[82] In 1994, President Clinton initiated a policy review that expanded non-hardware programs with Taiwan, including exchanges on defense planning, C4I, air defense, maritime capability, antisubmarine warfare, logistics, joint force integration, and training.[83] According to official DoD sources,

> These non-hardware programs serve multiple purposes. Functional non-hardware initiatives address many of the shortcomings in Taiwan's military readiness that were identified in the February 1999 *DoD Report to Congress on the Security Situation in the Taiwan Strait*. They allow Taiwan to better integrate newly acquired systems into its inventory and ensure that the equipment Taiwan has can be used to full effectiveness. These initiatives provide an avenue to exchange views on Taiwan's requirements for defense modernization, to include professionalization and organizational issues, and training. Exchanges and discussions enhance our ability to assess Taiwan's longer term defense needs and develop well-founded security assistance policies. Such programs also enhance Taiwan's

---

[81]Department of Defense, "Executive Summary of Report to Congress on Implementation of the Taiwan Relations Act," 18 December 2000.

[82]To fill the gap, the Taiwan military reportedly tried using retired U.S. military officers with mixed success. See Philip Finnegan, "Taiwan Seeks Tighter U.S. Military Relations, Increased Pressure From China Drives Taipei Strategy," *Defense News*, 27 March 2000.

[83]Department of Defense, "Executive Summary of Report to Congress on Implementation of the Taiwan Relations Act," 18 December 2000.

capacity for making operationally sound and cost effective acquisition
decisions, and more importantly, to use its equipment more effectively for
self-defense.[84]

In the fall of 1997, Undersecretary of Defense for Policy Walter Slocombe and
Deputy Assistant Secretary of Defense for Asia-Pacific Kurt Campbell insisted
that the United States should continue its arms sales to Taiwan and
simultaneously expand and diversify the military relationship with Taiwan.[85]
The enhanced program, which focused on "helping Taiwan help itself," has
proceeded quietly since 1997. While officers on active duty were not allowed to
visit Taiwan until 1992, there are now reportedly more than 100 visits per year,
almost 10 times the number in 1994.[86] A significant portion of these exchanges
are sub rosa by design, and are therefore easier to manage than the public arms
sales process. Despite the increases, however, it is important to note that
elements in Taipei and Washington (e.g., members of both defense
establishments, pro-Taiwan legislators in the U.S. Congress) desire to expand
military-to-military contacts even further, proposing to raise the bar on the rank
of visiting officers to allow one-star generals to visit the island; to establish a
secure communications link between Pacific Command in Hawaii and the
General Staff Headquarters in Taipei; and to conduct joint interoperability
exercises between American and Taiwan forces.[87]

The ongoing set of contacts between mid-level officers from the Department of
Defense are also likely to be an additional source of information about BMD
systems under development, as well as a source of expert advice about necessary
changes in Taiwan's military system to accommodate elements of a possible
BMD architecture. For example, the various DoD study teams sent to Taiwan to
assess BMD-related areas, particularly the recent air defense, battle
management/C4I, and naval defense groups dispatched by the Joint Staff, likely
do more than simply observe the situation in Taiwan, but probably engage in
interactive discussions with their Taiwan counterparts about the issues under
review. The Taiwan side likely benefits from these discussions and resulting
reports, garnering a better sense about the needed policy reforms in its own
system. For example, the battle management/C4I delegation reportedly
expressed concern about Taiwan's ability to survive a "first strike" of Chinese
missiles, suggesting that the island's forces harden its C4I infrastructure and

---

[84]Ibid.

[85]Nadia Tsao, "US Strikes Balance with Taiwan Arms Sales," *Taipei Times,* 7 November 2000.
[86]Ibid.
[87]Interviews in Taipei and Washington.

enhance the protection of its important military installations.[88] In September 1999, a field study of Taiwan's air defense capabilities concluded that Taiwan was vulnerable to missile attack as well. In October 2000, one U.S. military officer involved in the arms sales process remarked at a Washington meeting that "the most important countermeasure [to Chinese missiles] is a survivable C4I architecture and robust passive defenses."[89] From these exchanges, the Taiwan side also develops a keener understanding of the BMD-related acquisitions required to carry out these reforms, and the relative likelihood of the approval of these acquisitions by Washington.[90] For example, the naval defense assessment ordered after the deferral of the AEGIS request in 1999 reportedly recommended the future sale of AEGIS to Taiwan, concluding that Taiwan had a clear need for the ships and would have no difficulty operating and integrating them into the ROC Navy.[91]

Perhaps the most important channel of influence, therefore, is the arms sales process. Active or residual American influence can be seen at every level of the process on the Taiwan side. First, Taiwan's defense planning and budgeting systems have been loosely based since 1975 on the Planning, Programming, and Budgeting System (PPBS) originally developed by the U.S. Department of Defense under former Defense Secretary McNamara. The inputs into this process are provided by the planning offices of the individual service headquarters, each of which maintain some ties with their American counterparts. These plans are regularly distorted by unexpected changes, particularly the sudden availability of previously unobtainable foreign weapons, which leads to a situation aptly characterized as "procurement directed planning and budgeting."[92] As one of Taiwan's only arms suppliers, for example, U.S. government decisions about the availability of individual weapons systems and components for sale to Taiwan can dramatically alter the latter's defense planning process and the security-related aspects of its foreign policy. Former President Lee Teng-hui, for instance, reportedly viewed U.S. arms sales as symbols of reassurance and resolve, not as key components of a larger force structure designed to attain genuine warfighting objectives, and valued U.S.-supplied systems in particular as critical indicators of greater U.S. support for Taiwan. An example of an unexpectedly

---

[88]Interviews with Taiwan military officers.

[89]Major Mark Stokes at the American Enterprise Institute, October 2000.

[90]These exchanges has also possibly had some potentially negative influences on the Taiwan military, encouraging them to pursue the BMD option preferred by U.S. forces; namely, attack operations against the missile sites themselves. This development, combined with rumors of interest in Taiwan of developing an MRBM capable of striking countervalue or counterforce targets on the Mainland, could be highly destabilizing.

[91]Nadia Tsao, "US Strikes Balance with Taiwan Arms Sales," *Taipei Times*, 7 November 2000.

[92]Huang (1997), p. 290.

pleasant surprise was the approval of the sale of F-16s to Taiwan, even though the Ministry of National Defense was then presented with the difficult logistical challenge of integrating this complex aircraft with the product of an indigenous fourth generation program (IDF) and a completely separate fourth generation import (Mirage 2000-5). By contrast, the ROC Air Force (ROCAF) originally resisted the unexpected offer of air-launched anti-ship Harpoons, which represented a dramatic improvement of Taiwan's ability to interdict Chinese naval assets. The ROCAF responded initially with a parochial argument that exposed the lack of jointness in the Taiwan military at that time, asserting that interdicting ships was a "naval mission" and that the ROCAF really wanted Maverick missiles for ground attack missions. These types of attitudes and the variability of weapons availability make it difficult if not impossible for the Taiwan defense establishment to carry out meaningful long-range planning.

Patterns of U.S. influence are especially visible in the context of theater ballistic missile defense systems. Since the mid-1990s, BMD-related systems have dominated most of the public debate over the Taiwan arms sales issue in the United States and Taiwan, especially long-range, early-warning radars, Patriot batteries, and destroyers equipped with the AEGIS combat system. Other, less publicized systems, particularly those related to the ongoing C3I modernization of the Taiwan military, have also been an important part of the process. The influence of the United States in Taiwan's decision-making about BMD systems comes from primarily two sources: (1) meetings between U.S. Department of Defense or diplomatic officials and ROC representatives or military officers, and (2) unofficial interactions between U.S. politicians and private businessmen and ROC government officials and politicians. The former set of interactions includes both informal ad hoc meetings during the early stages of the procurement process at which ROC officials have sought to inform U.S. officials which existing BMD-related systems (such as additional Patriot batteries) would likely be requested by Taiwan in a given year, and formal annual meetings at which U.S. officials inform ROC officials of their decisions about these sales.

But the latter set of interactions reportedly exerts a greater influence on ROC procurement decisions related to BMD, since the development of BMD is still a subject of ongoing debate within the U.S. government and some bureaucracies are therefore understandably reluctant to make promises about systems that are not yet proven. Members of Congress and defense industrial representatives, by contrast, are not constrained by programmatic considerations, and indeed some likely see the stoking of Taiwan's interest in these systems as providing additional justification for aggressive development of BMD by the Pentagon. The reasoning behind these strategies varies, depending on the source. Many U.S.

members of Congress have a very strong interest in Taiwan security affairs, responding to national security, ideological (i.e., support of democracy, opposition to the PRC), and parochial (narrower political and economic interests of their constituencies) reasons. Some members of Congress feel especially passionate about the provision of theater ballistic missile defenses to Taiwan, given the vulnerabilities of the island that were exposed during the 1995–1996 missile crisis. In addition, many U.S. defense industries, including those involved in BMD-related systems, have an obvious financial interest in expanding their levels of business with Taiwan through increased military sales to the island. Congress and defense industries also maintain a somewhat symbiotic relationship. For example, defense-industrial production of high-profile BMD-related weapons systems, including AEGIS-equipped destroyers and Patriot missile batteries, is spread among many states so as to broaden the basis of political support for greater arms sales, both foreign and domestic. Thus, U.S. political representatives and businesses often take an active interest in the type and origin of various weapons systems available to Taiwan and will at times express their preferences regarding such systems to ROC officials. In general, this type of informal and indirect U.S. involvement has frequently influenced the procurement process, according to knowledgeable individuals, including the planning and budgeting related to BMD.[93]

Congressional Intervention

While Congress has been a periodic participant in U.S.-Taiwan relations, it has been a key driver of the arms sales process from the beginning, primarily through such legislation as the Taiwan Relations Act and the aborted Taiwan Security Enhancement Act. An analytic chronology of Capitol Hill's measures reveals an increasingly activist agenda, emboldened by perceived splits in the Executive Branch between those wishing to delay or deny arms to Taiwan, and those seeking to accelerate Taiwan's acquisition of arms and expand the U.S.-Taiwan military relationship. In recent years, theater ballistic missile defenses have become a central focus for Congress, despite the paucity of available systems for sale to Taiwan.

In November 1997, the U.S. House of Representatives passed the "United States-Taiwan Anti-Ballistic Missile Defense Cooperation Act" (H.R. 2386). The act declares that it is in the national interest of the United States that Taiwan be included in any effort at ballistic missile defense cooperation, networking, or

---

[93]Interviews with DoD officials and industry representatives.

interoperability with friendly and allied nations in the Asia-Pacific region. The act's findings state that

> The People's Republic of China is currently engaged in a comprehensive military modernization campaign that is enhancing the power-projection capabilities of the People's Liberation Army, including the introduction of advanced ballistic and cruise missiles that could alter the current balance of power in the Taiwan Strait and in the greater Asia-Pacific region;

> the early development and deployment of an effective United States theater ballistic missile defense system to the Asia-Pacific region, and the adjustment of United States policy to include Taiwan, including the Penghu Islands, Kinmen, and Matsu, under the protection of such defense system; and

> the early deployment of a United States theater anti-ballistic missile system in the Asia-Pacific region would maintain a balance of power in the Taiwan Strait and deter the People's Republic of China from resorting to military intimidation tactics to coerce or manipulate the people and freely-elected Government of Taiwan in the future.

Based on these findings, the proposed act required the Secretary of Defense to carry out a study by July 1, 1998, of the architecture requirements for the establishment and operation of a theater ballistic missile defense system in the Asia-Pacific region that would have the capability to protect Taiwan from ballistic missile attacks. Finally, the act contained a non-binding "sense of Congress" that the President, if requested by the Government of Taiwan and in accordance with the results of the DoD study, should transfer to the government of Taiwan appropriate defense articles or defense services for the purpose of establishing and operating a local-area ballistic missile defense system to protect Taiwan, including the Penghu Islands, Kinmen, and Matsu, against limited ballistic missile attacks. The bill was never acted upon in the Senate.[94]

During March 1999, the Senate passed the "Taiwan Security Enhancement Act" (S.693), jointly sponsored by Senate Foreign Relations Chairman Jesse Helms, (R-North Carolina) and Sen. Robert G. Torricelli (D-New Jersey). In May, Benjamin Gilman, Chairman of the International Relations Committee of the U.S. House of Representatives, and Thomas Delay, Majority Whip of the House, jointly initiated a similar bill (H.R. 1838) in the House. The bill sought to increase military cooperation with Taiwan, including introduction of additional missile defense systems. In particular, it authorized the sale of a broad array of BMD-related defense articles, including missile defense systems, satellite early warning data, and appropriate platforms for naval-based missile defense, such as

---

[94] Based on entries in THOMAS, the Library of Congress's online database for legislative information (http://thomas.loc.gov).

destroyers equipped with the AEGIS combat system. The bill passed in the House on 1 February 2000 by a vote of 341-70, but was not voted upon in the Senate. A revised version later passed that did not include weapons.

Congress has also indirectly strengthened the justification for BMD in Taiwan by mandating a number of Pentagon reports on cross-Strait issues, including assessments of Chinese military modernization, the security situation in the Taiwan Strait, and the implementation of the Taiwan Relations Act. The published, unclassified versions of these studies have had an important impact on Taiwan's foreign and defense policymaking, and in some cases have refocused the public line of the Ministries of Foreign Affairs and National Defense in Taipei. In February 1999, for instance, the Pentagon released a congressionally mandated report entitled "The Security Situation in the Taiwan Strait." The report stated that the PLA could attack Taiwan by air, by a blockade, or by full-scale military operation, and identified shortcomings in Taiwan's military readiness that the military-to-military programs were attempting to address. The study also asserted that "exclusive reliance on active missile defenses and associated BMD C4I will not sufficiently offset the overwhelming advantage in offensive missiles that Beijing is projected to possess by 2005." A leaked press account of the classified version of the report claimed that China would be able to field 650 missiles by 2005, a figure that immediately became the focus of the Taiwan government's public description of the China missile threat.[95]

In terms of theater ballistic missile defenses, the Department of Defense in May 1999 provided a "Report to Congress on Theater Missile Defense Architecture Options for the Asia-Pacific Region." The report responded to Congress' FY1999 National Defense Authorization Act, which directed the Secretary of Defense to "carry out a study of the architecture requirements for the establishment and operation of theater ballistic missile defense (BMD) systems for Japan, the Republic of Korea (ROK)[96] and Taiwan that would provide for their defense against limited theater ballistic missile attacks."[97] The report was carefully caveated, explicitly excluding discussions of the criteria (U.S. foreign policy interests, economic, domestic) for arms transfers to Taiwan and other countries in the region. It also avoided recommendations to any of the countries under review. Nonetheless, the technical analyses of "hypothetical options" were not

---

[95]Mure Dickie and Stephen Fidler, "Taiwan Voices Fears Over Arms Buildup," *Financial Times*, 11 February 1999.

[96]Since South Korea has not expressed an interest in BMD, the study focused primarily on Japan and Taiwan.

[97] "Report to Congress on Theater Missile Defense Architecture Options for the Asia-Pacific Region," May 1999, p. 1.

viewed as neutral number-crunching by Taiwan, which closely examined the DoD evaluation for operational guidance as well as possible clues about U.S. willingness to sell particular BMD-related systems. In particular, Taiwan analysts noted the assessment in the report that early warning surveillance assets for cueing purposes were "essential" for an effective missile defense, as well as the assertion that China's growing medium-range ballistic missile force would "preclude a high probability of intercept by lower-tier systems."[98] Though the report presented all of Taiwan's BMD options without bias in favor of one or the other, the prior analysis of the threat clearly implied that a system based solely on land-based, lower-tier systems would not be sufficient to meet the threat. It is not surprising, therefore, that Taiwan acquisition concerns since the issuance of the report have focused on AEGIS-equipped destroyers, which could theoretically be the base platform for a UT Navy Theater Wide System.

In February 2001, Congress began to prepare the political battlefield for the April 2001 arms talks between Washington and Taipei. A bipartisan letter, endorsed by members of both the House of Representatives and the Senate, urged President Bush to sell AEGIS-equipped destroyers, P-3 antisubmarine aircraft, and diesel-powered submarines to Taiwan.[99] The letter was drafted in January 2001 by Senator Jesse Helms, Chairman of the Senate Foreign Relations Committee, and Senator Robert Torricelli, both of whom are long-time supporters of Taiwan. The letter was co-signed by Senate Majority Leader Trent Lott and Senators Jon Kyl and Frank Murkowski. In the House, Representatives Chris Cox and David Wu were reportedly preparing a similarly worded document.

Postscript: The April 2001 Arms Decision

When the arms sales decision was finally announced in April, Taiwan received the most "robust" package of arms in years, although the Burke-class AEGIS ships were deferred for another year. Taiwan was approved to purchase four Kidd-class destroyers (previously built for the Shah of Iran and known as the "Ayatollah-class"), diesel submarines, P-3s, and artillery. Most of the debate over the decision centered on the decision to sell Kidds in lieu of AEGIS and the break with the past in the area of submarines. Clearly, there are groups in Taiwan who were disappointed with the decision to sell Kidds, which some viewed as another American "cast-off." Yet the Kidds, which were suggested by the U.S. side in the December 2000 round of the pre-talks, are highly capable ships, armed with some of the most advanced sensors and weapons systems in the U.S. Navy.

---

[98]Ibid.

[99]Nadia Tsao, "Arms Sales Find Support in US Capitol," *Taipei Times*, 18 February 2001.

Their addition could dramatically improve the Taiwan Navy's fleet air defense and antisubmarine capabilities. Second, the Kidds were an attractive choice because they would be available in 2003, while the earliest date for the Burkes would be 2007–2009. Some in the United States did not see the logic of paying the strategic costs with China of a Burke decision, while not providing Taiwan any real defensive benefit for more than a decade. Instead, it appears that the U.S. Navy will add four Burke-class ships to its order book, preventing any production delays should the United States in the future decide to sell the Burkes to Taiwan. Finally, it is important to note that most participants on the U.S. side do not view Kidds versus AEGIS as an either-or proposition, but instead see the ships as potentially complementary, with the Kidds replacing the ancient Gearing-class destroyers and the Burkes replacing the Knox-class ships in the future.

Submarines had long been rejected by the U.S. government as an inherently "offensive" system, and therefore excluded under the terms of the Taiwan Relations Act. Specifically, there were some who feared that the Taiwan side would not use the subs to run counter-blockade operations as they claimed, but would in fact be unable to resist the temptation to interdict Chinese naval forces in their bases on the Mainland. Yet the buildup of Chinese submarines, Sovremenny-class destroyers, and long-range cruise missiles like the SS-N-22 Sunburn was beginning to convince some participants in the debate that the advantage in the naval balance of forces was shifting to the Chinese side, requiring a rethinking on the issue of submarines. The April 2001 decision to approve the sale of eight diesel submarines to Taiwan was the final manifestation of this evolution in thinking. At the same time, it is difficult to ignore the possibility that part of the rationale for the submarine sale was to compensate for the deferment on the Burke-class destroyers. Yet at the time of this writing, it is not clear that Taiwan will ever receive any submarines. For a variety of political, bureaucratic and industrial reasons, the United States cannot autonomously build nonnuclear submarines. Instead, the U.S. side needs to implement one of the multiple existing license contracts with foreign submarine producers, but the representatives of the governments of the main candidates (Germany, Netherlands, Australia) have all publicly declared their unwillingness to sell submarines to Taiwan. Moreover, it is unlikely that a Taiwan shipyard could or would be allowed to produce the subs in Taiwan. This episode highlights the political difficulties inherent in the arms sales process with Taiwan, as well as the constraint imposed on Taiwan in having to rely on a limited number of arms suppliers.

Conclusions

This chapter has argued that the United States and Japan currently wield substantial influence over Taiwan's foreign and defense policymaking. This influence is partly a function of history, but it also reflects the realities of Taiwan's geographic, economic, political, and military circumstances. For Taipei, the United States has always been its most critical backer, providing political, military, economic and ideological guidance and material assistance of various forms for more than 100 years. Japan, by contrast, was a military opponent of the KMT on the Mainland and a colonial occupier of the island for fifty years. Like most post-colonial entities, however, Taiwan still enjoys deep ties to Japan, mainly cultural but also deeply economic and political.

The United States employs a mixture of encouragement and restraint in its interactions with the Taiwan defense policymaking apparatus. On the one hand, the Taiwan Relations Act encourages elements of the U.S. government to take an active interest in Taiwan's defense plans, requirements, and programs. The actual level of assistance and coordination, however, has varied widely over time. In recent years, the expansion of the military-to-military relationship with Taiwan suggests that the increased threat from China has indeed brought Taipei and Washington closer together, though there is still significant reluctance to re-initiate a full-blown, quasi-alliance relationship with joint interoperability and planning. Nonetheless, interviews in Taiwan suggest that the enhanced level of exchange between the two militaries may be encouraging some of the DPP policy initiatives, particularly with regard to offensive operations against the Mainland. One illustrative example is theater ballistic missile defense, where Taiwan interlocutors point out that the U.S. Air Force's preferred method of BMD is "attack operations," not active defenses like PAC-2 or passive defenses like hardening of facilities. On the other hand, U.S. policy tends to discourage the Chen government from pursuing some policies. For example, it is likely that the U.S. government would oppose the deployment of an MRBM or similar offensive-oriented weapon, for fear that such weapons would have little strategic utility and would in fact further exacerbate tensions with the Mainland.

Japan and especially the United States exercise considerable influence over Taiwan decision-making about BMD acquisition and deployment. Since Japan is a close ally of the United States and is widely believed to have the right of first refusal on BMD, Taiwan carefully observes Japanese moves in the BMD area for signals about American commitment to regional deployment, regional assessments of the Chinese missile threat, and regional calculations of PRC reactions to potentially destabilizing modernization programs. Taiwan might also view Japan as a testbed for BMD and BMD-related systems that the ROC military might want to acquire, including conventional platforms and C3I systems.

The United States is clearly the dominant influence on Taiwan's decision-making about theater ballistic missile defenses. This suasion is exercised informally through advice and support from pro-Taiwan elements inside and outside of the U.S. government, including former officials, think tankers, industry representatives, and congressional members and staffers. Despite the constraints of de-recognition, there are also formal channels of influence, including unofficial government-to-government contacts through the AIT, the BMD-related arms sales process, the military-to-military exchange process, and formal congressional legislation. These official and quasi-official government channels provide BMD information and source documents to the Taiwan government and are a source of expert advice about necessary changes in Taiwan's military system to accommodate elements of a possible BMD architecture. Non-Executive Branch channels, including Congress, outside experts, and the defense industrial base, lobby both sides on behalf of political, ideological, and financial interests.

6. The Future of Taiwan's Foreign and Defense Policies and Its Implications for the United States

Taiwan's foreign and defense policies have undergone enormous changes over the past two decades. The transition from authoritarianism to democracy, increasing social prosperity, the emergence of a distinctive Taiwan identity, the resulting exacerbation of military and political tensions with Beijing, and associated changes in U.S. and Japanese policies toward both sides of the Taiwan Strait have all contributed significantly to this ongoing process of policy evolution. It is likely that Taiwan's foreign and defense policies will continue to evolve in significant ways, given the dynamic nature of these factors.

At the same time, the five core national security objectives of the Taiwan government presented at the beginning of this study will likely remain relevant far into the future. Moreover, the emergence of a pragmatic mainstream set of values and perspectives among both the Taiwan's public and most political elites also suggest that one should not assume that sudden or radical policy departures will become the norm. However, continuing dramatic domestic political shifts, Beijing's intense (and arguably growing) dissatisfaction with Taiwan's existing foreign, defense, and cross-Strait policies, intensifying domestic and cross-Strait economic pressures and incentives, and an increasing emphasis by the United States and China on the military dimensions of the Taiwan issue also suggest that further significant changes in foreign and defense policies cannot be ruled out.

Thus far, few major foreign and defense policy initiatives have emerged from the Chen Shui-bian government, in large part because of the general pattern of political paralysis engendered by the ongoing, sharp rift between the government and the opposition, the relative inexperience of the Chen leadership, the distractions created by Taiwan's persistent economic woes, and the above-outlined problems in Taiwan's constitutional structure. In addition, the Chen government does not currently possess the flexibility or political will to make far-reaching concessions on cross-Strait relations, while internal and foreign constraints prevent Beijing from undertaking any serious initiatives to ameliorate relations with Taiwan. The result is a standoff, with both sides appealing to outside constituencies to facilitate a deal. Given the reluctance of Washington to directly mediate talks between the two sides, there is little prospect for improvement in ties.

This policy paralysis and stalemate will likely continue through 2001, thereby impeding consensus and eliciting great caution on every major issue. However, some elements of Taiwan's foreign and defense policies could change significantly as a result of further basic shifts in the balance of power among political parties and internal party factions. Over the near term, the current deadlock might be broken if Chen Shui-bian and Lee Teng-hui are able to form a strong, workable majority coalition following the December 2001 legislative and county-level executive elections. Such a coalition might have the power and influence to undertake greater initiatives in foreign affairs, perhaps along the lines of those features associated with the DPP position outlined above. Conversely, a weak Chen-Lee coalition, or the emergence of a counter-coalition among the opposition (e.g., in the form of a KMT-PFP alliance) could result in a protracted period of governmental—and hence policy—deadlock.

Over the long term, future policy shifts are more likely—at least in the areas of cross-Strait relations and foreign relations—because of the basic divide that continues to exist on issues of national identity and state legitimacy between the KMT and PFP on the one side, and the DPP (and perhaps the TSU) on the other. This is the case despite common movement by the major parties toward a more moderate political center. The emergence of a KMT- or PFP-led government could produce new policy initiatives designed to reduce tensions with the Mainland and at the same time to expand Taiwan's international influence and presence. Eventually, the potential for policy volatility will probably diminish greatly, however, if one party or coalition achieves a position of sustained dominance over the system or if all major political actors more fully observe the norms of the democratic process and more readily compromise to govern effectively. Under such circumstances, it is likely that the moderate, cautious elements within all major parties will increase in strength.

In addition to domestic politics, a second constraint on the conduct of Taiwan's foreign policy is foreign influence and pressure, particularly from China. Although Beijing has thus far adopted a "wait-and-see" stance toward the policies and actions of the Chen regime, many outside observers believe that the Chinese leadership has adopted an increasingly fatalistic attitude about the prospects for an eventual peaceful resolution of the Taiwan issue. As a result, China is placing significant political pressure on the Chen Shui-bian government through the united front strategy described above. In the defense arena, China's increasing emphasis on strengthening the credibility of its military options against Taiwan is of growing concern to Taipei, especially the ongoing and destabilizing deployment of additional SRBMs in the Nanjing Military Region.

This element of Beijing's policy, and the resulting threat it poses to Taiwan and Asian stability, are being used by the ROC government to obtain greater levels of weaponry and related military assistance from the United States, and to develop closer military and political relations between Taipei and Washington. The latter includes efforts ranging from substantial exchange of military intelligence to the establishment of direct and secure communications as preparation for actual operational links with both U.S. and Japanese forces. The possible acquisition from the United States of ballistic missile defense systems and their related support infrastructure or platforms in particular provide an increasingly important means for Taiwan to advance its objectives. However, the future course of action is by no means clear. As indicated above, internal debates have developed within Taiwan defense policy circles over the dangers, costs, and opportunities presented by the Chen government's policy proposals, including the adoption of offensive strike capabilities and/or by the construction of sophisticated active defense measures such as various types of theater ballistic missile defense systems. This debate will likely shape those basic contours of Taiwan's future defense policy of greatest interest to the United States.

In the area of ballistic missile defense, the key priorities of Taiwan's response to the Chinese missile threat are "early warning, immediate response, multiple-layer interception, and decisive destruction."[1] To achieve these goals, Taiwan's BMD-related procurement and modernization are currently governed by the following set of principles: "lower levels to higher ones, expansion from points to areas, west coast before the east, equal emphasis on land and sea."[2] In concrete terms, this policy is likely to have five major features. First, Taiwan will seek to acquire Lower Tier interceptors, as well as both LT- and UT-capable early warning systems and C3I infrastructure. The primary focus will be on land-based systems, unless the United States approves the sale of AEGIS systems. To this end, Taiwan will likely acquire key elements for joint early warning radars, sensors, and C3I components. The stated goal is 70 percent coverage of Taiwan, excluding largely uninhabited areas. Second, Taiwan will avoid open advocacy of U.S.-ROC integration, but will favor closer ties, particularly in the military-to-military realm. Third, Taipei will likely delay decisions on acquiring Upper Tier systems, avoiding public statements on the issue. Fourth, the ROC will likely avoid R&D cooperation with the United States on an Upper Tier BMD system. If

---

[1] 2000 Defense White Paper.
[2] 2000 Defense White Paper.

the United States presses, Taiwan will likely demur and promise to "study" the problem. Finally, internal pressure will lead Taiwan to continue to hedge its bets and proceed with the development of an offensive tactical missile.

Overall, we expect token, slow acquisition of UT at best, probably following the U.S. lead. Taiwan is likely to avoid any decision on UT until the United States deploys, assuming that the United States deploys by 2007 as planned. The deployment of the systems is unlikely to alter the strategic balance in Northeast Asia because it will be too slow and too incomplete. But BMD deployment could alter the political balance, especially Chinese perceptions of the regional security environment in Asia.

Implications for Asian Stability and U.S. Policy

Taiwan's evolving foreign and defense policies have a profound impact on U.S. relations with both Taiwan and China, whose current political and military impasse across the Taiwan Strait poses one of the single greatest challenges to U.S. security policy in the region. Some specific issues with important implications for U.S. policymakers include (1) Taiwan's perception of the nature and extent of U.S. support, particularly in Congress, for "pragmatic diplomacy"; (2) the perceived role of U.S. military intervention in Taiwan's foreign and defense planning, and the extent to which previous U.S. actions, such as the carrier deployments in March 1996, have emboldened Taipei to pursue more aggressive policies; (3) the perceived security impact of BMD deployments on Taiwan and attitudes about future deployments; and (4) the strategic implications of a Taiwan ballistic missile program.

Taiwan's Perception of U.S. Support for Pragmatic Diplomacy

The first important implication of this study on Taiwan's foreign and defense policymaking concerns Taiwan's perception of the nature and extent of U.S. support for "pragmatic diplomacy." American public opinion and political elites are strongly divided over the issue of Taiwan. This can be seen most clearly in the interaction between the U.S. Congress and the Executive Branch. In the years since de-recognition, Taiwan has proven adept at generating political support in Congress, beginning with the Taiwan Relations Act in 1979 and culminating in the June 1995 visit of Lee Teng-hui to Cornell. During the latter crisis, the debate over the issuance of a visa to President Lee exposed the lack of Executive Branch consensus on the Taiwan issue, leaving the final decision in the hands of the generally Taiwan-friendly Congress. Although the Clinton administration eventually recovered the policy initiative during the 1995–1996 crisis, in part by sending two carriers to the area near Taiwan in March 1996, our research confirmed that Taiwan's policymakers continue to believe that there are notable differences on Taiwan policy between Congress and the Executive Branch. The Bush administration should therefore instead seek to forge a united front with Congress on cross-Strait policy, reducing the incentives of those who would seek to exploit cleavages in the system.

U.S. Military Intervention

The second important implication of this study on Taiwan's foreign and defense policy concerns the perceived role of U.S. military intervention. Although U.S. government officials generally regard the deployment of two carrier battle groups to the Taiwan area in March 1996 as a success because it showed U.S. determination to enforce a peaceful resolution of the Taiwan problem, some U.S. officials privately fear that the deployments may embolden Taiwan to pursue more aggressive policies. Specifically, they are concerned that the Taiwan authorities perceive that they have been given a "blank check" guaranteeing U.S. military intervention in a conflict between China and Taiwan. The impression that Taiwan has been provided with the equivalent of a U.S. security guarantee was further strengthened when newly elected President George W. Bush stated in spring 2001 that the U.S. government would "do whatever it took" to defend Taiwan in the event of a Chinese attack.[3] These developments undermine the United States' stated policy of "strategic ambiguity" regarding possible U.S. military actions in the event of a cross-Strait conflict. This policy was designed to deter provocative behavior by either side and to allow the United States to retain some decision-making autonomy in a crisis.

Ballistic Missile Defense

The third important implication of this study on Taiwan's foreign and defense policymaking concerns the proposed U.S.-authorized deployments of BMD systems to Taiwan. Early on, the Taiwan government and military did not want the enhanced Patriot anti-aircraft batteries now stationed in Taiwan, because they were expensive and post–Gulf War analyses had cast doubt on their effectiveness against ballistic missiles. Although these systems are now deployed, they are not supported by the sensor and cueing systems necessary to give them a limited

---

[3]See http://www11.cnn.com/2001/ALLPOLITICS/04/25/bush.taiwan.04/ for a report on Bush's remarks. Although Bush and other administration officials subsequently insisted that the remarks did not amount to a change in U.S. policy toward Taiwan, many observers nonetheless received the impression that the United States had strengthened its defense commitment to Taiwan.

BMD capability. As a result, there are forces in both Taiwan and the United States pressing for Taiwan participation in the development of BMD systems planned for Japan and Korea, such as THAAD and Navy Upper Tier.

In the abstract, there are roughly three options for acquisition of a BMD capability in Taiwan, although any possible mixture of the options can also be envisioned. The first involves the sale or transfer of BMD systems to Taiwan itself. These systems could be either land-based systems (THAAD) or sea-based systems (NTW or Navy Area Wide). The land-based system would require the construction of radar installations and missile batteries around Taiwan's major cities and military facilities. A Pentagon study on theoretical BMD architectures concluded that Taiwan would need at least 12 Lower Tier land-based batteries for full coverage of the island, although this could be a mixture of Patriot systems and indigenous TK-2 Sky Bow batteries.[4] The sea-based system would require the transfer of AEGIS combat systems to Taiwan, integrated on Taiwan ships. Together, these systems (either alone or in combination) would complement the existing Patriot batteries (PAC-2+ now, perhaps PAC-3 in the future) to provide Taiwan with a layered defense.[5] There are two main obstacles to this option: (1) The United States must agree to sell the systems, despite Beijing's objections. Taiwan, along with its allies in the United States, strongly opposes a U.S. "deal" with the PRC over BMD and missile deployments. (2) Such a system would require unprecedented levels of systems integration among services, as well as extensive C3I modernization. With these two obstacles removed, the only major constraint on capability would be the effectiveness of the systems themselves.

The second option for BMD in Taiwan does not involve the transfer of equipment or systems. Instead, the U.S. Navy could deploy a NTW system on its own ships, which can then be sent to the waters surrounding Taiwan during a crisis. This option has one major drawback and one major advantage over Taiwan-based systems. The drawback is that the ships would require a set period of time to reach the theater, during which Taiwan would be completely vulnerable to Chinese missile attack. The advantage of a U.S.-based system is that Washington would retain an element of control over both Taiwan's behavior and the level of escalation of the crisis.

---

[4]DoD TMD Architecture Study.

[5]Theoretically, such a system would work as follows. Taiwan radar systems or U.S. satellites would detect the launch plume of a Chinese missile. As the missile entered its exoatmospheric stage, the "upper tier" components of the TMD system (THAAD, NTW, or both) would engage, attempting to destroy the missile with a "hit-to-kill" missile. If they missed, the last shot at the missile would come from the "lower tier" elements of the TMD system, such as Patriot, Navy Area Wide, or any indigenous Taiwan system.

A third, perhaps mid-term, option for BMD on Taiwan is that the United States would transfer only the BMD early warning apparatus to Taiwan, while upgrading Taiwan's C4I infrastructure through military-to-military exchanges. This might arise out of a bargain in which the United States promises China that it will not sell Taiwan either land- or sea-based BMD systems. To ameliorate Taiwan's security concerns, the United States might transfer AEGIS combat systems to improve Taiwan's naval warfighting and air defense capability but not transfer the BMD missiles and other pieces of the architecture. In the case of a crisis, Taiwan's early warning capability might be useful to U.S. forces deploying to the region, serving as a forward radar picket for U.S. BMD ships. At the same time, such an arrangement would be difficult to defend, as China could persuasively argue that the United States is recreating the U.S.-Taiwan defense alliance in all but name.

At least one interlocutor in Taiwan identified how this third option might prove to be a logical strategy, albeit counterintuitive, for Taiwan's leaders. In this scenario, the actions of the PRC are critical. Taiwan will continue to do studies of the threat and use these studies to keep DoD and the U.S. military close, but not too close. These interactions must remain lively so that the United States does not lose interest. For as long as possible, Taiwan will demur on the issue of actual procurement of missile defense batteries, but work very hard to advance its C4ISR, long-range radars, sensors, and tracking capability. The overall goal is an alliance with the United States, not BMD. Thus, Taiwan would seek a BMD system under U.S. control, with the United States directly controlling certain information sensors in Taiwan. Those data links would bring the alliance closer together, with Taiwan serving as a "quiet partner." Underpinning this strategy is a belief that the United States will not move quickly to defend a Taiwan that has acquired its own limited missile defense infrastructure, but will move rapidly to defend the island if it has simply engaged in low-profile, unprovocative early warning and C3I modernization.

A fourth, relative unlikely, option for BMD on Taiwan is indigenous development of a missile defense capability. The Chungshan Institute is reportedly working on a missile defense variant of the Tien-Kung (TK)-2 or Sky Bow air defense missile system, with mixed success. According to Taiwan interlocutors, the Sky Bow system will take eight years to equal PAC-3 level capability. Given limitations on indigenous development and the clear preference for politically symbolic acquisitions from the United States, however, this option seems the most remote of all, and would only be considered in extreme circumstances.

In light of the evidence presented above, we offer five policy recommendations for missile defenses and Taiwan. First, the United States should not press Taiwan to participate in joint development of the systems. The technical and financial benefits would be minimal, while the potential damage to Sino-U.S. relations would be high. Moreover, Taiwan itself does not seek this type of development, and it should not be forced upon Taiwan for fiscal reasons. Second, Taiwan should be discouraged from making any Upper Tier–related announcements. There is no useful purpose served by such an action. Third, the United States should make a clear distinction between UT interceptors and support systems. Regarding the latter, a high priority should be a careful evaluation of the implications of a UT system for ROC-U.S. C3I integration. Fourth, the best option seems to be Lower Tier with long-range radar, plus the indigenous Sky Bow system. This configuration requires much better C3I integration than Taiwan currently possesses. Finally, any EACS/AEGIS sale should explicitly preclude future Upper Tier capability.

Taiwan's Reported Ballistic and Cruise Missile Programs

As discussed above, interviews in Taiwan suggest that there is an active program of research on a tactical ballistic missile with a maximum 1,000-km range, plus a possible land-attack variant of the Hsiung-Feng II cruise missile. The alleged purpose of these missiles is to degrade the PLA's strike capability, including missile infrastructure and non-missile infrastructure (airfields, harbors, missile sites, etc.), with the hope of counterstriking against China to either deter it from further action or improve Taiwan's position in a post-exchange negotiation. Taiwan advocates argue that the MRBM program is not designed to be strategic in character (i.e., is a limited threat to coastal cities), is not viewed as a substitute for BMD, and is viewed as less provocative to PRC if developed indigenously without U.S. assistance.

Nonetheless, there are nagging concerns in Taiwan over feasibility, effectiveness, and the U.S. stance toward such a step. Specifically, the stated strategic and operation dilemmas include the difficulty of testing missiles without alerting U.S. intelligence, the inability of such systems to deal with a large number of PRC targets, the relative inaccuracy of such a weapon, the weakened deterrence effect of missiles incapable of hitting Beijing, the reduced utility of the systems without WMD warheads, and the vulnerability of the Taiwan missile infrastructure to either Chinese missile or special forces attack.

Although the U.S. government would likely detect any testing or deployment of these missiles and could press to stop the program, policymakers in Washington should be alerted to the possibility that the program is actually a "card" to be dealt away in exchange for specific weapons systems (AEGIS or Upper Tier) or enhanced defense commitments.